COUNTERTRANSFERENCE AND REGRESSION

COUNTERTRANSFERENCE AND REGRESSION

L. Bryce Boyer, M.D.

Edited by Laura L. Doty, Ph.D.

A JASON ARONSON BOOK

ROWMAN & LITTLEFIELD PUBLISHERS, INC.
Lanham • Boulder • New York • Toronto • Oxford

A JASON ARONSON BOOK

ROWMAN & LITTLEFIELD PUBLISHERS, INC.

Published in the United States of America
by Rowman & Littlefield Publishers, Inc.
A wholly owned subsidary of The Rowman & Littlefield Publishing Group, Inc.
4501 Forbes Boulevard, Suite 200, Lanham, Maryland 20706
www.rowmanlittlefield.com

PO Box 317, Oxford, OX2 9RU, UK

British Library Cataloguing in Publication Information Available

Library of Congress Cataloging-in-Publication Data

Boyer, L. Bryce.
    Countertransference and regression / L. Bryce Boyer ; edited by Laura L. Doty.
      p. cm.
    "This second volume of collected papers supplements the contents of The regressed patient (Boyer, 1983)"—Author's introductory note.
    Includes bibliographical references and index.
    ISBN 1-56821-706-4 (alk. paper)
    1. Regression (Psychology). 2. Countertransference (Psychology).
    3. Psychoanalysis. I. Doty, Laura L. II. Boyer, L. Bryce. Regressed patient. III. Title.
    [DNLM: 1. Countertransference (Psychology)—collected works. 2. Regression (Psychology)—collected works. 3. Psychoanalytic Therapy—methods—collected works. 4. Psychoanalytic Theory—collected works.
    WM 62 B789c 1998]
    RC489.R42B69 1998
    616.89'17—dc21
    DNLM/DLC
    for Library of Congress   97-51669

Printed in the United States of America

The paper used in this publication meets the minimum requirements of American National Standard for Information Sciences—Permanence of Paper for Printed Library Materials, ANSI/NISO Z39.48-1992.

For my dear friends and mentors
Thomas H. Ogden, David Rosenfeld, and Vamık D. Volkan
with love and gratitude

Contents

Foreword   ix
James S. Grotstein, M.D.

Foreword   xiii
 David Rosenfeld, M.D.

Contributors   xvi

About the Author   xvii

Introduction   xix

1. Countertransference: Brief History and Clinical Issues with Regressed Patients   1

2. Psychoanalytic Treatment of the Borderline Disorders Today   23

3. Regression and Countertransference in the Treatment of a Borderline Patient   39

4. Christmas "Neurosis," Reconsidered   59

5. On Man's Need to Have Enemies   81

6. Approaching Cross-Cultural Psychotherapy   103

7. Psychoanalysis with Few Parameters in the Treatment of Regressed Patients, Reconsidered   113

8. Thinking of the Interview As If It Were a Dream   139

9. Regression in Treatment: On Early Object Relations   147

10. Countertransference, Regression, and an Analysand's Uses of Music   171
    with the assistance of Laura L. Doty

11. Countertransference and Technique in Working with the Regressed Patient: Further Remarks   203

12. The Verbal Squiggle Game in Treating the Seriously Disturbed Patient   225

13. A Conversation with L. Bryce Boyer   241
    Sue von Baeyer

Credits   251
Index   253

Foreword

JAMES S. GROTSTEIN, M.D.

The title of this work, *Countertransference and Regression*, epitomizes the main thematics that have emerged from L. Bryce Boyer's distinguished career in psychoanalyzing psychotics and other primitive mental disorders. This is the second volume of collected papers, the first being *The Regressed Patient* (1983). Part autodidact and part Promethean, he has arrived at a place where he has become a legend in his own lifetime and a place where his contributions support that legend. Once existing in the outback of traditional psychoanalytic respectability, he has lived long enough to witness the widespread acceptance of his ideas that were once heretical, at least in this country. He was one of a very few courageous analysts who pioneered the psychoanalytic treatment for schizophrenia, manic-depressive illness, and other primitive mental disorders, which were once categorized as "narcissistic neuroses" and, by a fiat from Freud himself, supposedly untreatable by psychoanalysis. In the course of enduring the isolation that his early career entailed in treating these patients, he explored the clinical phenomenon of cataclysmic regression. What he learned about "psychotic regressions" has become an important legacy to today's psychoanalysts and psychotherapists. First, he was able tolerate them, and then he interpreted them — successfully! He was like Canute, halting the onrushing tide of the sea.

His work on countertransference is especially noteworthy. The change in our present attitude toward countertransference is due in no small measure to Bryce's courageous persistence in validating it. He was critical of those who only emphasized its resistant aspects and believed that there was an absolute interdependence of transference and countertransference. That the analyst's unconscious was able to reconstruct his patient's unconscious was one of his deepest and all-abiding convictions. We all know today what was largely behind the resistance in the formal acceptance of the positive clinical worth of countertransference. Analysts lost their protective barrier of neutrality and consequently their sense of safety from intersubjective intimacy and emotional counter-involvement.

In his conception of countertransference responses he cited the importance of the patient's bodily experience as a form of communication and a form of memory and included "dermal, muscular, sensory, and visceral sensations, as well as daydreams." Technique for him is "working through the countertransference." Further, he believes that the analytic session is to be considered as if it were a dream. Bryce also extends the concept of countertransference in a very interesting and provocative way. He states: "The analyst develops a form of deep love for his patient, one that has both maternal and paternal aspects . . ." and "the patient's introjection of the loving object provides . . . patients with a self that *can* be analyzed. The introjected love 'allows' the patient to take risks in the form of experiencing thinking and symbolizing aspects of experience that had formerly been unthinkable."

Bryce's sensitivity to his patients is a fundamental part of his legend. Anyone who knows him, whether patient, colleague, family member, or friend, would not deny that he has ESP! His sensitivity and prescience are nothing less than a marvel. His emotional and sensory-motor states operate as a high-fidelity receiver, not only of his patient's preconscious feeling states per se, but of their unconscious fantasies and historic narrative scenarios as well. The reader of this present work, which represents key selected works from his publications across the years, will have ample opportunity to confirm my impressions of this gift of his. He put this countertransference sensitivity to good use, not only in treating his patients but also in validating this once condemned entity as a valuable tool for psychoanalytic technique. In that regard one can accurately say that he was a pioneer in the area of what is now called intersubjectivity.

As these achievements were not enough, there is yet another dimension to him worthy of note, that of his psychoanalytically-informed anthropological career, along with his wife Ruth, among tribes within the Apache nation. He studied some of these Native Americans with Rorshach tests and treated others with psychoanalytic psychotherapy. I recall a conference many years ago in which he spoke in Los Angeles on the treatment of primitive mental disorders. In that presentation he poignantly and graphically described the psychoanalysis he had conducted on a medicine woman in which her "penis envy" came to light. The audience burst out laughing—for a variety of reasons, as I was ultimately able to learn. Some feminists in the crowd were upset, and therefore some of the laughter was due to their nervous irritation. Others laughed because the very notion of penis envy made this arcane Apache medicine woman one with the rest of humanity. Her acceptance of his interpretation had removed racial and historic differences and seemed to validate the universality of psychoanalysis and of the unconscious itself. His work in anthropology deserves some comment.

Bryce was able to bring both a clinical and a theoretical psychoanalytic perspective, a perspective that was to have a strong influence on that field. He was able to maintain his influence there as an editor of that discipline's official journal. His anthropological work also fitted hand-in-hand with his psychoanalytic technique, which was that of "orthodox" analysis, the latter of which I shall discuss shortly. Whereas analysts today rely heavily on infant development research for understanding the primitive aspects of their patients, Bryce's anthropological and Rorschach studies of the rituals and customs of the Apaches gave him first-hand awareness of primitivity in the real world.

Bryce is unique in even another way. He is one of the few remaining analysts I know of who speaks that now all but lost "ancient" tongue of "orthodox" analysis, otherwise known as *id analysis*. When I listened to his lectures and read his publications, I could easily detect his use of primary process interpretations to his patients. One has only to read his clinical case presentation in Chapter 3 to confirm this impression.

Another feature of his character is his readiness to learn from other psychoanalytic contributors. Although originally an orthodox analyst, he also now borrows from ego psychological ("classical") concepts. His technique today reveals the influence of the British object relations schools, especially of Klein and Winnicott, but the two current individuals who most influence him are David Rosenfeld and Thomas Ogden.

A word must be said about Bryce, the scholar. When I pick up an article or book to read, I almost invariably scrutinize the author's list of references to see whom he has selected to influence or to inform his/her contribution. A glance at almost any one of the chapters in this book will reveal some idea of the extent of Bryce's scholarship. I counted 139 references in Chapter 1, 131 for Chapter 2, and 165 for Chapter 5; I then looked at the names of each reference and satisfied myself that he had pretty well covered the significant literature in the field that related to his contribution. This is diligence of a rare order as well as a token of respect for other contributors to the subject at hand. That respect is one of his seldom-mentioned high points.

But that is L. Bryce Boyer, an analyst, a scholar, a courageous innovator, a "shaman," and a gentleman, all of rare order.

Foreword

It is impossible to overstate how greatly honored I felt when Bryce Boyer, my admired teacher, asked me to write a foreword to this book. I would like to begin by discussing what it means to be a teacher. We say Bryce Boyer is a teacher, but this cannot be said lightly of anyone. A teacher is a person whose thinking is original, who does not repeat what others have said. This is probably his core feature. Bryce Boyer was always at our side, helping us to reflect, both as psychoanalysts and human beings. He helped us to become aware of our own feelings and apply them to psychoanalytic technique, especially in the use of countertransference with severely disturbed and psychotic patients.

Bryce Boyer challenged all dogmatic premises that assumed certain patients could not be helped by psychoanalysis. Why should we not think as psychoanalysts when confronted with all patients, including drug addicts and those with borderline and psychotic disorders?

Thus Bryce Boyer helped us think for ourselves, independently and autonomously. We must remember that when Galileo asked: "Why do you not look through the telescope, to see for yourselves the things I talk and write about?" the Inquisitors answered: "We do not need to do it, because Aristotle has explained all this before in his philosophy." Bryce Boyer taught us to be like Galileo, to look through the telescope of transference–countertransference and write about our findings.

In 1964, in San Diego, at a meeting of the West Coast Psychoanalytic Societies, Bryce Boyer organized the first national conference on the psychoanalytic treatment of psychoses; together with Harold Searles, Peter

Giovacchini, James Grotstein, Vamık Volkan, and other gifted psycho-analysts, he has organized many subsequent congresses. He has written or co-written numerous books and perhaps a hundred articles, many of which have become international classics on the psychoanalysis of severely re-gressed patients; his writings have been translated into seven languages. His papers on countertransference are milestones for the teaching and learning of its use in the treatment of patients. For the past eighteen years he has co-directed with Thomas Ogden, the Center for the Advanced Study of the Psychoses in San Francisco.

Psychoanalysis has changed significantly during the past twenty years and for this change we must thank Bryce Boyer, Harold Searles, Frieda Fromm-Reichmann, Otto Kernberg, Edith Jacobson, James Grotstein, Vamık Volkan, and Thomas Ogden in the United States, and many others in England, France, and Italy, as well as many in South America, in particular Argentina.

Bryce Boyer was co-editor of *The Psychoanalytic Study of Society* from 1976 through 1984 and editor-in-chief of the last nine volumes, from 1985 through 1994. In these volumes he published many of his profound and fascinating articles combining cultural anthropological, psychoanalytic, and projective psychological studies of two major tribes of Apache Indians, the Mescaleros and the Chiricahuas; the Tanaina and Upper Tanana Indians and Yukon Delta Eskimos in Alaska; and Laplanders of Northern Finland, studies that involved his actual fieldwork, done over a period of some thirty-five years with his wife, Ruth Boyer, at times accompanied by other anthropologists. Ruth Boyer has written the most important book to date on the transmission of culture and mythology that takes place in Indian tribes in the Americas from grandparents to grandchildren. The Boyers' life with the Apaches led to his work with the Rorschach test and work on the psychology and the unconscious cultural codes of tribal family structures. This experience produced some of the most fascinating work ever done by a psychoanalyst, such as "Effects of Acculturation on the Vicissitudes of the Aggressive Drive among the Apaches of the Mescalero Indian Reservation" (*Psychoanalytic Study of Society*, 1972, 5:40–82). The Apaches considered him to be a shaman; he successfully treated them using only interpretations.

His awards are too numerous to count. A sample follows.

I am especially pleased that, in 1985, the Argentine Psychoanalytic Association struck a medal in honor of his teaching. He is a founding and honorary member of the Mexican Psychoanalytic Association. The Uni-versity of California Medical School gave him the J. Elliott Royer Award in

1987 as the outstanding psychiatrist in Northern California; a Lifetime Achievement Award was created for him in 1994 at the 11th Symposium for the Psychological Treatment of Schizophrenia. He directs the Boyer House Foundation, a hospital for the psychoanalytic treatment of seriously disturbed patients that was established in his honor in 1984; he has also headed the Boyer Research Institute since its establishment in 1980.

I would like to conclude by saying that beyond a foreword to a book, these lines pay homage to a teacher who, together with others, has changed our view concerning the types of patients who could benefit from psychoanalysis. Bryce Boyer changed our mental attitude toward psychoanalysis, one of the most difficult tasks in this impossible profession.

You will find in this volume psychoanalytic studies that are milestones for the future of psychoanalysis. They will become the classics, an indispensable part of the fundamental texts to be studied in our discipline.

Last, but not least, I cannot close without saying that Bryce Boyer is a man endowed with the greatest warmth and humanity, which he has chosen to devote to both the science of psychoanalysis and to his colleagues and beloved family.

Contributors

Laura L. Doty, Ph.D., received her doctorate from the Wright Institute in Berkeley, California. She maintains a private practice in forensic psychology and psychoanalytic psychotherapy and assessment in Santa Rosa, CA.

James S. Grotstein, M.D., is Clinical Professor of Psychiatry at UCLA School of Medicine and Training and Supervising Analyst at The Los Angeles Psychoanalytic Institute/Society and The Psychoanalytic Center of California, Los Angeles. Author of 200 contributions to the literature and author, editor, or co-editor of five books, he is in private practice in West Los Angeles.

David Rosenfeld, M.D., is Professor of Psychiatry, School of Medicine, University of Buenos Aires, Argentina. Former vice president of the International Psychoanalytic Association, he received the Sigourney Award of the American Psychoanalytic Association in 1996.

Sue von Baeyer, Ph.D., is Director of Training and Education and a supervisor at Boyer House Foundation, an affiliate member of the San Francisco Psychoanalytic Institute, and is in private practice in Berkeley, CA. She has been a member of the Center for the Advanced Study of the Psychoses, co-chaired by Drs. Thomas H. Ogden and L. Bryce Boyer. Her clinical work has been supervised by Dr. Boyer for some eight years.

About the Author

L. Bryce Boyer, M.D., is Co-Director of the Center for the Advanced Study of the Psychoses, San Francisco, and Director of the Boyer Research Institute and the Boyer House Foundation (for the inpatient psychoanalytic treatment of seriously disturbed patients). He is Training and Supervising Analyst for the Psychoanalytic Institute of Northern California and the San Francisco Institute for Psychoanalytic Psychotherapy and Psychoanalysis and faculty member of the San Francisco Psychoanalytic Institute.

Dr. Boyer has authored and co-authored, edited and co-edited numerous books, including *Psychoanalytic Treatment of Schizophrenic, Borderline, and Characterological Disorders,* 2 editions; *The Regressed Patient; Technical Factors in the Treatment of the Severely Disturbed Patient; Childhood and Folklore: A Psychoanalytic Study of Apache Personality; Master Clinicians on Treating the Regressed Patient, Vols. 1 and 2;* Vols. 7–19 of *The Psychoanalytic Study of Society: A Rorschach Handbook for the Affective Scoring System,* 3 editions; and numerous articles. Many of his books and articles have been translated into such languages as German, Italian, Spanish, Portuguese, Norwegian, and Finnish. Dr. Boyer maintains a private practice in Berkeley.

Introduction

This second volume of collected papers supplements the contents of *The Regressed Patient*, published in 1983. Reading that book revealed that there had been a gradual change in my theoretical and technical orientation regarding countertransference. As is detailed in the preface of that book and in Dr. von Baeyer's last chapter of this one, my training organization was utterly opposed to the psychoanalytic treatment of the narcissistic neuroses and ridiculed any psychoanalytic orientation that questioned the intellectual ego psychology advocated especially by Hartmann. The rigid attitude of my training analysts was that psychoanalysis was not to be used in the treatment of the narcissistic neuroses and that the first permissible interpretations should deal with oedipal conflicts. Most of them taught also that the analyst was to respond almost solely to the patient's verbal communications. Additionally, countertransference was not to be understood except as a deficiency in the analyst, of which he was to rid himself, in some mysterious manner.

My personal background included a severely disturbed mother whom I had learned to understand fairly well and whose rages and paranoid episodes I could modify by interpretations when still a preschool child, and I had learned that her bodily and visceral actions and reactions conveyed clear messages and might be more significant than what she said. Viewed retrospectively, I learned our interactions—emotional, visceral, and skeletomuscular—were mutually interdependent. Unable to believe anything she said, threatened or promised, I became a truly investigatory scientist early in life, playing hookey to study nature.

It was many years before I learned that she consciously tried to be a good person and did the best that her unconscious masters permitted her to do. This of course, contributed profoundly to my belief that seriously disturbed patients do their utmost during treatment and that their apparent actings-out may be the sole way they can recall vital past experiences for which they do not yet have words. I believe analysts frequently focus solely on their resistive aspects.

Knowing that my childhood interpretations obviously modified my mother's psychotic behavior, I did not believe Freud's position that psycho-analysis was contraindicated in the treatment of the narcissistic neuroses and, in the loneliness of my position in my training institute, determinedly sought to treat individuals who suffered from such disorders.

To my great good fortune, Peter Giovacchini, who held theoretical positions similar to my own and underwent similar experiences in his training institute, read some of my earliest papers (Boyer 1956a,b, 1957a,b, 1960) and communicated with me.

We shared thoughts, experiences, and publications (Boyer and Gio-vacchini 1967, 1990, 1993, Giovacchini and Boyer 1982, Giovacchini et al. 1975). His support and ideas were invaluable in my development. In his words, "We grew up together" (personal communication).

Not being satisfied with ego psychology or object relations theory as explanatory or even helpful at times, I tried to incorporate the ideas of Klein and some of her intimates into my theoretical and technical compre-hension and practice, ideas I had ridiculed in an earlier book through my own ignorance (Boyer 1967).

Fortunately for the broadening of my theoretical position and for my comfort and optimism in working with patients who have serious psycho-logical disturbances, Thomas Ogden and I have worked together for the past twenty years, first in the setting of a psychiatric teaching hospital and, beginning in 1981, as co-conductors of the Center for the Advanced Study of the Psychoses. We have listened together to some 200 cases presented to us. We have discussed thoroughly the writings of Klein, Bion, Winnicott, and their followers, and, of course, significant others; I continue to learn from Ogden. It is well known that Tom has spent his professional life clarifying, expanding, and enhancing the clinical usefulness of their think-ing and has integrated it with that of the most insightful contributions of North American analysts, such as Loewenwald (Ogden 1982, 1986, 1989, 1994, 1997a).

Having become convinced of the absolute interdependence of trans-ference and countertransference, I have come to agree with Rosenfeld

(1987) that the interaction of analysand and analyst can best be understood if we think of the analyst as introjecting the patient's unconscious projective identifications and vice versa. The analyst's comprehension of this interchange will depend on his capacity to understand the symbology or metaphorical meaning of the projection, whether it be produced in words, actions, or visceral and/or sensorial perceptions.

Many of our supervisees and seminar members have voiced the opinion that, during the past twenty years, I have become profoundly courageous and optimistic. My own sense is that, while courage was evident during the years when I was unsure of the outcome of analytic treatment of such patients, it is scarcely an element today.

In addition to supervising therapists' work with Tom, I have been engaged in teaching many other psychotherapists to do such work. In 1982, without my knowledge, a grateful patient donated a large sum of money, which some of my students and supervisees used to establish the Boyer House Foundation, an inpatient service where therapists were to be trained in the psychoanalytic treatment of seriously regressed patients in a milieu therapy situation. During the seventeen years of the Foundation's existence, the vast majority of the patients have improved remarkably, as substantiated clinically and by repeated projective psychological tests, particularly the Rorschach test given and scored in a manner that permits quantification of affectual responses. (Boyer et al., in press). Today, I believe the seeds of my optimism arose in my interactions with my mother and that its authenticity has been amply substantiated in clinical experience.

The analyst must have the courage to speak the truth and to hear the truth. It may be that my more than thirty years of studying the personalities of so-called "native" peoples in the field has contributed to my certainty that this is so. (In conjunction with my cultural anthropologist wife, I have worked psychotherapeutically with and done Rorschach tests on members of three Apachean tribes in New Mexico, and studied and procured Rorschach protocols from the Upper Tanana and Tanaina Indians and the Inuits of the Yukon Delta region of Alaska as well as Laplanders in Northern Finland. Thus are included Chapters 5 and 6.)

During the past decade or more I have come to believe that in a successful analysis, the analyst develops a form of deep love for his patient, one that has both maternal and paternal aspects. The love is never stated directly or acted out in terms of violations of the analytic frame. Nonetheless, the love is experienced by the analysand and introjected as a good, but not idealized, internal object. Sometimes I think that the patient's introjection of the loving object provides such patients with a self that *can* be analyzed. The introjected love, as Ogden (1997b) states, "allows the patient to take risks in the form of experiencing thinking and symbolizing aspects of experience that had formerly been unthinkable. It has been my impression that this valuing of the positive transference and countertransference (in a way that is for the most part unspoken by the analyst) has come to occupy as central a place in Bryce's clinical thinking as the necessity of recognizing and squarely addressing the full intensity of the negative transference."

I cannot emphasize too strongly that the analyst must be aware of and interpret the patient's bodily experience as a form of communication and a form of memory. If the domain of psychoanalysis does not include the patient's bodily sensations, there is little hope that the primitive aspects of the patient's experience can be attained.

An intrinsic element of my technique in dealing with such patients is to do what I call "working through the countertransference." Because, like Freud, I have the patient lie down so that I can be less distracted by his movements and expressions and observations of my reactions, I can frequently enter a state of reverie during which, while a part of me remains in contact with the patient's and my behavior, another part is freer to experience a sort of daydream, or to become more aware of dermal, muscular, sensory, and visceral experiences and daydreams; meanwhile, I continue to observe the interactions between the patient and me. I assume that my experience reflects my introjective identification with the patient's projective identifications, modified, of course, by my own physical and mental propensities. On the basis of the product of my lowered consciousness experience, I formulate interpretations or questions that lead to previously unknown important data.

As an example, in this book I write of a man whose analysis had become stalemated, dead, until during a reverie I heard a humming inside my head (Chapter 10). My question to him as to whether he was hearing music led to his revealing that indeed this was so. This information restored life to our work together and led to the recovery of vital, very early experiences and a most successful analysis.

Two other chapters that are included here resulted from exhilarating and surprising experiences.

It is well known that poets sometimes dream lines before writing them and scientists have made momentous discoveries in dreams. It is not infrequent that I awaken, aware that my dream has been a continuation of an effort to further understand an unresolved transference–countertransference issue. I was both moved and startled when I awoke, realizing that I had dreamed that one could profitably think of an interview as though it were a dream. The dream, with my morning, half-conscious elaboration of it, was almost as it has been reproduced here in Chapter 8.

The idea of understanding the interview as if it were a dream has been very valuable in my individual work and has benefited many of my supervisees immensely. Simply put, every communication given by the patient is presumed to be related symbolically or metaphorically to the dominant unresolved transference–countertransference issue of the last session or series of sessions, the "day residue" of the hypothetical dream. Such communications may be an action, a movement, or a verbal statement; they may be a sensation, whether dermal or muscular or visceral or a fantasy of any of them, or an experience, recollection, or fantasy of the therapist. We think again of Rosenfeld's notion of the reciprocal introjective and projective identifications of the therapist and the patient.

The *awareness* that a "squiggle game" can occur during concurrent reveries of analyst and analysand (Chapter 12) came as a pleasant surprise. Retrospectively, certain analysands and I had had similar experiences, of varying intensity, for some months before I recognized the similarity of our interchanges with Winnicott's "squiggle game" (1971, pp. 121–123). The verbal squiggle game occurs while both analyst and analysand are both in states of reverie and have greater access to repressed material than at other times. The game is intersubjective play between analyst and analysand, in which a generative space is available to each, through which new understanding and conceptualizations can emerge, the creativity to which Winnicott often refers. Often, deep regression occurs with recovery of early psychological traumata; the transient psychosis, in my experience, has always been limited to the analytic session.

In 1955 (Chapter 4) I had learned that in some people the Christmas season reawakens unresolved sibling rivalries. They unconsciously compare themselves to Christ, the favorite son of the Christian world, and become depressed or suffer other psychological illnesses. The subject stirred worldwide interest; more than forty years since its initial publication, I continue to receive requests for reprints each Yuletide, in recent years principally from Slavic countries.

A review of all my analytic case material for the succeeding thirty years reaffirmed the earlier observations and also revealed that some patients suffered from similar problems at Eastertime. Most interesting was the finding that frequently, when a patient begins to talk of or remember with emotion Christmas or Easter experiences at any time of the year, reawakened sibling rivalry problems reemerge. Religious persuasion of such patients was of no importance whatsoever.

From 1976 until its publication ceased, I was co-editor of *The Psychoanalytic Study of Society*, senior co-editor of Volumes 11 (1985) through 19 (1994). An award in my name for excellence of psychoanalytic–anthropological writing was established by the Society for Psychological Anthropology, a division of the American Anthropological Association.

Chapters 5 and 6, "On Man's Need to Have Enemies" and "Approaching Cross-Cultural Psychotherapy," were written by request for Brazilian psychoanalytic–anthropological conferences and are included here to reflect my continuing interest in psychoanalytic anthropology.

References

Boyer, L. B. (1956a). Ambulatory schizophrenia: some remarks about the diagnosis. *Kaiser Foundation Medical Bulletin* 4:467–470.

——— (1956b). On maternal overstimulation and ego defects. *Psychoanalytic Study of the Child* 11:236–256.

——— (1957a). Uses of delinquent behavior by a borderline schizophrenic. *Archives of Criminal Psychodynamics*, Summer, pp. 542–571.

——— (1957b). The meaning of insulin therapy to a schizophrenic patient. *Journal of the Hillside Hospital* 6:3–6.

——— (1960). A hypothesis concerning the time of appearance of the dream screen. *International Journal of Psycho-Analysis* 41:114–122.

——— (1967). Historical development of psychoanalytic therapy of the schizophrenias: contributions of the followers of Freud. In *Psychoanalytic Treatment of Schizophrenic and Characterological Disorders*, by L. B. Boyer and P. L. Giovacchini, pp. 80–142. New York: Science House Press.

——— (1983). *The Regressed Patient*. New York: Jason Aronson.

Boyer, L. B., Dithrich, C. W., Harned, H., et al. (in press). *A Rorschach Handbook for the Affective Inferences Scoring Systems—Revised*. Berkeley, CA: Boyer Research Institute.

Boyer, L. B., and Giovacchini, P. L. (1967). *Psychoanalytic Treatment of Schizophrenic and Characterological Disorders*. New York: Science House Press.

———, eds. (1990). *Master Clinicians on Treating the Regressed Patient*. Northvale, NJ: Jason Aronson.

———, eds. (1993). *Master Clinicians on Treating the Regressed Patient, Vol. 2*. Northvale, NJ: Jason Aronson.

Giovacchini, P. L., and Boyer, L. B., eds. (1982). *Technical Factors in the Treatment of the Severely Disturbed Patient*. New York: Jason Aronson.

Giovacchini, P. L., Flarsheim, A., and Boyer, L. B., eds. (1975). *Tactics and*

Techniques in Psychoanalytic Therapy. Vol. 2: Countertransference. New York: Jason Aronson.

Ogden, T. H. (1982). *Projective Identification and Psychotherapeutic Technique.* New York: Jason Aronson.

———— (1986). *The Matrix of the Mind: Object Relations and the Psychoanalytic Dialogue.* Northvale, NJ: Jason Aronson.

———— (1989). *The Primitive Edge of Experience.* Northvale, NJ: Jason Aronson.

———— (1994). *Subjects of Analysis.* Northvale, NJ: Jason Aronson.

———— (1997a). *Reverie and Interpretation: Sensing Something Human.* Northvale, NJ: Jason Aronson.

———— (1997b). Some reflections on my work with Dr. Bryce Boyer. *Arquivos de Psiquiatria, Psicoterapia e Psicanalise* (in press).

Rosenfeld, H. R. (1987). *Impasse and Interpretation: Therapeutic and Anti-Therapeutic Factors in the Treatment of Psychotic, Borderline and Neurotic Patients.* London/New York: Tavistock.

Winnicott, D. W. (1971). *Playing and Reality.* New York: Basic Books.

Countertransference: Brief History and Clinical Issues with Regressed Patients

INTRODUCTION

This chapter discusses the development of modern attitudes toward countertransference and its use in the psychoanalytic treatment of regressed patients. There is a large literature pertaining to countertransference reactions in the analyses of patients with neurotic disturbances, including a number of reviews (Glover 1955, Langs 1976, Orr 1954, A. Reich 1951). A sharply curtailed history of attitudes toward countertransference follows, adding to other studies, as those of Boyer (1979a, 1983), Davis (1991), Epstein and Feiner (1979), Etchegoyen (1991), and Scharff (1992). It must be stressed that prior to the middle of the present century, very few contributors disagreed with the view that countertransference must be considered solely an interference in the analytic procedure. Those such as Ferenczi, who communicated their emotional reactions to their patients in word or action, were reprimanded severely (M. Balint 1968, Stärcke 1920).

As is well known, Freud (1910) introduced the term *countertransference* in the context of disapproval. Although the subject continued to concern him, he never devoted a specific study to the phenomenon, nor was a theory of countertransference elaborated until much later.

Freud seldom if ever totally renounced any theoretical position he had introduced. For example, he continued in his last works to combine the topographical and the structural theories as explanatory models (Freud 1933a). We shall see that this holds true with regard to countertransference as well. Freud never recanted his position that countertransference was an undesirable impediment. In 1912, in a letter written to Ferenczi, he implied that his failure to overcome his positive, paternal countertransference had made impossible the interpretation to Ferenczi of a negative transference. It is hard to know whether Freud had his tongue in his cheek, when, in 1937, he spoke of a patient who had complained that the mentor had not interpreted the negative transference, to whom Freud replied if it had not been interpreted, it had not appeared (Jones 1955).

Heimann (1950) suggested that Freud's discovery of resistance was based on his countertransference, his feeling that he was meeting a resistant force in the patient. Boyer agrees with Grotstein (1992) that it is more profitable in therapeutic situations to think of many so-called resistances as communications.

It is well known that Freud's clinical failures sometimes were the products of countertransference interferences (Binswanger 1956, Boyer 1967). Freud (1910) introduced the word *countertransference* when writing technical advice to unanalyzed and largely untrained physicians who were practicing psychoanalysis, doubtlessly in the hope that the danger of the clinician's emotional involvement and acting out with the patient could be reduced. He defined countertransference as a function of the analysand, the product of the influence of the patient's verbal and nonverbal communications on the unconscious of the analyst. Two years later he (Freud 1912) specifically recommended training analysis,[1] urging that the "therapist turn his own unconscious like a receptive organ towards the transmitting unconscious of the patient . . . so that the doctor's unconscious is able . . . to reconstruct the patient's unconscious" (pp. 115–116). This is an example of Freud's ambivalence or reflection of his dialectical mode of thinking of which he was largely unconscious, a position that continues to underscore the disagreement between the classical and the totalistic approaches to countertransference. At the same time that Freud insists that

---

1. There seems ample evidence that Freud, at least at times, had disappointing clinical results because of unresolved countertransference problems (Boyer 1967). May (1990) has suggested that much of Freud's formulations, technique, and style demonstrated in the case history of the Wolf Man were products of unanalyzed transference–countertransference phenomena.

the analyst be purified so that he has no blind spots, he says that the analyst's unconscious should be in contact with that of the analysand.

Probably having been influenced by Janet while studying with Charcot (Jones 1953), Freud was much interested in the subject of telepathy, publishing on related subjects in 1899, 1904, and 1921. Soon after the appearance of Stekel's (1920) *The Telepathic Dream*, Freud (1922) wrote specifically about telepathy; other publications appeared later on (1925 and 1933b).[2] In his earliest article on telepathy, Freud (1921) wrote,

> Psychoanalysts . . . study occult material only because they hope that this would enable them to eliminate once and for all the creations of the human wish from the realm of material reality. . . . If, in the course of his work, [the psychoanalyst] is on the lookout for occult phenomena, he runs the risk of overlooking everything which is closer at hand. . . . The analyst's self-discipline can protect him against the subjective risk of having his interest absorbed by occult phenomena. Things are different, however, as regards the objective danger. It is probable that the study of occult phenomena will result in the admission that some of these phenomena are real. . . . [p. 58]

His attitudes did not change in subsequent articles.

In his survey of Freud's contributions to psychoanalysis and telepathy, Eisenbud (1953) wrote, "What Freud says, in effect, is: 'Distortion of perception is one of the characteristics of mental functioning dominated by unconscious needs. But this distortion is purposeful and occurs along dynamic, deterministic lines. There is no reason to suppose that telepathic perceptions should be free from this universal effect'" (p. 9).

The Telepathic Dream was based on Stekel's dreams while working with neurotic patients, dreams that today would be strongly suspected by analysts as being associated with countertransference phenomena (Bollas 1987, McDougall 1978, 1989, Racker 1960). But a footnote to Freud's 1922 article acknowledging his awareness of Stekel's book makes no allusion to countertransference. In all of Freud's communications the question of the validity of extrasensory perception remained open. Oddly, the word *countertransference* does not appear in any of Freud's communications dealing with telepathy and the occult. One wonders whether Freud thought, perhaps unconsciously, that telepathy constituted some aspect

---

2. Excerpts of his first two articles and his last three contributions appear in Devereux (1953).

of transference–countertransference interactions.[3] Surely many other analysts have implied a similar belief, namely, that unconscious communication involves extrasensory perception.[4] In his summary of the theories of István Hollós, Devereux (1953) writes, "Telepathic incidents became especially numerous during a difficult period in the analyst's life" (p. 200), surely linking them with countertransference, although the word was not used by Hollós or Devereux in this context.

Analysts have long been concerned with the means by which the psychological attributes of one person are assumed by another. Many, following Freud's (1915) lead, have written about the influence of patients' introjection of analysts' attributes on the transference relationship. Fenichel (1945) was the first to note that analysts' countertransferences are largely determined by the influences on their unconscious conflicts by introjections of patients' attributes, a frequently affirmed observation (Federn 1952, Fliess 1953, Weigert 1954).

Meltzer (1978) called introjection "the most important and mysterious concept in psycho-analysis" (p. 14) and said we have not yet described the process by which the child's experience of the external object is taken in. Menzies-Lyth (1983) added that "introjection and introject have in no way found in the psycho-analytical literature a place comparable to projection and project" (p. 1). In agreement with Meissner (1987) and countless others, she notes, "Projection turns out to be more exciting, more innovative, more illuminating, to our understanding of normal and pathological development" (p. 3). Hinting, perhaps, at a reason that many analysts have been so reluctant to study countertransference, preferring instead to investigate "intuition" and "enactment," Menzies-Lyth suggests that the introjective process has been underinvestigated because of interference from the effects of selective introjection by the patient of the analyst's narcissism. Scharff (1992) would add that the analyst's narcissism may affect what the patient finds available for introjection, suggesting that "the analyst censors

---

3. It was long common for many Kleinian psychoanalysts, particularly in Latin America, to speak of projective identification as constituting the patient's actual rather than fantasied projection into the analyst, a phenomenon that surely resembles telepathy (Garma 1962, Goldberg 1979).

4. This material has been reviewed at great length in Devereux (1953), where relevant articles by Helene Deutsch, Hitschmann, Róheim, Schilder, Zulliger, and others are republished and the Eisenbud-Pederson-Krag-Fodor–Ellis controversy is reviewed, and in book 10 of *Confrontation: Telepathie* (Major 1983), where several of those articles and later contributions by Bergson, Costa de Beauregard, Derrida, Dumas, Farrell, Mignotte, and others are reprinted.

the introjective process before and after it occurs, because it is gratifying inside the self" (p. 52).

The study of introjection has proceeded from the beginnings of psychoanalysis; it has been determined that the means by which the analyst and the analysand may introject the other's qualities are legion. In "The Psychopathology of Everyday Life" Freud (1901) commented on sensory preference in referring to forms of memory, and in "Instincts and Their Vicissitudes" (1915) he noted that every perceptive mode is related to introjection. In 1917 he introduced the concept of oral incorporation as a step in identification, as did Abraham (1924) that of oral incorporation, affirming the inferences of van Ophuijsen (1920) and Stärcke (1920), who had written independently of the enema as the infantile prototype of the paranoid's equation of persecutor and feces. Abraham (1924) found epidermal incorporation to correspond to feces-smearing; later, Lewin (1930) viewed it to be an equivalent of oral incorporation. Leonard (1961) wrote of visual incorporation. Fenichel (1931) made respiratory incorporation a special study and stated that the respiratory tract has an autonomous erotogenicity. It is common knowledge that every perceptive mode can also be used in the service of projection; Malcolm (1970) wrote of the use of vision for the attempted unification of fragmented internal objects.

It has long been assumed that countertransferences are determined largely by the analyst's introjection of qualities of the patient that come into contact with the therapist's unresolved infantile conflicts (Federn 1952, Fenichel 1945, Fliess 1953). In Giovacchini's (1989) experience and my own (Boyer 1986, 1988, 1989, 1992), like that of Searles (1979) and Volkan (1981), both the most effective interpretations and the recovery of the most relevant repressed memories are based frequently on information gathered through countertransference reactions, that is, interpreting through the countertransference. Until the past few years, interpreting through the countertransference appears to have been very unusual in the practice of North American analysts, if not limited to the four analysts cited above, but not uncommon among neo-Kleinians.[5]

There were almost no direct studies of countertransference for approximately forty years following the introduction of the term. To my knowledge, the first to suggest that the analyst's reactions to the patient's productions could be used as *helpful* data was Hann-Kende (1933). Sharpe (1927) had earlier reported a clinical case concerning countertransferential

---

5. As illustrated by the case presentations in Spillius (1988).

reactions to the patient, yet, rather than elaborating a theory of counter-transference, confined herself to discussing the analyst's resistances to Kleinian methods.

While countertransference was not investigated, curiosity about intu-ition was active, as it remains today. Throughout his works, Reik (1933, 1948, 1953) indicated that if the analyst has a receptive attitude and trusts intuition more than mere reasoning, he will be surprised with a sudden understanding of a message from the analysand's unconscious, an intuitive grasp from unconscious to unconscious, as Freud (1912, 1915) had indi-cated previously. When Reik (1924) mentions countertransference, he views it as a resistance and does not indicate that the analyst's response is nourished by a conflict of his own. Similarly, W. Reich (1933) refers to his own affective reactions as intuitions. Racker (1953) would rename them as countertransferential reactions, and Etchegoyen (1991) wrote that "the analyst's *métier* consists in listening to and scrutinizing his countertransference—that is his intuition" (p. 163).

MELANIE KLEIN'S CONTRIBUTION TO THE UNDERSTANDING OF COUNTERTRANSFERENCE

Analysts have sought to understand what constitutes Reik's (1948) *listening with the third ear*, or Isakower's *analyzing instrument*.

The vast majority of today's authors who write about transference–countertransference interactions use one or another version of Klein's (1946) concepts of splitting and projective and introjective identification,[6] in their attempts to understand the phenomena. This is true whether their dominant orientation stems from the ideas about object relations deriving from the structural theory, or from theories of the British independent school. Although Melanie Klein herself firmly held the traditional view that countertransference constituted solely an obstacle to treatment (Grosskurth 1986), "her work has been the most powerful single influence" for the "shift of perspective" (O'Shaughnessy 1983, p. 281) that has led to interpretations now being directed toward the interaction of patient and

---

6. As does Ogden (1982, 1994), I use the term *projective identification* to refer to a wide range of psychological-interpersonal events, including the earliest forms of mother–infant communication (Bion 1962), fantasied coercive incursions into and occupation of the personality of another person, schizophrenic confusional states (Rosenfeld 1952), and healthy "empathic sharing" (Pick 1985, p. 45).

analyst at an intrapsychic level. This shift potentiated modern understanding of countertransference, with its emphasis on the positive therapeutic uses of the analyst's reactions to the patient's verbal and nonverbal productions. Obviously, the importance of Bion's (1962) extension of Klein's work must also be recognized: particularly his finding projective identification to be not only a defense mechanism, but also simultaneously an infant's first way of communicating with his objects, and the role of the mother and the analyst as metabolizing containers (see also Winnicott 1958, 1965).

As early as 1961, Stone ascribed to the neo-Kleinian Racker's (1952, 1960) work the growing appreciation of the countertransference as an affirmative instrument facilitating perception, enhancing sensitive awareness of the analyst's incipient reactions to the patient, leading to a richer and more subtle understanding of the patient's transference striving. More recent Kleinian contributors to this area of analytic thought include Grinberg (1957, 1962, 1979), Joseph (1975, 1982), Meltzer (1966, 1978), Money-Kyrle (1956), O'Shaughnessy (1983), and Segal (1981).

Through the inclusion of views of countertransference discussed below, views traceable to influences of neo-Kleinian thinking, the psychoanalytic treatment of regressed patients is becoming revolutionized in North America, despite the seemingly adamant opposition of many Hartmann-influenced ego psychologists who also oppose regression to primitive states during treatment.[7]

COUNTERTRANSFERENCE AND INTROJECTION SINCE MIDCENTURY

We turn now to the definition of countertransference as it is used here and a history of the development of that view. Our concept of transference–countertransference follows Rosenfeld's (1987) contribution, detailing the

---

7. A similar revolution is gaining impetus among the thinking and field techniques of investigators of culture and personality development. Over thirty years passed between the writing and the publication of Devereux's (1967) landmark *From Anxiety to Method in the Behavioral Sciences*, due to the unpopularity of his introducing the theme of countertransference distortions into anthropological fieldwork, as had Racker and Boyer into psychoanalytic treatment. Since then, influenced by similarly psychoanalytically knowledgeable anthropologists, the understanding and even the techniques of fieldwork have been influenced heavily by their increasingly taking into account the effects of countertransference (Crapanzano 1980, Good et al. 1982, Kracke 1981, R. Levine 1966, S. Levine 1981, Parsons 1969, Stein 1994, Tobin 1986).

constant interplay between analyst and analysand involving their mutual introjection of the other's projective identifications. Regarding countertransference, projective identification functions as a means of communication in learning from the patient what he cannot think consciously. The analyst seeks to find words to bridge the subjective states of the analyst and the patient, while understanding that the space that separates them is the most potentially powerful link between the patient's dissociated states.

Faimberg (1992) argues that what the analysand cannot say through parapraxes, dreams, silences, and symptoms can be heard only from the countertransference position of the analyst. As Bromberg (1991) suggests, when words are found and negotiated, they can become part of the patient's creative effort to symbolize and enunciate what he had no way of expressing. Bromberg finds the patient not to be in need of insight that will correct faulty reality, but in need of a relationship with another person through which words can be found for that which has no verbal language. As the patient finds words that represent his experience, he "knows" himself. E. Balint (1991) adds that as the patient knows about mutual experience, he knows about the analyst, too. She holds that in the transference–countertransference relationship, another person is there to enable the patient to put himself together, provided that the analyst can use his emotional responses to the patient's communications without countertransference distortion.

A major thread in the development of analytic understanding of the interdependence of transference and countertransference emerged from Winnicott's ideas concerning the interdependence of the subjectivities of mother and infant (1965) and the creation of a "third area of experiencing" in the potential space "that exists (but cannot exist) between the baby and the object" (1971a, p. 107). Subsequent authors have significantly expanded the understanding of the analytic process as taking place in the "overlap of two areas of playing, that of the patient and that of the therapist" (Winnicott 1971b, p. 38; see also Ogden 1992). Winnicott (1960) held there to be "no such thing as an infant [apart from the maternal provision]" (p. 39, fn.) and Ogden believes there to be no such thing as an analysand apart from the relationship with the analyst or an analyst apart from his relationship with the analysand. Ogden (1994) has developed the concept of the analytic third. He writes,

> the intersubjective entity described as the analyst–analysand coexists in dialectical tension with the analyst and analysand as separate individuals with their own thoughts, feelings, sensations, corporal reality, psy-

chological identity and so on. Neither the intersubjectivity of the mother–infant nor that of the analyst–analysand (as separate psychological entities) exists in pure form. The intersubjective and the individually subjective each create, negate and preserve the other. In both the relationship of mother and infant and the relationship of analyst and analysand, the task is not to tease apart the elements constituting the relationship in an effort to determine which qualities belong to each individual participating in it; rather, from the point of view of the dialectical interdependence of subject and object, the analytic task involves an effort to describe as fully as one can the specific nature of the interplay of individual subjectivity and intersubjectivity. [p. 4]

The Gaddinis (E. Gaddini 1981, R. Gaddini 1985, 1990) and Boyer (1990) have discussed and demonstrated with case examples the emergence of words during complementary regression of patient and therapist.

It is held here that whatever the analyst experiences during the analytic session constitutes his idiosyncratic introjection of the patient's verbal and nonverbal communications, containing the patient's projections, and the analyst's predominantly unconscious reactions to those introjections. In addition, the analyst exists as a part of the analytic third, experiencing and simultaneously observing himself, the analysand, and the analytic third as they interact with one another. We should not be misled into thinking our stray, apparently unrelated thoughts, fantasies, physical or emotional reactions can be dismissed as idle preoccupations, taking us away from the business at hand, interfering with our free-floating or evenly hovering attention.

Drowsiness is a reaction of the analyst that has been discarded often as irrelevant or explainable by "rational" reasons. McLaughlin (1975) and others have emphasized its countertransference implications, and I (Boyer 1989, 1992) illustrated how sleepiness provided highly important clues to patients' unconscious conflicts.

It is obvious that the analyst's prevailing emotional state and individual conflicts, repressed or otherwise, will determine his degree of openness to the analysand's projections.

The mental set of the analyst is firmly embedded in his life history, which will strongly influence his receptivity. To cite a few examples suffices. My lifelong experiences with psychotic people have conditioned me to be *automatically* aware of very early stages of regression as possibly premonitory of psychotic outbreak. Here I note only subtle manifestations, leaving aside such obvious events as slips of the tongue and the insertion into speech or action of false memories or of fantasies momentarily held to be facts. When a person who regularly uses good grammar begins to use pronouns incorrectly, such as saying "to *him* and *I*," I become alerted and keep track of possible repetitions and the circumstances in which they occur. Frequently, my eventually calling the analysand's attention to the erroneous use of (for instance) *I* rather than *me* leads to his awareness that his incorrect use of *I* signals a potential profound regression, a speaking from a position in which he had not yet become differentiated into an *I* and a *me*. Similarly, when an analysand begins to use scatological language, I am especially aware of relevant bodily sensations and their potential meanings.

We all know of Freud's holding that some dreams cannot be interpreted on the basis of the patient's associations; yet that the analyst is certain that he understands significant elements. My many years of field research in anthropology and study of folklore and the cross-cultural use of the Rorschach test (Boyer 1979b, De Vos and Boyer 1989) have led me to firmly believe that each symbol has at least one basic meaning, apparently inborn, in addition to whatever additional meanings have been added by learning. My automatic subliminally thinking "female–mother" when a patient began to be preoccupied with the wood of furniture near him in the consultation room led me to make an interpretation that both relieved my inner tension and lifted him from a deep, sudden psychotic regression (Boyer 1983). Automatically thinking of sibling rivalry when patients begin to talk of tiny animals or insects (Boyer 1979b) or Christmas or Easter (Boyer 1985), of dentate vaginas when they mention furry spiders (Boyer et al. 1989), often leads to a quickened introjection and understanding of a projection.

The analyst's involvement in his countertransference may prove distracting at times, especially when his patients succeed each other in tandem or after but a few minutes. It may be difficult for the analyst to make the internal changes requisite for undistorted perception of the conflicts and emotional states of the second patient who enters the consultation room. This is more true if the patients' characterological structures and the contemporary nature of the transference–countertransference relationships are similar.

For example, two women had suffered similarly severely traumatic infancies and childhoods, and each had undergone frequent catatonoid episodes, involving intense withdrawal and obviously psychotic thinking, until they left home to attend school. Subsequently, each withdrew from stressful situations with similar episodes that might last for days or weeks. Neither had been hospitalized, but both had undergone repeated psychotherapy and psychoanalysis in the care of highly respected training analysts in North America. Neither considered her analyses to have been useful clinically; each had stopped them voluntarily when their analysts made regression impossible in the service of treatment. An extreme example follows. When one asked why she was being discouraged from attempting to recover fantasies that immediately preceded a frightening dissociated state while on the couch, her analyst, as she reported to me, had said that the recovery of the fantasies might lead to her suicide. It was more usual for the analyst to discourage covertly the patient's attempt to regress, usually by asking questions that changed the subject. It has long been common knowledge that the therapist often seeks to relieve his own anxiety in this way (Gill et al. 1954).

Winnicott (1971a) and Ogden (1985, 1986, 1989) have stressed the need of the analyst to be able to allow the existence of potential space in which creativity can occur, and Bion (1967), the need for the analyst to enter into a "reverie" allowing a similar development. I find my most exhilarating and productive periods when working with regressed patients to occur during those unusual occasions when, while in a slight state of reverie, I play Winnicott's (1971a) "squiggle game" with the patient. We do not use pencils, but instead create our "drawings" verbally through associating to each other's associations. It is at these times that the thinking of both analysand and analyst most easily switches without conflict to the simultaneous use of the autistic-contiguous, schizo-paranoid, and depressive modes of generating experience (Ogden 1989). It is most doubtful that such an interchange could take place in a therapeutic endeavor in which the analytic frame had not been consistently maintained, or in which the therapist was uncomfortable during the patient's sometimes psychotic regressions.

Especially important in this interchange, according to Spillius (1988), are the distinctive features of the depressive position "as the integration of part objects to form the whole object and the painful recognition by the individual that his feelings of love and hate are directed to the same, whole object. The theme of concern for the object is central to the idea" (p. 4). There is also recognition of the object's separateness, as well as the intrinsic relationship between the depressive position, symbolic thought, and creativity (Segal 1952, 1957, 1974).[8] At such times both analysand and analyst

---

8. While this interchange between analyst and analysand can be thought of as involving combinations of primary and secondary process thinking (Spiro 1992), viewing

retain sufficient objectivity that a part of their minds can observe the interplay among primitive mental functions. During such a period, one of the female patients mentioned above laughed aloud and said that were any other analyst she knew to listen in on our conversation, he or she would surely deem us mad.

For a few months, these patients had tandem sessions one day each week, their other four hours being at separate times of the day. During that period, each had bravely regressed to a primitive state during her interviews, which both frightened and greatly encouraged her because she deemed it as necessary reliving in the service of her analysis. For several days, each had been playing a verbal squiggle game with me, during which our interactions created a state that we found to be similar to the potential space of which Winnicott and Ogden wrote, within which creations occur when mother and infant are properly attuned. It is my impression that many analysts become uneasy with the onset of reverie and seek to terminate the state.

One night, after one of the women and I had experienced such an episode, I dreamed that she and I were Siamese twins, connected solely by our occipital cortices. One of my waking associations was that we had been seeing "eye to eye" and did indeed share visual cortices. For me, the women had indeed become Siamese twins, connected by my head.

The following day I told the patient my dream, an act I had never performed previously with any analysand, only to remember subsequently and secretly that I had in fact had the dream about the other patient.

In this instance, no harm was done. However, on other occasions I have felt foolish and delayed analytic progress when I have unwittingly carried my emotional state and preoccupation with the former transference–countertransference interactions into the successive hour.

Such experiences, among others, led me to seek to view each analytic session as though it were a dream, in which the major unresolved transference–countertransference issue of the last or last few sessions composes the day residue (Boyer 1988). Accordingly, I assume that *every* communication of the interview is in some way related to that day residue in the context of the ensuing "dream" and am particularly interested in the symbolic meanings of the opening verbal and/or nonverbal communications. Often, to refresh my memory, I review my notes in advance of the

---

the interchange in these terms fails to convey the richness inferred by Ogden's (1989) trilogy.

interview, notes that include my own fantasies, emotional experiences, and physical sensations.

Countertransference interpretations can even enable a reactively hostile frightened patient to *begin* treatment. A woman was convinced that her characterological disturbance and multiple psychosomatic symptoms, predominantly gastrointestinal, were products of her having been sexually molested during her early childhood, although she had no memory of such an event. She refused to enter psychotherapy with any of a series of analysts whom she consulted after drug therapy had proved ineffective, because none would vouchsafe that he believed that her symptomatology was the result of such early molestation. Finally, I chose not to deal with her demand at face value but instead depended on my experiencing internal anxiety and gastrointestinal cramping while listening to her litany and observing her tension and underarm perspiration. I told her that I could not know on the basis of her stated history or my medical and psychiatric knowledge that her belief was accurate, but that I felt certain that she had been severely psychically traumatized while very young on the basis of my emotional and physical reactions to her presentation of her complaints. Relieved and intrigued, she promptly entered psychoanalytic treatment, which was remarkably successful.

Analysts suddenly began to present and publish studies devoted specifically to countertransference at midcentury, perhaps beginning with Winnicott's (1947) "Hate in the Countertransference," but soon to be followed by contributions such as those of Lacan (1951), Little (1951, 1957), Nacht (1963), and A. Reich (1951).

Many psychoanalysts agree that the earliest systematic and valuable work toward developing a theory of countertransference was done by Heiman (1950, 1960) and Racker (1952, 1953, 1957, 1960), who apparently worked independently, each without knowledge of the thinking of the other. The contributions of Rosenfeld (1965, 1987) have been overlooked by many. This may be because he did not use the word *countertransference* in any title until very late in his career. While depicting himself as an orthodox Kleinian, in his earliest publication dealing with psychotic states, Rosenfeld (1947) notes his use of countertransference reactions as guides to interpretation. He first uses the word *countertransference* in 1952 while discussing the difficulties in interpreting to schizophrenics: "Our countertransference is frequently the only guide" (p. 126). No doubt Rosenfeld wanted to protect his relations with Melanie Klein (his analyst), who was so incensed with Paula Heimann that their previously cordial relationship was terminated when Heimann delivered her 1950 paper at the Zurich conference (see De Paola 1993). Similarly, Klein was hostile toward Little (1951) following her advocating the use in treatment of countertransference reactions, as, it has been said, she would be eventually toward Hanna Segal (Conran 1991).[9] The Balints' (E. Balint 1974, M. Balint 1957, Balint and Balint 1959) advocating in the early 1950's the conscious use in therapy by the analyst of his emotional reactions to patients has also been overlooked (see also M. Balint 1968).

SUMMARY

During the past half century, countertransference has come to be seen as a valuable tool in our therapeutic armamentarium, rather than solely as an impediment to psychoanalytic treatment. This change of attitude resulted from psychoanalysts' coming to view their own task to be to interpret the interactions of both patient and therapist on an intrapsychic level, rather than about the patient's intrapsychic dynamics, and understanding those interactions in terms of the constant interplay between analysand and analyst, involving their mutual introjection of the other's projective identifications. An important element in the change in therapists' attitudes regarding the types of patients who should be included as analytic subjects is the increased understanding of the nature of the interaction between therapist and patient during the inevitable regressions in the service of treatment, an understanding that can be usefully interpreted.

Although Freud is generally understood to have originally viewed countertransference solely as an impediment to analysis, from the outset he was ambivalent in regard to this issue and may have believed that there was a relationship between transference and countertransference and extrasensory perception.

Heiman and Racker are credited generally with having the major roles in the development of a systematic theory of countertransference, and the important work of others, notably Rosenfeld and Balint, has probably been underplayed.

---

9. It may be that Segal's (1981) overtly advocating the use of countertransference only followed Klein's death.

References

Abraham, K. (1924). A short study of the development of the libido, viewed in the light of mental disorders. In *Selected Papers of Karl Abraham*, pp. 418–479. London: Hogarth, 1948.

Balint, E. (1974). A portrait of Michael Balint: the development of his ideas on the use of the drug "doctor." *International Journal of Psychiatric Medicine* 5:211–222.

——— (1991). Commentary on Philip Bromberg's "On Knowing One's Patient Inside Out." *Psychoanalytic Dialogue* 1:423–430.

Balint, E., and Balint, M. (1959). On transference and counter-transference. *International Journal of Psycho-Analysis* 20:223–230.

Balint, M. (1957). *The Doctor, His Patient and the Illness*. London: Pitman.

——— (1968). *The Basic Fault. Therapeutic Aspects of Regression*. New York: Brunner/Mazel, 1979.

Binswanger, H. (1956). Freuds psychosentherapie. *Psyche* (Heidelberg) 10: 357–366.

Bion, W. R. (1962). *Learning from Experience*. London: Heineman.

——— (1967). *Second Thoughts; Selected Papers on Psycho-analysis*. New York: Jason Aronson.

Bollas, C. (1987). *The Shadow of the Object: Psychoanalysis of the Unknown Thought*. London: Free Association.

Boyer, L. B. (1967). Historical development of psychoanalytic therapy of the schizophrenias: contributions of the followers of Freud. In *Psychoanalytic Treatment of Schizophrenic and Characterological Disorders*, ed. L. B. Boyer and P. L. Giovacchini, pp. 80-142. New York: Science House.

——— (1979a). Countertransference with severely regressed patients. In *Countertransference: The Therapist's Contribution to the Therapeutic Situation*, ed. L. Epstein and A. H. Feiner, pp. 347–374. New York: Jason Aronson.

——— (1979b). *Childhood and Folklore. A Psychoanalytic Study of Apache Folklore*. New York: Library of Psychological Anthropology.

——— (1983). *The Regressed Patient*. New York: Jason Aronson.

——— (1985). Christmas "neurosis" reconsidered. In *Depressive States and Their Treatment*, ed. V. Volkan, pp. 297–316. Northvale, NJ: Jason Aronson.

——— (1986). Technical aspects of treating the regressed patient. *Contemporary Psychoanalysis* 22:25–44.

——— (1988). Thinking of the interview as though it were a dream. *Contemporary Psychoanalysis* 24:275–281.

——— (1989). Countertransference and technique in working with the regressed patient: further remarks. *International Journal of Psycho-Analysis* 70:701–714.

——— (1990). Introduction: psychoanalytic intervention in treating the regressed patient. In *Master Clinicians on Treating the Regressed Patient*, ed. L. B. Boyer and P. L. Giovacchini, pp. 1-32. Northvale, NJ: Jason Aronson.

———— (1992). Roles played by music as revealed during countertransference facilitated transference regression. *International Journal of Psycho-Analysis* 73:55–70.

Boyer, L. B., Boyer, R. M., Dithrich, C. W., et al. (1989). The relation between psychological states and acculturation among the Tanaina and Upper Tanana Indians of Alaska. *Ethos* 17:387–427.

Bromberg, P. M. (1991). Reply to Enid Balint's commentary on Philip Bromberg's "On Knowing One's Patient Inside Out." *Psychoanalytic Dialogue* 1:431–437.

Conran, M. (1991). Personal communication.

Crapanzano, V. (1980). *Tuhami: Portrait of a Moroccan.* Chicago: University of Chicago Press.

Davis, D. M. (1991). Review of the psychoanalytic literature on countertransference. *International Journal of Short-Term Psychotherapy* 6:131–143.

De Paola, H. F. B. (1993). Contributions and limitations of Kleinian theory to the analysis of psychotic patients. In *Master Clinicians on Treating the Regressed Patient, Vol. 2,* ed. L. B. Boyer and P. L. Giovacchini, pp. 143–169. Northvale, NJ: Jason Aronson.

Devereux, G. (1967). *From Anxiety to Method in the Behavioral Sciences.* The Hague: Mouton.

————, ed. (1953). *Psychoanalysis and the Occult.* New York: International Universities Press.

De Vos, G. A., and Boyer, L. B. (1989). *Symbolic Analysis Cross-Culturally.* Berkeley, CA: University of California Press.

Eisenbud, J. (1953). Psychiatric contributions to parapsychology; a review. In *Psychoanalysis and the Occult,* ed. G. Devereux, pp. 3–15. New York: International Universities Press.

Epstein, L., and Feiner, A. H., eds. (1979). *Countertransference: The Therapist's Contribution to the Therapeutic Situation.* New York: Jason Aronson.

Etchegoyen, R. H. (1991). *The Fundamentals of Psychoanalytic Technique.* London: Karnac.

Faimberg, H. (1992). The countertransference position and the countertransference. *International Journal of Psycho-Analysis* 73:541–547.

Federn, P. (1952). *Ego Psychology and the Psychoses.* New York: Basic Books.

Fenichel, O. (1931). Respiratory introjection. In *The Collected Papers of Otto Fenichel,* pp. 221–240. New York: W. W. Norton, 1953.

———— (1945). *The Psychoanalytic Theory of the Neuroses.* New York: W. W. Norton.

Fliess, R. (1953). Counter-transference and counter-identification. *Journal of the American Psychoanalytic Association* 1:268–284.

Freud, S. (1899). A premonitory dream fulfilled. *Standard Edition* 5:623–625.

———— (1901). The psychopathology of everyday life. *Standard Edition* 6.

———— (1904). Premonitions and chance. (An excerpt.) In *Psychoanalysis and the*

Occult, ed. G. Devereux, pp. 52–55. New York: International Universities Press, 1953.

——— (1910). The future prospects for psycho-analytic therapy. *Standard Edition* 11:139–152.

——— (1912). Recommendations to physicians practicing psycho-analysis. *Standard Edition* 14:109–120.

——— (1915). Instincts and their vicissitudes. *Standard Edition* 14:108–140.

——— (1917). Mourning and melancholia. *Standard Edition* 14:237–260.

——— (1921). Psychoanalysis and telepathy. In *Psychoanalysis and the Occult*, ed. G. Devereux. New York: International Universities Press, 1953. Originally published with no title in "Schriften aus dem Nachlass," *Gesammelte Werke* 17:25–44, London: Imago. See also *Standard Edition* 18:175–194.

——— (1922). Dreams and telepathy. *Standard Edition* 18:195–220.

——— (1925). The occult significance of dreams. *Standard Edition* 19:135–140.

——— (1933a). New introductory lectures. *Standard Edition* 22:3–184.

——— (1933b). Dreams and occultism. New introductory lectures. *Standard Edition* 22:31–56.

Gaddini, E. (1981). Il problema mente-corpo en psicoanalisis. *Rivista di Psicoanalisi* 27:3–29.

Gaddini, R. (1985). Early psychosomatic symptoms and the tendency toward integration. *Journal of the Squiggle Foundation* 1:49–56.

——— (1990). Regression and its uses in treatment. In *Master Clinicians on Treating the Regressed Patient*, ed. L. B. Boyer and P. L. Giovacchini, pp. 227–244. Northvale, NJ: Jason Aronson.

Garma, A. (1962). *El Psicoanálisis: Teoría, Clínica, y Técnica*. Buenos Aires: Paidós.

Gill, M. M., Newman, R., and Redlich, F. C. (1954). *The Initial Interview in Psychiatric Practice*. New York: International Universities Press.

Giovacchini, P. L. (1989). *Countertransference Triumphs and Catastrophes*. Northvale, NJ: Jason Aronson.

Glover, E. (1955). *The Technique of Psycho-Analysis*. London: Balliére Tindall and Cox.

Goldberg, L. (1979). Remarks on the transference–countertransference in psychotic states. *International Journal of Psycho-Analysis* 60:347–356.

Good, B. J., Herrara, H., Good, M. J. D., and Cooper, J. (1982). Reflexivity and countertransference. *Culture, Medicine and Psychiatry* 6:281–303.

Grinberg, L. (1957). Perturbaciónes en la interpretación por la contraidentificación proyectiva. *Revista de Psicoanálisis* 14:23–28.

——— (1962). On a specific aspect of countertransference due to the patient's projective identification. *International Journal of Psycho-Analysis* 43:436–440.

——— (1979). Countertransference and counteridentification. *Contemporary Psychoanalysis* 15:226–247.

Grosskurth, P. (1986). *Melanie Klein: Her World and Work*. New York: Knopf.

Grotstein, J. S. (1981). *Splitting and Projective Identification*. New York: Jason Aronson.

———— (1992). Personal communication.

Hann-Kende, E. (1933). On the role of transference and countertransference in psychoanalysis. In *Psychoanalysis and the Occult*, ed. G. Devereux, pp. 158–167. New York: International Universities Press, 1953.

Heimann, P. (1950). Counter-transference. *International Journal of Psycho-Analysis* 31:81–84.

———— (1960). Counter-transference. *British Journal of Medical Psychology* 33:9–15.

Jones, E. (1953). *The Life and Work of Sigmund Freud, 1856–1900. The Formative Years and the Great Discoveries*. New York: Basic Books.

———— (1955). *The Life and Work of Sigmund Freud, 1901–1919. Years of Maturity*. New York: Basic Books.

Joseph, B. (1975). The patient who is difficult to reach. In *Tactics and Techniques in Psychoanalytic Therapy. Vol. 2: Countertransference*, ed. P. L. Giovacchini, with the collaboration of A. Flarsheim and L. B. Boyer, pp. 205–216. New York: Jason Aronson.

———— (1982). Addiction to near death. *International Journal of Psycho-Analysis* 63:449–456.

Klein, M. (1946). Notes on some schizoid mechanisms. In *Envy and Gratitude and Other Works, 1946–1963*, pp. 1–24. New York: Delacorte Press/Seymour Laurence, 1975.

Kracke, W. (1981). Kagwahiv mourning: dreams of a bereaved father. *Ethos* 9:258–275.

Lacan, J. (1951). Intervention sur le transfert. In *Écrits*, pp. 215–226. Paris: Éditions du seuil, 1966.

Langs, J. (1976). *The Therapeutic Interaction. Vol. 2: A Critical Overview and Synthesis*. New York: Jason Aronson.

Leonard, M. (1961). Problems in identification and ego development in twins. *Psychoanalytic Study of the Child* 16:300–320. New York: International Universities Press.

Levine, R. A. (1966). *Dreams and Deeds*. Chicago: University of Chicago Press.

Levine, S. (1981). Dreams of the informant about the researcher. *Ethos* 9:276–293.

Lewin, B. D. (1930). Kotschmieren, Menses und weibliches Ueber-Ich. *Internationale Zeitschrift für Psychoanalyse* 16:43–56.

Little, M. I. (1951). Counter-transference and the patient's response to it. In *Transference Neurosis and Transference Psychosis*. New York: Jason Aronson, 1981.

———— (1957). "R"—the analyst's total response to his patient's needs. *Transference Neurosis and Transference Psychosis*. New York: Jason Aronson, 1981.

Major, R., ed. (1983). *Cahiers Confrontation*. No. 10. Paris: Aubier-Montaigne.

Malcolm, R. R. (1970). El espejo: una fantasía sexual perversa en una mujer, vista como defensa contra un derrumbe psicótico. *Revista de Psicoanálisis* 27:793–826. Translated and published in *Melanie Klein Today. Developments in theory and practice. Vol. 2: Mainly Practice,* ed. E. B. Spillius, pp. 115–137. London: Routledge, 1988.

May, R. (1990). The idea of history in psychoanalysis: Freud and the "Wolf-Man." *Psychoanalytic Psychology* 7:163–183.

McDougall, J. (1978). Countertransference and primitive communication. In *Plea for a Measure of Abnormality,* pp. 247–298. New York: International Universities Press.

———— (1989). *Theaters of the Body. A Psychoanalytic Approach to Psychosomatic Illness.* New York: W. W. Norton.

McLaughlin, J. T. (1975). The sleepy analyst: some observations on states of consciousness in the analyst at work. *Journal of the American Psychoanalytic Association* 23:363–382.

Meissner, W. W. (1987). Projection and projective identification. In *Projection, Identification, Projective Identification,* ed. J. Sandler, pp. 27–49. Madison, CT: International Universities Press.

Meltzer, D. (1966). The relation of anal masturbation to projection identification. *International Journal of Psycho-Analysis* 47:335–342.

———— (1978). A note on introjective processes. In the *Bulletin of the British Psycho-Analytical Society,* October 14–21, privately circulated.

Menzies-Lyth, I. (1983). Some pathological aspects of introjection. Unpublished paper read at the 9th Brazilian Psychoanalytic Congress.

Money-Kyrle, R. (1956). Normal counter-transference and some of its deviations. *International Journal of Psycho-Analysis* 37:360–366.

Nacht, S. (1963). *La presence du psychanalyse.* Paris: Presses Universitaires France.

Ogden, T. H. (1982). *Projective Identification and Psychotherapeutic Technique.* New York: Jason Aronson.

———— (1985). On potential space. *International Journal of Psycho-Analysis* 66:129–142.

———— (1986). *The Matrix of the Mind: Aspects of Object Relations Theory.* Northvale, NJ: Jason Aronson.

———— (1989). *The Primitive Edge of Experience.* Northvale, NJ: Jason Aronson.

———— (1992). The dialectically constituted/decentred subject of psychoanalysis: II. The Contributions of Klein and Winnicott. *International Journal of Psycho-Analysis* 73:613–626.

———— (1994). The analytic third: working with intersubjective clinical facts. *International Journal of Psychoanalysis* 75:3–20.

Orr, D. W. (1954). Transference and countertransference: a historical survey. *Journal of the American Psychoanalytic Association* 2:621–670.

O'Shaughnessy, E. (1983). Words and working through. *International Journal of Psycho-Analysis* 64:281–290.

Parsons, A. (1969). *Belief, Magic, and Anomie: Essays in Psychosocial Anthropology.* New York: The Free Press.

Pick, I. (1985). Working through in the counter-transference. In *Melanie Klein Today. Vol. 2: Mainly Practice,* ed. E. Spillius, pp. 34–47. London: Routledge, 1988.

Racker, E. (1952). Observaciones sobre la contratransferencia como instrumento técnico; comunicación preliminar. *Revista de Psicoanálisis* 9:342–354.

———— (1953). A contribution to the problem of countertransference. *International Journal of Psycho-Analysis* 34:313–324.

———— (1957). The meanings and uses of countertransference. *Psychoanalytic Quarterly* 26:303–357.

———— (1960). *Transference and Countertransference.* New York: International Universities Press, 1968. (Published originally as *Estudios sobre Técnica Psicoanalítica.* Buenos Aires: Paidós.)

Reich, A. (1951). On Counter-transference. *International Journal of Psycho-Analysis* 32:25–31.

Reich, W. (1933). *Character Analysis.* New York: Orgone.

Reik, T. (1924). Some remarks on the study of resistances. *International Journal of Psycho-Analysis* 5:141–154.

———— (1933). New ways in psychoanalytic technique. *International Journal of Psycho-Analysis* 14:321–334.

———— (1948). *Listening with the Third Ear.* New York: Farrar-Straus.

———— (1953). *The Haunting Melody. Psychoanalytic Experiences in Life and Music.* New York: Farrar, Straus & Young.

Rosenfeld, H. A. (1947). Analysis of a schizophrenic state with depersonalization. *International Journal of Psycho-Analysis* 28:130–139.

———— (1952). Notes on the psycho-analysis of the superego conflict of an acute schizophrenic patient. *International Journal of Psycho-Analysis* 33:111–131.

———— (1965). *Psychotic States: A Psycho-Analytic Approach.* London: Hogarth.

———— (1987). *Impasse and Interpretation.* London: Tavistock.

Scharff, J. S. (1992). *Projective and Introjective Identification and the Use of the Therapist's Self.* Northvale, NJ: Jason Aronson.

Searles, H. F. (1979). *Countertransference and Related Subjects.* New York: International Universities Press.

Segal, H. (1952). A psycho-analytical approach to aesthetics. *International Journal of Psycho-Analysis* 33:196–207. Also in *The Work of Hanna Segal,* pp. 185–206. New York: Jason Aronson, 1981.

———— (1957). Notes on symbol formation. *International Journal of Psycho-Analysis* 38:391–397. Also in *The Work of Hanna Segal,* pp. 49–65. New York: Jason Aronson.

———— (1974). Delusion and artistic creativity. *International Review of Psycho-Analysis* 1:135–141. Also in *The Work of Hanna Segal,* pp. 207–216. New York: Jason Aronson, 1981.

——— (1981). *The Work of Hanna Segal.* New York: Jason Aronson.

Sharpe, E. F. (1927). Symposium on child-analysis. *International Journal of Psycho-Analysis* 8:380–384.

Spillius, E. B., ed. (1988). *Melanie Klein Today. Developments in Theory and Practice. Vol. 1: Mainly Theory.* London: Routledge.

Spiro, M. E. (1992). The "Primary Process" revisited. In *The Psychoanalytic Study of Society* 17:171–180, ed. L. B. Boyer and R. M. Boyer; assoc. ed. S. M. Sonnenberg. Hillsdale, NJ: Analytic Press.

Stärcke, A. (1920). A reversal of the libido sign in delusions of persecution. *International Journal of Psycho-Analysis* 1:231–234.

Stein, H. F. (1994). Massive social change and the experience of loss: a study in the cultural psychology of mourning in a North American Great Plains community. *Psychoanalytic Study of Society* 19:273–310.

Stekel, W. (1920). *Der telepathische Traum.* [*The Telepathic Dream.*] Berlin: Johannes Baum.

Stone, L. (1961). *The Psychoanalytic Situation.* New York: International Universities Press.

Tobin, J. (1986). (Counter)transference and failure in intercultural therapy. *Ethos* 14:120–143.

van Ophuijsen, J. H. W. (1920). On the origin of the feeling of persecution. *International Journal of Psycho-Analysis* 1:235–239.

Volkan, V. D. (1981). Transference and countertransference. An examination from the point of view of internalized object relations. In *Object and Self: A Developmental Approach*, ed. S. Tuttman, C. Kaye, and M. Zimmerman, pp. 429–451. New York: International Universities Press.

Weigert, E. (1954). Counter-transference and self-analysis. *International Journal of Psycho-Analysis* 35:242–246.

Winnicott, D. W. (1947). Hate in the countertransference. *Collected Papers: Through Paediatrics to Psycho-analysis*, pp. 194–203. New York: Basic Books, 1958.

——— (1958). *Collected Papers: Through Paediatrics to Psycho-analysis.* New York: Basic Books.

——— (1960). The theory of the parent–infant relationship. In *The Maturational Processes and the Facilitating Environment*, pp. 37–55. New York: International Universities Press, 1965.

——— (1965). *The Maturational Processes and the Facilitating Environment.* New York: International Universities Press.

——— (1971a). The place where we live. In *Playing and Reality*, pp. 104–110. New York: International Universities Press.

——— (1971b). Playing: a theoretical statement. In *Playing and Reality*, pp. 38–52. New York: International Universities Press.

2

Psychoanalytic Treatment of the Borderline Disorders Today

Prior to perhaps thirty years ago, most of those psychoanalysts whose dominant theoretical orientation was that of ego psychology and the structural theory held that near-classical psychoanalysis should be used solely in the therapy of neurotics and that individuals whose personality structure lay nearer the psychotic end of the continuum of psychopathological states were best treated by other means. Subsequently, in the United States, psychoanalysis with relatively few parameters (Eissler 1953) has come to be used more commonly in the treatment of people who are afflicted with at least the less primitive varieties of those conditions that have come to be subsumed under the rubric *borderline personality* (Meissner 1984). It is the thesis of this chapter that a major reason for this change is to be found in the infusion into the thinking of the ego psychologists of portions of the thinking of the so-called British schools of psychoanalysis concerning the development of object relations and a resultant better understanding of transference–countertransference phenomena. My conclusion was reached impressionistically rather than through a systematic literature review.

In my opinion, Kernberg, who migrated to the United States from Chile, has been the person most influential in two significant areas. First, from his position of respectability in the Menninger Foundation, with its ego psychological-structural point of view, he made aspects of the thinking of some members of the British schools, especially the Kleinians, palatable to ego psychologists, something the English writers themselves had been unable to do (Kernberg 1972, 1975a, 1976, 1980). To my knowledge, no United States psychoanalytic training institution gave courses in the thinking of the British schools prior to Kernberg's synthetic clarifications; even now, some do not. Second, standing on the shoulders of others and in a changing therapeutic climate, he finally made more acceptable to United States therapists the psychoanalytic treatment of borderline patients.

Two other Latin American psychoanalysts, the Argentinians Racker and Grinberg, through their writings in English, have enhanced, with Kernberg, ego psychologists' comprehension of the uses and functions of the primitive defensive mechanisms *splitting* and *projective identification*, and the use of the therapist as a container of the fantasied externalizations (Barchillon 1963, Grinberg 1962, 1976, 1979, Racker 1953, 1957, 1959, 1960, 1968). In the United States literature on countertransference that appeared before the late 1970s, I have found their writings to be cited more often than those of English members of the British object relations theorists, with the exception of Winnicott.

HISTORICAL CONSIDERATIONS

Although adequate historical reviews of the borderline personality disorder and its treatment appear in English (Langs 1976, Mack 1975, Meissner 1984), the most thorough summation that has come to my attention is that of Paz and colleagues (1975, 1976a,b; see Boyer 1980).

While Morel (1857), Kahlbaum (1863), Kraepelin (1883), and Magnan (1893) attempted to define psychopathological conditions that lie between the psychoses and the neuroses, the United States psychiatrists Hughes and Rosse, in 1884 and 1890, were the first to use the term *borderline insanity*. The term *borderline psychosis* appeared in the English literature written prior to the middle of this century, but it seems that Eisenstein (1951), Wolberg (1952), and Knight (1953) first wrote of "borderline states and conditions" in the 1950s. Knight clearly equated them with borderline psychoses. The name most frequently given previously to the group of patients now called borderline was Bleuler's (1911) *latent schizophrenia*. Many other titles have had limited use, such as Claude's (1930) *schizomanie*, Zilboorg's (1941) *ambulatory schizophrenia*,

Deutsch's (1942) *as-if personalities*, Freud's (1938) *grave neurosis*, Merenciano's (1945) *psicosis mitis*, Mahler's (Mahler et al. 1949) *benign psychosis*, Frosch's (1964) *psychotic character*, and Eisenstein's (1958; Bergeret 1974, Timsit 1971) *etats-limities*.

These disorders were generally assumed to be constitutionally generated until Hendricks (1936) and Deutsch (1942) stressed developmental defects and particularly deficiencies in identificatory processes and suggested that faulty socialization contributed significantly to the causation of such disorders.

THE DIAGNOSIS

Concerning the diagnosis borderline personality disorder, I need remind you only that it is now used internationally, following particularly the contributions of Kernberg (1967, 1975a), Grinker and colleagues (1968), and Gunderson (Gunderson and Kolb 1978, Gunderson and Singer 1975) concerning adults, and those of Ekstein and Wallerstein (1954), Geleerd (1958), and S. K. Rosenfeld and Sprince (1963) to children (see also Shapiro 1978, Shapiro et al. 1975, Zinner and E. Shapiro 1975). Very briefly, the term is applied to a group of people who share a chronic and stable condition that has a variable but similar symptomatic constellation, a specific pathological characterological organization, a particular configuration of internalized objects and object relations, and genetic and dynamic characteristics, which often occur only at times of stress. Transient psychotic episodes are fairly common. Some psychiatrists today diagnose schizophrenia only if a psychotic regression persists for six months.

PSYCHOPATHOLOGY

Borderline pathology is related to difficulties in management of impulse and affect, is perceived most typically in interpersonal relationships, and emerges most clearly in unstructured situations. In treatment there is diagnostic relevance in the development of transference psychoses (Boyer 1970, Kernberg 1975a, Peto 1967, Timsit 1971). Indeed, it is common for analysis to be undertaken with a presumed neurotic whose diagnosis is changed because of a primitive transference reaction. These patients have difficulties in interpersonal relationships, experiencing in particular a pervasive sense of loneliness and believing that their problems arise from outside themselves. Sexual deviancy is common, and many of these patients have antisocial tendencies. They may be distinguished from schizophrenics by a greater capacity for reality testing, by an incapacity to be alone, and by having heightened rather than flattened affect. They may have severe neurotic and perverse symptomatology stemming from varying levels of psychosexual development, and psychosomatic problems are common. There is a selectively deficient modulation of drives in regressed patients and many observers have stressed the central conflict related to the presence of untamed aggression (Fromm-Reichmann 1950, Hartmann 1953, Jacobson 1967, Klein 1946, Lidz and Lidz 1952). The vicissitudes of the expression of primitive aggression result in therapists' empathically experiencing eeriness, anxiety, and confusion.

In my practice a high percentage of these patients suffer also from a severe narcissistic personality disorder, one more serious than is found in the patients described by Kohut (1971).

It is my impression that most therapists who treat these patients psychoanalytically have come to agree with Rosenfeld (1965) that they use a constellation of primitive defenses, characteristically including splitting and projective identification (Garma 1978, Giovacchini 1975a,b, 1979, 1986, Grotstein 1975, 1981, Kernberg 1975a, 1976, Malin and Grotstein 1966, Ogden 1982, 1986). All observers agree that the borderline outcome results from a specific failure in ego development characterized by a fixation at an early stage in the development of internalized object relations and that this has resulted in large part, if not totally, to the mothering person's inability to provide an adequate facilitating environment (Winnicot 1965). With the successful negotiation of the rapprochement subphase of separation-individuation (Mahler et al. 1975), the child develops the capacity for ambivalence and object constancy. Most investigators agree that the borderline has failed to traverse the rapprochement phase. On the basis of careful observation of the transference relations developed by borderline patients of more primitive varieties, Giovacchini (1984, 1986) demonstrates the psychopathology of these patients to be at times rooted in earlier periods of development.

COUNTERTRANSFERENCE

In 1910 Freud introduced the concept of countertransference, deeming it to be the repetition in the therapeutic relationship of the analyst's irrational, previously acquired attitudes. Prior to Hann-Kende's suggestion in 1933 that the emotional responses of the therapist could be used as facilitators of the analytic process, psychoanalysts uniformly viewed countertransference in a pejorative light (Ferenczi 1919, Gruhle 1915, Stern 1924). I believe that the next therapist to recommend the use of countertransference as an analytic tool was Little in 1951. My own conscious efforts to use my emotional responses to the patient in the service of treatment encompass a period of more than twenty-five years (Boyer 1986).

There is a large literature pertaining to countertransference reactions in the analyses of neurotic patients, including extensive reviews (Glover 1955, Langs 1976, Orr 1954, Reich 1960). During the past forty-odd years, increasing attention has been paid to the role of countertransference in the treatment of regressed patients, both as an impediment to and as a facilitator of the therapeutic process (Arbiser 1978, Bion 1967, 1973, Epstein and Feiner 1979, Giovacchini et al. 1975, Kernberg 1975b, Kusnetzoff and Maldovsky 1977, Meissner 1986, Modell 1968, Nadelson 1977, Prado Galvão 1966, Searles 1979, Volkan 1976, 1982). Therapists who use analytic treatment for regressed patients note that their emotional responses with them differ greatly from those experienced with neurotic patients.

Analysts have been long concerned with the means by which the psychological attributes of one person are assumed by another; many have written about the influence of patients' introjection of analysts' attributes on the transference relationship (Fairbairn 1952, Freud 1915, Giovacchini 1975a, Guntrip 1961, Hartmann 1939, Loewald 1960, Schafer 1968). Fenichel (1945) was the first to note that the analysts' countertransferences are determined largely by their introjection of patients' attributes; subsequent authors have corroborated his observation (Federn 1952, Fliess 1953, Weigert 1954).

Although I treated borderline patients successfully prior to my understanding and incorporating some of the thinking of the British schools, a review of my detailed records reveals that before then, the incidences of impasses due to unresolved countertransference issues was higher and such impasses were more serious and at times led to the termination of treatment. Since I have understood the transference–countertransference interaction in terms of patients' use of the primitive defense mechanisms splitting and projective identification, no impasse has proceeded thus far. I have been more at ease with patients and believe their analyses have been more successful.

The use of splitting involves reversion to an omnipotent fantasy that parts of the personality or internal objects can be split, projected into external objects, and controlled (Klein 1946). In their transference these patients split the love and hate associated with internalized relationships to avoid the anxiety that would result if they were experienced simultaneously (Kernberg 1975a). During treatment, the patient's use of splitting is generally fairly obvious and causes the experienced analyst little difficulty.

It is much more difficult to deal with projective identification. An ever-growing number of therapists turn to the concept of projective identification to understand their countertransference responses and to use those responses as facilitators of therapeusis (Bio 1967, Carpinacci et al. 1963, Cesio 1973, Giovacchini 1975b, Grinberg 1957, 1962, Grotstein 1981, D. Rosenfeld and Mordo 1973, Siquier de Failla 1963, Zinner and R. Shapiro 1972).

Once the patient has fantasized his projection of an unwelcome aspect of himself into the therapist, he thereby maintains unconscious connection to the therapist but consciously perceives the analyst to be different from himself. Usually the uncomfortable projected aspect involves primitive aggression and the patient's fear of its potential effects on others or himself, but love that is thought to be destructive is treated similarly at times (Boyer 1982, Giovacchini 1984, Klein 1946, Searles 1958). Racker (1968) wrote of concordant and complementary countertransference identifications. In the former the analyst identifies with the corresponding part of the patient's psychical apparatus, that is, ego with ego and superego with superego, and can behave empathically because he experiences as his own the central emotion being experienced by the patient. In complementary countertransference, the analyst identifies with the internalized transference object of the patient. On the basis of the therapist's unresolved internal conflicts, he cannot perceive the projection as a product of the patient's transference and analyze it objectively and in a timely manner. He cannot serve as a safe container for the projection until it has been modified by the patient's analysis and it is possible for the patient to reaccept it as a relatively comfortable part of himself. An example of complementary counteridentification is one in which the analyst unconsciously identifies with a superego formation connected with a forbidding father, seeks aggressively to control the patient, and probably causes a therapeutic impasse (Boyer 1983, Giovacchini and Boyer 1975). Grinberg (1979) holds that in complementary counteridentification, analysts always react in ways that correspond with their own unconscious conflicts. He also describes projective counteridentification and illustrates how it may lead to treatment impediments.

Space does not allow further elucidation of this fascinating area or clinical material to demonstrate adequately how understanding the primitive defensive mechanisms splitting and projective identification make countertransference more understandable and more easily manageable. Suffice it to say that during recent years I have come to assume that many of my own emotional reactions, physical sensations, and fantasies that occur during the therapeutic hour, and sometimes in nighttime dreams, give me information about the problems my patients are dealing with that I have been unable to understand otherwise. Inquiries and interpretations made on the basis of my understanding of those personal phenomena facilitate the therapeutic process (Boyer 1986).

CONCLUSION

Early on, I commented that Kernberg was most instrumental in making acceptable the psychoanalytic treatment of borderline patients by United States therapists, and that the analytic climate had become more or less ready for his impact. I shall close this chapter by describing very briefly that climate and its development, which I believe to have two closely interwoven roots, the first essentially pragmatic and the other a continuing effort at diagnostic refinement.

Many analysts seem unaware that although Freud at one time declared psychoanalytic therapy to be unsuitable for patients with narcissistic disorders, he himself continued to use psychoanalysis to treat patients who would today be called borderline and, in at least one instance, a man whom he deemed to be "always psychotic" (Boyer and Giovacchini 1980). Many therapists sought to treat seriously regressed patients psychoanalytically during the period when the curative effect was presumed to result from making the unconscious conscious (Boyer and Giovacchini 1980), but met with scant success. Following the advent of the structural theory, an occasional pioneer such as Waelder (1924), Garma (1931), and Bullard (1940) qualifiedly recommended psychoanalytic treatment for regressed patients and indeed many tried again. However, with very few exceptions, such as Laforgue (1935), psychoanalytic therapists included many nonanalytic elements in their treatment methods. At the same time, an occasional analyst whose patients developed transference psychoses during their analytic regressions continued the classical approach without making an issue of his actions in print (Jacobson 1954, 1967, Lewin 1950). In England and South America, therapists were encouraged to work analytically with psychotics by the thinking and actions of the British schools and in the

United States by Sullivan, surely one of the earliest object relations theorists, despite the opacity of much of his writing (Greenberg and Mitchell 1983, Jacobson 1955). It seems almost redundant to mention the immense contributions of some of the Chestnut Lodge workers, such as Fromm-Reichmann (1950), Searles (1965), and Will (1964).

In the late 1940s and early 1950s a few young United States analysts, having noted empirically that Freud's idea that regressed patients were incapable of developing clinically usable transference relationships was wrong, set out to work experimentally with the psychoanalytic treatment with few parameters of those patients. Their work was reported in a panel discussion of the West Coast Psychoanalytic Societies in 1964. That discussion resulted in Giovacchini's and my first book (Boyer and Giovacchini 1967), recommending such treatment for many regressed patients, including selected schizophrenics who would now probably be called borderline. Its message was received with much interest and we were invited to present our ideas widely. They were greeted initially with strongly ambivalent reactions. Kernberg's contributions followed shortly and were greeted with less initial scepticism and surely less violent hostility.

Diagnoses have always carried predictive therapeutic implications. Patients who are labeled schizophrenic have been assumed to be treatable, if at all, largely by organic means, whether by Metrazol, insulin, electro-convulsive therapy, or, more recently, drugs. The inclusion of insight-oriented elements in the accompanying psychological treatment has been considered to have very limited applicability, except by a few, such as Bellak (1948), Federn (1952), and Nunberg (1948). By contrast, the inclusion of some interpretation of resistance and transference has been approved for patients diagnosed as severe characterological disorders and borderline conditions.

During the past forty-odd years a concerted effort has been made to develop criteria for establishing diagnostic categories for regressed patients. The effort has been largely successful, and as a result many patients who would have been denied insight-oriented therapy because they had been diagnosed as schizophrenic are now deemed eligible for such treatment.

References

Arbiser, A. (1978). Patología de la contratransferencia en los tratamientos interminables. *Revista de Psicoanálisis* 34:753–765.

Barchillon, J. (1963). Review of *Estudior Sobre Técnica Psicoanalítica* by Heinrich Racker. Buenos Aires: Paidos, 1960. *Psychoanalytic Quarterly* 32:427–431.

Bellak, L. (1948). *Dementia Praecox: The Past Decade's Work and Present Status. A Review and Evaluation.* New York: Grune & Stratton.

Bergeret, J. (1974). *La Depression et les Etats-Limites.* Paris: Payot.

Bion, W. R. (1967). *Second Thoughts.* London: Heinemann.

—— (1973). *Elements of Psychoanalysis.* New York: Jason Aronson.

Bleuler, E. (1911). *Dementia Praecox, or the Group of Schizophrenias.* New York: International Universities Press, 1950.

Boyer, L. B. (1970). Estados fronterizos: Una revisión del concepto y sus aplicaciones (Relatos de mesas redondas). *Revista de Psicoanáluis* 27:865–886.

—— (1980). Review of *Estructuras y Estados Fronterizos en Niños, Adolescentes y Adultos.* I. *Historia y Conceptualización* (1975), II. *Casuistica y Consideraciones Teorias* (1976), III. *Investigación y Terapeutica* (1976) by C. A. Paz, M. L. Pelento, and T. Olmos de Paz. Buenos Aires: Nueva Vision. *Journal of Nervous and Mental Diseases* 168:118–122.

—— (1982). Analytic experiences in work with regressed patients. In *Technical Factors in the Treatment of the Severely Disturbed Patient*, ed. P. L. Giovacchini and L. B. Boyer, pp. 65–106. New York: Jason Aronson.

—— (1983). *The Regressed Patient.* New York: Jason Aronson.

—— (1986). Technical aspects of treating the regressed patient. *Contemporary Psychoanalysis* 22:25–44.

Boyer, L. B., and Giovacchini, P. L. (1967). *Psychoanalytic Treatment of Schizophrenic and Characterological Disorders.* New York: Science House.

—— (1980). *Psychoanalytic Treatment of Schizophrenic, Borderline, and Characterological Disorders.* New York: Jason Aronson.

Bullard, D. M. (1940). Experiences in the psychoanalytic treatment of psychoses. *Psychoanalytic Quarterly* 9:493–504.

Carpinacci, J., Liberman, D., and Schlossberg, N. (1963). Perturbaciones en la comunicación y neurosis de contratransferencia. *Revista de Psicoanalisis* 20:63–69.

Cesio, F. (1973). Los fundamentales de la contratransferencia. *Revista de Psicoanálisis* 30:5–16.

Claude, H. (1930). Schizomanie a forme imaginative. *Encephale* 25:715–727.

Deutsch, H. (1942). Some forms of emotional disturbance and their relationship to schizophrenia. *Psychoanalytic Quarterly* 11:301–321.

Eisenstein, V. W. (1951). Differential psychotherapy of borderline states. *Psychiatric Review* 25:379–401.

—— (1958). Psychotherapie differentielle des etats-limites. In *Techniques Specialisées de la Psychotherapie*, ed. G. Bychowski and J. L. Desperet. Paris: Presses Universitaires de France.

Eissler, P. R. (1953). The effect of the structure of the ego on psychoanalytic technique. *Journal of the American Psychoanalytic Association* 1:104–143.

Ekstein, R., and Wallerstein, J. (1954). Observations on the psychology of borderline and psychotic children. *Psychoanalytic Study of the Child* 9:344–369. New York: International Universities Press.

Epstein, L., and Feiner, A. H. (1979). *Countertransference: The Therapist's Contribution to the Therapeutic Situation.* New York: Jason Aronson.

Fairbairn, W. R. D. (1952). *An Object Relations Theory of Personality.* New York: Basic Books.

Federn, P. (1952). *Ego Psychology and the Psychoses.* New York: Basic Books.

Fenichel, O. (1945). *The Psychoanalytic Theory of Neurosis.* New York: Norton.

Ferenczi, S. (1919). On the technique of psycho-analysis. IV. The control of the countertransference. In *Further Contributions to the Theory and Technique of Psycho-Analysis,* pp. 186–189. London: Hogarth, 1950.

Fliess, R. (1953). Counter-transference and counter-identification. *Journal of the American Psychoanalytic Association* 1:268–284.

Freud, S. (1910). The future prospects of psycho-analytic therapy. *Standard Edition* 11:139–157.

———— (1915). Observations on transference-love. *Standard Edition* 12:159–171.

———— (1938). Splitting of the ego in the process of defense. *Standard Edition* 23:275–279.

Fromm-Reichmann, F. (1950). *Principles of Intensive Psychotherapy.* Chicago: University of Chicago Press.

Frosch, J. (1964). The psychotic character: clinical psychiatric considerations. *Psychiatric Quarterly* 38:91–96.

Garma, A. (1931). La realidad exterior y los instinctos en la esquizofrenia. *Revista de Psicoanálisis* 2:56–82.

———— (1978). La esquizofrenia. In *El Psicoanálisis, Teoria, Clínica y Técnica,* pp. 191–216. Buenos Aires: Paidos.

Geleerd, E. R. (1958). Borderline states in childhood and adolescence. *Psychoanalytic Study of the Child* 13:279–295. New York: International Universities Press.

Giovacchini, P. L. (1975a). Self-projections in the narcissistic transference. *International Journal of Psychoanalytic Psychotherapy* 4:142–166.

———— (1975b). *Psychoanalysis of Character Disorders.* New York: Jason Aronson.

———— (1979). *Treatment of Primitive Mental States.* New York: Jason Aronson.

———— (1984). *Character Disorders and Adaptive Mechanisms.* New York: Jason Aronson.

———— (1986). *Developmental Disorders: The Transitional Space in Mental Breakdown and Creative Integration.* Northvale, NJ: Jason Aronson.

Giovacchini, P., and Boyer, L. B. (1975). El "impasse" psicoanalitico como un hecho terapeutico inevitable. *Revista de Psicoanálisis* 32:143–176.

Giovacchini, P., Flarsheim, A., and Boyer, L. B. (1975). *Tactics and Techniques in Psychoanalytic Therapy. II: Countertransference.* New York: Jason Aronson.

Glover, E. (1955). *The Technique of Psychoanalysis.* New York: International Universities Press.

Greenberg, J., and Mitchell, S. (1983). *Object Relations in Psychoanalytic Theory*. Cambridge: Harvard University Press.

Grinberg, L. (1957). Perturbaciones en la interpretación por la contratransferencia. *Revista de Psicoanálisis* 14:23–28.

———— (1962). On a specific aspect of countertransference due to the patient's projective identification. *International Journal of Psycho-Analysis* 43:436–440.

———— (1976). *Teoría de la Identificación*. Buenos Aires: Paidos.

———— (1979). Countertransference and projective counteridentification. *Contemporary Psychoanalysis* 15:226–247.

Grinker, R., Werble, B., and Drye, R. (1968). *The Borderline Syndrome: A Behavioral Study of Ego-Functions*. New York: Basic Books.

Grotstein, J. (1975). A theoretical rationale for psychoanalytic treatment of schizophrenia. In *Psychotherapy of Schizophrenia*, ed. L. R. Mosher and J. G. Gunderson. New York: Jason Aronson.

———— (1981). *Splitting and Projective Identification*. New York: Jason Aronson.

Gruhle, H. W. (1915). Selbstschilderung und Einführung; zugleich ein Versuch der Analyse des Falles Bantung. *Zeitschrift für die Gesamte Neurologic und Psychiatric* 28:148–231.

Gunderson, J. G., and Kolb, J. (1978). Discriminating features of borderline patients. *American Journal of Psychiatry* 135:792–796.

Gunderson, J. G., and Singer, M. (1975). Defining borderline patients. *American Journal of Psychiatry* 132:1–10.

Guntrip, H. (1961). *Personality Structure and Human Interaction*. New York: International Universities Press.

Hann-Kende, F. (1933). On the role of transference and countertransference in psychoanalysis. In *Psychoanalysis and the Occult*, ed. G. Devereux, pp. 158–167. New York: International Universities Press, 1953.

Hartmann, H. (1939). *Ego Psychology and the Problem of Adaptation*. New York: International Universities Press, 1958.

———— (1953). Contribution to the metapsychology of schizophrenia. In *Essays on Ego Psychology: Selected Problems in Psychoanalytic Theory*, pp. 182–206. New York: International Universities Press, 1964.

Hendricks, I. (1936). Ego development and certain character problems. *Psychoanalytic Quarterly* 5:320–346.

Hughes, C. H. (1884). Borderland psychiatric records—prodromal symptoms of psychic impairment. *Alienist and Neurologist* 5:85–91.

Jacobson, E. (1954). Contribution to the metapsychology of psychotic identifications. *Journal of the American Psychoanalytic Association* 2:239–262.

———— (1955). Sullivan's interpersonal theory of psychiatry. *Journal of the American Psychoanalytic Association* 3:102–108.

———— (1967). *Psychotic Conflict and Reality*. New York: International Universities Press.

Kahlbaum, K. (1863). *Die Gruppierung der Psychischen Krankheiten und die Einteilung der Seelenstorungen.* Danzig: A. W. Kaufman.

Kernberg, O. (1967). Borderline personality organization. *Journal of the American Psychoanalytic Association* 15:641–685.

——— (1972). Critique of the Kleinian School. In *Tactics and Techniques in Psychoanalytic Therapy*, ed. P. L. Giovacchini, pp. 62–93. New York: Science House.

——— (1975a). *Borderline Conditions and Pathological Narcissism.* New York: Jason Aronson.

——— (1975b). Transference and countertransference in the treatment of borderline patients. *Strecker Monograph Series, No. XII.* Philadelphia: Institute of Pennsylvania Hospital.

——— (1976). *Object Relations Theory and Clinical Psychoanalysis.* New York: Jason Aronson.

——— (1980). *Internal World and External Reality.* New York: Jason Aronson.

Klein, M. (1946). Notes on some schizoid mechanisms. *International Journal of Psycho-Analysis* 27:99–110.

Knight, R. P. (1953). Borderline states. In *Selected Papers of Robert P. Knight*, ed. S. C. Miller, pp. 208–222. New York: Basic Books, 1972.

Kohut, H. (1971). *The Analysis of the Self. A Systematic Approach to the Treatment of the Narcissistic Disorders.* New York: International Universities Press.

Kraepelin, E. (1883). *Dementia Praecox and Paraphrenia.* Edinburgh: Livingston, 1925.

Kusnetzoff, J., and Maldovsky, D. (1977). Aportes el estudio de una paciente borderline de base esquizoide. Analisis componencial y consideracion de los "lugares psiquicos." *Revista de Psicoanalisis* 34:803–842.

Laforgue, R. (1935). Contribution à l'etude de la schizophrenie. *Evolution Psychiatrique* 3:81–96.

Langs, R. J. (1976). *The Bipersonal Field.* New York: Jason Aronson.

Lewin, B. (1950). *The Psychoanalysis of Elation.* New York: W. W. Norton.

Lidz, R. W., and Lidz, T. (1952). Therapeutic considerations arising from the intense symbiotic needs of schizophrenic patients. In *Psychotherapy with Schizophrenics*, ed. E. B. Brody and F. C. Redlich, pp. 168–178. New York: International Universities Press.

Little, M. (1951). Counter-transference and the patient's response to it. *International Journal of Psycho-Analysis* 32:32–40.

Loewald, H. (1960). On the therapeutic action of psycho-analysis. *International Journal of Psycho-Analysis* 41:16–33.

Mack, J. E., ed. (1975). *Borderline States in Psychiatry.* New York: Grune & Stratton.

Magnan, V. (1893). *Leçons Classiques sur les Malades Mentale*, 2nd ed. Cited by A. Dureau, *La Grande Encyclopedie: Inventaire Raisonne des Sciences, des lettres et des Artes*, 19:950. Paris: H. Lamirault, 1886–1902.

Mahler, M., Pine, F., and Bergman, A. (1975). *The Psychological Birth of the Human Infant*. New York: Basic Books.

Mahler, M., Ross, J. R., and DeFries, Z. (1949). Clinical studies in benign and malignant cases of childhood psychosis (schizophrenia-like). *American Journal of Orthopsychiatry* 19:295–305.

Malin, A., and Grotstein, J. (1966). Projective identification in the therapeutic process. *International Journal of Psycho-Analysis* 47:26–31.

Meissner, W. W. (1984). *The Borderline Spectrum: Differential Diagnosis and Developmental Issues*. New York: Jason Aronson.

——— (1986). *Psychotherapy and the Paranoid Process*. Northvale, NJ: Jason Aronson.

Merenciano, M. (1945). *Psicosis Mitis*. Madrid: Diana Artes Graficas.

Modell, A. (1968). *Object Love and Reality*. New York: International Universities Press.

Morel, B. (1857). *Traite des Degenerescences Physiques: Intellectuelles et Morales de l'espèce Humane*. Cited in *A History of Medical Psychology*, ed. G. Zilboorg and G. W. Henry, p. 402. New York: W. W. Norton, 1942.

Nadelson, T. (1977). Borderline rage and the therapist's response. *Archives of General Psychiatry* 134:748–751.

Nunberg, H. (1948). *Practice and Theory of Psychoanalysis*. New York: Nervous and Mental Disease Publishing.

Ogden, T. (1982). *Projective Identification and Psychotherapeutic Technique*. New York: W. W. Norton.

——— (1986). *The Matrix of the Mind, Aspects of Object Relations Theory*. Northvale, NJ: Jason Aronson.

Orr, D. (1954). Transference and countertransference. A historical survey. *Journal of the American Psychoanalytic Association* 2:621–670.

Paz, C. A., Pelento, M. L., and Olmos de Paz, T. (1975). *Estructuras y Estados Fronterizos en Niños, Adolescentes y Adultos. I. Historia y Conceptualización*. Buenos Aires: Nueva Visión.

——— (1976a). *Estructuras y Estados Fronterizos en Niños, Adolescentes y Adultos. II. Casuística y Consideraciones Teorías*. Buenos Aires: Nueva Visión.

——— (1976b). *Estructuras y Estados Fronterizos en Niños, Adolescentes y Adultos. III. Investigación y Terapeútica*. Buenos Aires: Nueva Visión.

Peto, A. (1967). Dedifferentiation and fragmentation during analysis. *Journal of the American Psychoanalytic Association* 15:534–550.

Prado Galvão, L. (1966). Contratransferencia frente a regressão. *Revista Brasileira de Psicanálise* 2:22–34.

Racker, E. (1953). A contribution to the problem of countertransference. *International Journal of Psycho-Analysis* 34:313–324.

——— (1957). The meanings and uses of countertransference. *Psychoanalytic Quarterly* 26:303–357.

———— (1959). Countertransference and interpretation. *Journal of the American Psychoanalytic Association* 6:215–221.

———— (1960). *Estudios Sobre Técnica Psicoanalítica.* Buenos Aires: Paidos.

———— (1968). *Transference and Countertransference:* New York: International Universities Press.

Reich, A. (1960). Further remarks on countertransference. *International Journal of Psycho-Analysis* 41:389–395.

Rosenfeld, D., and Mordo, E. (1973). Fusión, confusión, simbiosis e identificacion proyectiva. *Revista de Psicoanalisis* 30:413–422.

Rosenfeld, H. A. (1965). *Psychotic States: A Psycho-Analytical Approach.* London: Hogarth.

Rosenfeld, S. K., and Sprince, M. P. (1963). An attempt to formulate the meaning of the concept "borderline." *Psychoanalytic Study of the Child* 18:603–635. New York: International Universities Press.

Rosse, I. C. (1890). Clinical evidences of borderland insanity. *Journal of Nervous and Mental Disease* 17:669–683.

Schafer, R. (1968). *Aspects of Internalization.* New York: International Universities Press.

Searles, H. A. (1958). Positive feelings in the relationship between the schizophrenic and his mother. In *Collected Papers on Schizophrenia and Related Subjects*, pp. 216–253. New York: International Universities Press, 1965.

———— (1979). *Countertransference and Related Subjects.* New York: International Universities Press.

Shapiro, E. R. (1978). The psychodynamics and developmental psychology of the borderline patient: a review of the literature. *American Journal of Psychiatry* 135:1305–1315.

Shapiro, E. R., Zinner, J., Shapiro, R. L., and Berkowitz, D. A. (1975). The influence of family experience on borderline personality development. *International Review of Psychoanalysis* 2:399–411.

Siquier de Failla, M. (1963). Transferencia y contratransferencia en el proceso analitico. *Revista de Psicoanálisis* 23:450–470.

Stern, A. (1924). On the counter-transference in psychoanalysis. *Psychoanalytic Review* 11:165–174.

Timsit, M. (1971). Les états-limites. Evolution des concepts. *Evolution Psychiatrique* 36:679–724.

Volkan, V. D. (1976). *Primitive Internalized Object Relations. A Clinical Study of Schizophrenic, Borderline and Narcissistic Patients.* New York: International Universities Press.

———— (1982). A young woman's inability to say no to needy people and her identification with the frustrator in the analytic situation. In *Technical Factors in the Treatment of the Severely Disturbed Patient*, ed. P. L. Giovacchini and L. B. Boyer, pp. 439–466. New York: Jason Aronson.

Waelder, R. (1924). The psychoses: their mechanisms and accessibility to treatment. *International Journal of Psycho-Analysis* 6:254–281.

Weigert, E. (1954). Counter-transference and self-analysis. *International Journal of Psycho-Analysis* 35:242–246.

Will, O. A., Jr. (1964). Schizophrenia and the psychotherapeutic field. *Contemporary Psychoanalysis* 1:1–29.

Winnicott, D. W. (1965). *The Maturational Processes and the Facilitating Environment.* New York: International Universities Press.

Wolberg, A. R. (1952). The borderline patient. *American Journal of Psychotherapy* 6:694–710.

Zilboorg, C. (1941). Ambulatory schizophrenias. *Journal of Nervous and Mental Disease* 94:201–204.

Zinner, J., and Shapiro, R. A. (1972). Projective identification as a mode of perception and behavior in families of adolescents. *International Journal of Psycho-Analysis* 53:523–530.

Zinner, J., and Shapiro, E. R. (1975). Splitting in families of borderline adolescents. In *Borderline States in Psychiatry*, ed. J. E. Mack. New York: Grune & Stratton.

3

Regression and Countertransference in the Treatment of a Borderline Patient

The case presented in this chapter demonstrates a borderline personality disorder that falls near the psychotic boundary on the continuum of psychopathological states. While there has been some debate about what constitutes a valid diagnosis of borderline personality disorder, the psycho-analytic treatment of patients whose character structures place them near the psychotic end of the continuum of psychopathological states has become increasingly accepted in North America during the past twenty-five to thirty years. (For historical reviews of the concept, see Boyer 1980, Mack 1975, and Paz et al. 1975.) Before this acceptance of greater flexibility at the edges of the borderline definition, many patients were relegated to the category of untreatable—victims of a rigid adherence to diagnostic labels in selecting methodologies of treatment. I believe this greater flexibility has resulted from the synergistic contributions of three lines of research (although I would not venture to rate the relative influences of the three). I refer to child analysis, longitudinal studies of mother–child interactions, and the persevering efforts of those few analysts who disagreed with Freud's stand that people who suffer from the so-called narcissistic neuroses are incapable of developing therapeutically useful transferences.

Everyone has a predominant character structure of his or her own that contains various areas of normality and abnormality, various degrees of fixation along with more mature, better-organized facets. Among psychotics and people who suffer from borderline personality disorders, there are, in addition, developmental arrests. For the most part, character structure tends to be stable. However, the borderline character structure has been described as one of "stable instability," varying from day to day and from moment to moment, both depending on ego states and external circumstances. As an additional aid in placing the borderline disorder on a continuum, we should consider the views of those who claim that some successfully analyzed schizophrenic patients may become borderline on the way to neurosis (Boyer 1961, Searles 1979).

Patients such as a Mrs. X, whose case will be discussed in detail, are now almost uniformly considered to suffer from ego defects in addition to fixations from which regression takes place in the face of heightened conflicts. (Of course, those defects may themselves serve defensive purposes and also be used for secondary gain.) The primary therapeutic task has long been considered to be the development and restoration of a reasonable ego and superego, and it is generally agreed that this goal may be accomplished through the mutually enhancing effects of interpretation and development of object relationships.

The last phase of a successful psychoanalysis of a schizophrenic or borderline patient proceeds like the analysis of a neurotic. This occurred in the case of Mrs. X, who had a mixed schizoid and hysterical personality disorder with an immense capacity to regress. Under the influence of chronic alcohol poisoning, her acute, serious regressions became schizophrenic in nature. When she responded to therapy, where she received her first experience of adequate mothering, she was able to renounce her bounteous alcohol intake. During the course of the therapy to be described, she moved from schizoid trends to gradual manifestation of a neurotic hysterical personality.

A consensus is growing that the successful psychoanalytic treatment of such conditions depends on a clear understanding of the influences of early pregenital experiences on the formation of character and on the patient's being allowed to relive those experiences (Giovacchini 1979, 1981), obviously modified in the controlled holding environment provided by the analytic situation (Modell 1968, Winnicott 1965). There is growing agreement that when those experiences have been adequately worked through and interpreted, the patient will have progressed sufficiently to allow oedipal interpretations to be made meaningfully, and the analysis will proceed in the manner that customarily occurs in the treatment of the transference neuroses (Boyer 1966, Ornstein and Ornstein 1975, Rosenfeld 1966, Volkan 1981). Such reliving may involve the development of psychosomatic disorders (Atkins 1967, Wilson 1968).

The possibility of reliving those pregenital experiences clearly depends not only on the patient's character structure but also on the analyst's capacity to tolerate controlled regression and to use the transference–countertransference interaction in a therapeutically constructive manner and thereby obviate the potentially destructive nature of the impasses that inevitably arise in the treatment of such patients (Boyer 1981, Giovacchini and Boyer 1975).

Analysts have long been concerned with the means by which the psychological attributes of one person are assumed by another, and many have written about the influence of introjection and identification with actual aspects of the analyst on the transference and developing object relationships (Fairbairn 1952, Freud 1915, Giovacchini 1975, Guntrip 1961, Hartmann 1939, Loewald 1960, 1979, Ogden 1980, Schafer 1968). Fenichel (1945) first noted in 1926 that countertransferences are determined to a high degree by the analyst's introjection of his patient's attributes, and Federn (1952), Fliess (1953), and Weigert (1954) were among the first to agree. The combination of the regressed patient's tendency to use defenses that involve projection and the introjective aspects of countertransference contributes heavily not only to the greater countertransference involvement of therapists working with such patients but also to the special characteristics of the involvement.

With successful negotiation of the rapprochement phase, the child develops the capacity for ambivalence and object constancy (Frailberg 1969, Mahler et al. 1975, Settlage 1979). Although Boyer and Giovacchini (1980), Giovacchini (1981), and Lindon (1981) believe the psychopathology of the borderline patient often has its roots in earlier periods of development, and others believe it to be rooted in the transitional object phase (Spiro and Spiro 1980), most observers think the difficulty lies in the patient's failure to satisfactorily traverse the rapprochement phase (Carter and Rinsley 1977, Mahler 1972, Masterson 1972, 1976, Shapiro et al. 1975, Zinner and Shapiro 1975). Like Gunderson (1981), I am impressed by repeated trauma or deprivation during all periods of infancy and childhood, and frequently also during adolescence, in the history of the borderline patient.

While the neurotic patient projects primarily his superego into the therapist, the borderline patient projects his sick self, his "bad," primitive, internalized object relations (Kernberg 1975, Volkan 1976). The therapist must be an indestructible container of the patient's illness and may eventually serve as the transitional object (Winnicott 1953) that many, if not most, borderline patients seem to have lacked in their early development.

The case presentation that follows focuses on two aspects of the treatment of a successfully analyzed borderline patient. It shows how some of the many pregenital and subsequent traumas to which the patient was subjected were reenacted in the transference–countertransference situation and how resolution of countertransference-induced impasses enabled the treatment to proceed. The patient involved has been discussed previously from other viewpoints (Boyer 1977, 1979).

CASE PRESENTATION

When first interviewed, Mrs. X, a 53-year-old Caucasian, was a friendless filing clerk who lived alone. Previously abstemious, she had become a chronic alcoholic following the birth of her third child, an autistic, hyperactive, feces-smearing boy. Her first daughter had been born deaf. She had feared taking care of her children lest she harm them, and therefore nursemaids had always been retained. Her first husband, in medical school and residency in distant cities before and after his overseas military service, had never lived with her. He had tried to murder her because of her sexual passivity during their honeymoon, and his infrequent letters taunted her about her frigidity and his pornographic experiences with other women. He divorced her and institutionalized the children while completing his residency.

Following the divorce, Mrs. X became an inveterate bar habituée, customarily picking up men, taking them home, having sexual relations of all kinds with them, and then repressing these activities. She learned about her activities in the following way. On weekends, when her son was home from the psychiatric hospital in which he lived for several years, she hired a woman to be present because she had vague fears of being alone with the boy. As we later learned, such fears were based on unconscious incestuous and murderous wishes. On Mondays the hired woman sometimes told her she had brought men home and had performed sexual acts of all sorts with them in front of her son, thereby subjecting him to experiences she had had as a child.

Mrs. X's choice of men soon included African Americans. Before long, she seduced only black men, and finally needed to be with several rather than only one. She remembered various elements of her interactions with them, but totally repressed the sexual activities per se.

Her becoming an alcoholic was partially out of identification with her father, whose drunken neediness was rewarded sexually by her mother, despite the contempt it received from her and their four daughters (of whom the patient was the second). Her drunkenness also helped her repress her sexual activities and thereby be more like her mother, who praised sexual anesthesia as ladylike.

Often diagnosed as schizophrenic, Mrs. X had been under almost constant psychiatric care for some twenty years—receiving almost every imaginable type of treatment with the exception of electroconvulsive therapy—for continual aloofness, diffuse anxiety, incapacitating anxiety attacks, impulsivity, and chronic alcoholism. She had been jailed often—masturbating, smearing feces and menstrual effluvia, and screaming endlessly while in the "drunk tank"—and had been hospitalized many times.

Between the ages of 16 and 22 Mrs. X went through a catatonic episode, from which she withdrew without psychotherapy. Following this she eagerly sought psychoanalysis but was refused by a number of famous analysts. She decided to try once again to obtain analysis when a therapist of her psychotic son said her interactions with the son kept him ill. Before her analysis began, she voiced the opinion that its success depended on her recovery of and understanding of the influences on her life of vaguely remembered childhood experiences and especially an early latency period involvement with a chauffeur.

Mrs. X had been at least average, and perhaps precocious, in her ability to do mathematics and to read before she went to school. By the end of the first school year, however, she had lost her capacity to do either. During all of her subsequent educational years, including those spent at a prestigious finishing school, she failed all examinations. This was of no concern to her parents, who relegated to their daughters the responsibility to become charming women and marry rich doctors.

Mrs. X's forebears were wealthy aristocrats who viewed and treated as subhuman people who were not affluent. The men of the family graduated from the most prestigious universities and were influential financiers and highly placed religious figures; the women attended finishing schools and were patrons of the arts. Her father, an alcoholic bond salesman, squandered his and his wife's fortunes; thus, beginning early in the patient's lifetime, the nuclear family lived on the grudging largesse of other relatives.

Following the birth of each child, it is likely that Mrs. X's mother suffered postpartum depression, which lasted for weeks or months. Although she tried to nurse one or two of the children, she was emotionally distant from her four daughters, and their care was left principally to a sanctimonious and doddering woman who had been the mother's nurse-maid. The old woman's philosophy of child rearing appeared to be studied neglect, in order to make babies Spartan, and the later systematic teaching of hypocrisy. Each in a series of young women who served as nursemaids under the old woman's guidance was discharged as soon as one or another daughter seemed to manifest preference for her over their mother—with whom they had contact almost exclusively at those dinners when she ate with the family (and at which she acted as though she were a queen), and when they obligatorily kissed her goodnight.

Mrs. X's constant conscious view of her mother was that she was perfect, and when she began her analysis, her idealization of her mother and mother surrogates was as uncritical as was her devaluation of her father and his "representatives," especially the Establishment, the military, and the police. Despite all the contradictory aspects of her attitudes toward me, she uncritically viewed me as a perfect mother surrogate until very late in her analysis, when she developed the capacity to mourn her maternal grandfather and acquired object constancy. At that point her mother became equated with the Establishment, and she was then able to evaluate critically previously idealized and devalued objects (see Kernberg 1975).

Throughout the patient's childhood, her mother spent entire days in bed for weeks on end, depressed, hypochondriacal, and unapproachable. Apparently she arose for only three events: preparation for gala social functions, for which she dressed elegantly and at which she behaved regally; her annual Grand Tour, made solely in the company of a personal maid; and the temper tantrums of two of her daughters. Mrs. X early learned that she received transient emotional rewards from her mother by being excep-tionally docile and by taking care of and soothing her anxiety-ridden sisters. During the daytime, her mother vacillated between two ego states. In one, she lay with her aching head covered with cold cloths, bemoaning her marital fate. In the other, she lay in reveries, reading romantic novels. While actually asleep or in a dreamy state, she allowed Mrs. X, until she was 3 or 4 years old, access to her body. The patient touched her naked breasts and genitals both manually and with her face; the mother did not appear to notice, although sometimes her breathing became hard and quivering.

In the evening Mrs. X's mother seemed to come to life, royally presiding over the dinner table and treating her husband like a vassal. He came home in a state of charming tipsiness during the evening, often becoming querulous and even somewhat belligerent. Then the mother would take him to bed and submit to sexual acts, apparently in the service of reestablishing peace.

Whether the mother's early emotional inaccessibility to Mrs. X seriously delayed her emergence from what Spitz (1945) has called coenesthetic organization, and therefore delayed her capacity to distinguish "inside" from "outside" and to begin to perceive external stimuli as being external, cannot be determined, in view of the presence of other caregivers. Nevertheless, evidence presented shortly indicates that Mrs. X, when regressed, lost her capacity to retain mental images of love objects. The literature is replete, of course, with statements related to psychopathological effects on infants of the mother's lack of accessibility (Anthony 1970, Belfer 1979, Bennett 1976, Blank 1976, McCluskey and Arco 1979, Mester et al. 1975, Spitz 1970, Spitz and Cobliner 1966).

The eldest of Mrs. X's sisters remains an alcoholic spinster, who has been under continuous psychiatric care from early adulthood and is still periodically hospitalized. The younger two are childless divorcees who live on lavish alimony and continue to have young lovers. Each is remarkably self-indulgent and socially irresponsible.

Mrs. X was incapable of saying no to anyone she perceived to be needy and arranged to be exploited by anyone who looked needful to her (see Volkan 1981). Her apartment was usually occupied by people who sponged on and stole from her; she did not resent their presence and felt guilty when they left because her resources no longer provided them with sustenance. Her altruism was partly in the service of maintaining her primitive denial that she had ever experienced anger or had an angry thought. She identified with needy people and sought to master, through giving to them, the trauma of having been helplessly emotionally deprived as a child. At the same time she saw the needful as sibling surrogates and continued with them a lifelong pattern of taking care of her sisters, not only with the unconscious expectation of maternal rewards but also in the service of denying the existence of her own hostility, which for her had magically destructive powers (as is so common with borderline and psychotic patients).

Dangerous as was her pattern of permitting strangers to live with her, another element of Mrs. X's lifestyle was even more perilous. She periodically went to black ghettos where she induced men to serially abuse her sexually. She submitted to any kind of sexual usage and acquiesced willingly to the black men taking her money and jewelry. This behavior ceased when she got married a second time, as will be discussed below.

During an early interview, Mrs. X said she remembered having been frightened on shipboard as a tiny girl, going to and being ignored by her mother, who was breakfasting with the captain, and being solaced by a black waiter who held her on his lap and gave her a lump of sugar. Late in her analysis, she remembered that around the same time she had gone into the lavatory and seen her father having intercourse *à tergo* with the children's nursemaid. Her stunned response included her feeling as though her face, in her words, slid off her head and lay on the floor like an emptied breast; then she perceived her father's face undergoing a similar transformation. Startled, he withdrew his erection, which she viewed as surrounded by light; at later times, when experiencing intracrural sensations, she sometimes saw a halo (Boyer 1971, Greenacre 1947). We can assume that this withdrawal of cathexis from the ability to perceive external reality, or, stated differently, regression to an ego defect, was defensive in nature; it is strikingly reminiscent of the phenomena described in 1938 by Isakower. The symbology of the emptied breast and the phenomenon of the facial image sliding off the head are strongly reminiscent of the dream screen and the wish to have a blank dream, signifying oral satiety (Boyer 1960, Lewin 1946).

During Mrs. X's analysis, after she had begun to develop emotional ties to me as a person rather than simply as a transference object, she lost the ability to retain a visual image of me as a person. Previously she knew me outside the consultation room and looked at me with pleasure when entering and leaving. Later, however, she appeared to look through me when she came into the room and never turned toward me upon departing. Outside the office, she quite literally bumped into me one day without recognition. During the period of a few months when she sometimes appeared to maintain a mental image of me but seldom did, she periodically looked at my reflection in a small mirror used to check her nonexistent makeup. She sought to determine whether I had turned into a vampire. The oral and projective aspects of that phenomenon are obvious. Her inability to maintain a mental image of me can be viewed as a defensive renunciation of a previously acquired psychological capacity, in the service of denying the growing importance I had to her both as a maternal grandfather and a good mother surrogate transference and as a real object (Loewald 1960).

During this same period, Mrs. X believed that it was I who wanted to fuse with her and gain her powers rather than she who wanted to enter my bloodstream, be with me at all times, invisibly watch my private activities with my wife and loved ones, share all my experiences, be necessary for my existence, and mysteriously satisfy all my sensuous needs. Later we would learn that one aspect of her touching her mother's breasts and genitalia was imitation of her father's actions in an attempt to replace him as her mother's lover. The idea seemed to be that if she could satisfy her mother's passion, she and her sisters would receive all of her mother's loving attention.

During four consecutive separations during her analysis, she forgot not only my mental image but also my existence until a day or so before our next scheduled interview.

Analysis of an episode of acting out the transference, in which Mrs. X spied on my toilet activities, led to her remembering that before her latency period she had slept with her sisters in a nursery separated from the master bedroom by a bathroom. Her sisters generally went to sleep soon after dark, but she remained awake, often hiding in the bathroom—from where she watched her parents' sexual activity, which involved fellatio, cunnilingus, and sodomy, as well as intercourse in many positions. Her heavily breathing and excited mother sometimes groaningly protested but at other times seemed to Mrs. X to absent herself, as she had done while being caressed by the patient during the daytime contacts. Mrs. X reacted to her observations in various ways: at times excitedly urinating and defecating, at other times experiencing terror lest one or the other of her parents be killed and imagining that both parents were endowed with the lethal genitals of both sexes. She desperately wanted both to join with her parents and share their excitement and to stop their actions, to preserve their lives. Sometimes she succeeded in interrupting them through noisy bathroom activities.

It was late in her analysis before Mrs. X was able to structuralize her sexual drives sufficiently to distinguish among urethral, anal, and genital sensations, thereby removing another ego defect. Only then was her previous relative anesthesia during compulsory and desperate masturbation and frantic intercourse, in which she generally insisted on assuming the superior position and believed she had the phallus, replaced by relatively calm enjoyment.

One interaction from Mrs. X's adolescence merits attention. Her father was out of work for some months or years and was persona non grata at home. He spent days boating alone. Mrs. X, perceiving his neediness and knowing of his drinking while aboard, decided to take care of him, despite her contempt for him. After he had drunk for a time, she would take the tiller and he would go to the cabin. Occasionally she would then observe him masturbating. To her awareness, the experience was merely an observation that elicited no emotional response. When, during her analysis, she developed the delusion that I was masturbating behind her, she was able to experience the vaginal and anal excitement she must have felt while watching her father, as well as rage in realizing that he preferred to masturbate rather than to use her as he had used her mother and the nursemaid.

Before her treatment began, Mrs. X was informed that six months thence I would be absent for a few weeks. Her anxiety regarding that separation led to a thorough analysis of her terrified reactions to her mother's yearly European jaunts and to her parents' short social absences. When I left, however, I had no inkling of what was to follow.

During my absence, Mrs. X seriously attempted suicide, her effort being thwarted only by chance. The analysis of that event uncovered a memory that she had had one dependable love object during her prelatency years—her mother's father. He had held her on his lap, obviously adored her, and taught her to read and do mathematics. He died during her first year of grammar school, but she never admitted his death to herself. She believed that she would find him alive in India or in some superior existence. Her attempt at suicide was based largely on her wish to join him, the one person to whom she could turn in her mother's absence. Her loss of the ability to read and do mathematics had been based in part on the philosophy that if she forgot what she had learned, she had never learned it; and while she had heard that her grandfather had died, she could erase the event by forgetting its existence. Subsequently, during the course of her analysis, she became a proficient college student.

Following the loss of her grandfather, Mrs. X turned for solace to a swarthy chauffeur who wore black gloves. She equated him with the caregiving black waiter on shipboard. The chauffeur held her on his lap and told her stories. Later he had repeatedly caressed her genitals and forced his phallus into her mouth, events she kept secret. One reason for her silence was that she viewed the chauffeur as needy, since he was treated as subhuman by her parents. Perhaps more impelling was her fear that if mother knew of her exciting and frightening involvement with the chauffeur, she would displace Mrs. X as his paramour.

Because Mrs. X lived entirely on alimony and handouts from relatives, one of her psychiatrists suggested she would have more self-esteem if she got a job. She became a practical nurse and worked at various psychiatric hospitals, where she showed some talent for caring for senile and psychotic people. Of course, she was frequently discharged because of her drunkenness.

In one of the hospitals she became involved with an alcoholic man who was her physical twin. She even wore his clothes. She soon began to live with him and adored him as she had her mother. She knew of his many faults, but that did not diminish her idealization of him. She felt complete and rapturous with him and at times believed they were not only psychological but physical continua. (We later learned that she had felt similarly complete while having sexual relations with the black male substitutes for her grandfather, who had been her sole dependable caregiving figure.) They married and the idyllic fusion persisted. Periodically they bought whiskey and went to bed, where they remained for days, engaging in polymorphous sexuality to the point of exhaustion, occasionally lying in their excreta. While she never had an orgasm, she felt complete. Such episodes were especially pleasing to her when she was menstruating and they were smeared with blood, which she also enjoyed eating. When he divorced her after nine years, she was bewildered, especially since she had supported him financially during the entire time.

During her analysis, when I was absent on two occasions, Mrs. X returned to him. The first time, they resumed their earlier style of life. On her return to treatment, she became aware that she had fantasized a similar union with me. Thereafter, she lost her need to fuse with him, me, and her mother and instead developed the wish to look after us as a loving caregiver. The second time, she did indeed serve only as his concerned nurse.

After she had been in analysis for just over two years, Mrs. X was a vastly changed woman, and it seemed to me that the principal remaining task was the mourning of the death of her mother's father. A termination date was agreed upon a year thence. Soon after the agreement was made, she became involved with a highly educated black gardener and again relived in her analysis her experiences with the chauffeur and various black men. Some months before the termination date, she went on a hiking tour of the Himalayas. On her return it became obvious that her involvement with the black man had been an unsuccessful attempt to avoid mourning her grandfather and that she had gone to India in hopes she would find him there and be able to rejoin him. On her return from India she brought religious objects, including fragments of stone from a shrine. She had not yet mourned her grandfather's death when we terminated her analysis, and a follow-up interview was therefore scheduled for six months later, at the beginning of the new year. On our second-to-last interview she brought me an Oriental bonsai tree decorated with one of the stone fragments. It was to remain with me and remind me of her while she imagined we were conversing. For some months before her termination her relationship with the gardener had diminished in intensity, and she began to feel almost ready to renounce it and begin to look for a suitable prospective husband.

Mrs. X did not call to schedule her follow-up interview. When I contacted her, she was vastly relieved. She had again forgotten about me. Her relationship with the black man had again intensified, and over Christmas, when two of her sisters and her mother visited her, she had developed the delusion that they were conniving to steal him from her, although in fact her mother did not know of his existence. We might recall that she had not told her mother of her childhood affair lest mother steal the chauffeur from her.

Mrs. X reentered analysis for a few weeks and returned for a week or two each year for the next three years. She eventually did mourn her grandfather, and when she departed, we had become like old friends. She sends letters once or twice a year, talking of her joy in living and in feeling alive, something she had begun to experience during the last year of her analysis.

THE USE OF THE ANALYST'S EMOTIONAL RESPONSE AS FACILITATORS OF THERAPY

I turn now to two examples of how understanding my own emotional responses enabled me to take therapeutically beneficial steps.

Following an early interview, to which Mrs. X came drunk, seeking through bizarre behavior to test my anxiety tolerance, seduce me, and establish a symbiotic union through sexual actions, she decided not to come again to the office intoxicated. Soon thereafter, she spontaneously vowed also to cease going to bars and picking up men; she promised, as she expressed it, "to be a good girl." Nevertheless, during the first four or five months of her treatment, on most Friday or Saturday nights she drank wine or beer at home and the following morning found herself either alone in a rumpled bed or in the company of a man whom she often could not recall having met. She had no memory of their activities. After a time she was able to recall the intervening step of going to bars until she found a man who was willing to be picked up. I understood her behavior as having a symbolic communication role in which she unconsciously sought to inform me of the meanings of past activities (Ekstein 1976). My initial trial interpretations of her behavior in transference terms, that is, my being a father surrogate, were confusing to her and were rejected. Eventually I comprehended that my transference role was that of an idealized phallic maternal surrogate.

On Mondays Mrs. X often presented dreams or fantasies in which a young animal or child was tortured or unjustly punished. I assumed that there was a connection between these fantasies and her weekend activities, and I silently hypothesized that the fantasies constituted an identification with what she had perceived to be aggression toward her when she had been exposed to parental sexual behavior as a child while her father was drunk, and her recollection that she had then felt tortured or unjustly punished. I knew I would have to wait a very long time to validate my hypothesis. Retrospectively, however, I believe I had begun effectively to ignore her as an adult and to perceive her only as a kind of puppet. Treatment stagnated, and she began to get drunk and pick up men during the week.

I found myself more and more annoyed with Mrs. X and feeling incompetent and helpless. I now doubted her claim that she had forgotten the sexual activities with the various men, and I felt she could not have been unaware of my accusing anger. During an interview, following my having subtly called her a liar, I became sleepy (McLaughlin 1975). While dozing, I pictured myself as a young child whose contradictory wishes to be good and bad controlled him unwillingly. With a start, I became alert and thought it had been necessary for Mrs. X to subject me to her emotional experience and that my own emotional needs were being satisfied by an empathic response. I briefly recalled Searles's oft-repeated statement that working with regressed people requires emotional growth from both patient and therapist. I then consciously put myself in her place and supposed that she was experiencing similar helplessness in the face of contradictory wishes. I further assumed that she experienced my repeated questions as accusations, that my actions had given support to her externalization of a self-punitive need, and that she had expected a reward for her vow to be a good girl but felt she had received none.

When I questioned Mrs. X about the validity of my assumptions, she became aware that they were true and that she had been disappointed at my having been previously unaware of what she was experiencing. She said that she must have been trying to put parts of herself into me and thus get rid of them. She then recalled going to a bar and being disappointed when a man refused her advances, saying she was "too old a pussy" for him. Later she dreamed that a boy put kerosene onto and lit the tail of a kitten, which ran away terrified, wanting to claw and bite her tormentor. In association with the dream, she recalled the early dramatic interview in which I had refused her crass sexual advance and she had wanted to claw my face, while also halfheartedly seeking to kick my genitals, to harm my "tail," which she had tried to put "on fire" with her gross seductive effort.

The foregoing events were followed by Mrs. X's ceasing to go to bars and by her becoming aware that she was angry both with the men who refused her seductive offers and the men who acceded to her endeavors to get them to misuse her, even though the sexual interactions remained repressed. It was a large step forward for her to become aware that she *had* anger and angry wishes that were not rationalized as stemming from altruistic motives. She did not yet, however, learn that her various disappointments with me also screened angry feelings toward me. I remained the forgiven, projected, uncritically idealized good-mother object.

Earlier I mentioned that Mrs. X seriously attempted to kill herself during the first period when I left her for more than a day or two. The resolution of the impasse just described was followed by her recovery of memories of her grandfather's involvement with her, memories of his death and her defensive denial of it. Then another impasse transpired, once again understandable as the product of my unconscious response to disturbing material of which she sought to rid herself by placing it within me.

It will be recalled that Mrs. X had subjected her son, during his home visits as a small boy, to exhibitions of her drunken sexual behavior with men. Sometimes, when she was unwittingly angry with me, she would return to her shameful memories of being confronted with those actions by her child's nursemaids. There came a few weeks during which her interviews were dominated by ruminations pertaining to this issue. I did not know why she was angry with me, albeit without her awareness of that anger, except in the most general of terms, and I felt frustrated that I could not understand why her expression of that repressed anger took the form of filling hours with seemingly endless, repetitious material that led nowhere.

I gradually noted that when she began her ruminative iterations, I responded with irritation and/or sleepiness. She reverted to her tales of seduction of men whom she picked up in bars, and our rapport all but disappeared. I regretted for the first time having accepted her in analysis and wondered, also for the first time, why I had done so. I found myself in a dreamy state during an interview, and when I became alert, I found that I had forgotten my fantasy. Over the years, I have come to the conclusion that the fantasies I have during interviews often represent my empathic response to what the patient is seeking to tell me or seeking to have me experience for whatever reason. Accordingly, in this case I thought that my fantasy had been forgotten because I needed to defend myself from internal conflicts that my relations with the patient were reawakening. On the night of the day in which I had fantasized during the interview, I had a dream that reminded me of my own past. I had learned previously that I had become an analyst with the unconscious motivation of curing an important love object of my childhood who had suffered from a regressive personality disorder. Analysis of my dream made me aware that another reason for my becoming an analyst was that I had sought to protect a younger sibling from the effect of that adult's personality disorder. I knew then that I had accepted Mrs. X in therapy not only to effect changes in her but to help her psychotic son as well.

I then became aware that underlying my conscious identification of Mrs. X with the disturbed love object of my past lay an unconscious identification of her abused son with my sibling and myself as a child, and that I was expressing my anger by withdrawal and refusal to recognize her, as her autistic son had done during several of the first years of his life. This knowledge permitted me to regain my objectivity. Finally, I could interpret to her her wish to provoke me to abuse her and to punish her for her treatment of her son and me. She responded by remembering dreams and hypnopompic fantasies in which she was forced to watch women being raped anally and having huge phalluses shoved into their mouths. This led to the recovery of memories of what had transpired between her and the black-gloved, swarthy chauffeur. She had equated him with a kind black waiter, and following her grandfather's death, she had sat on his lap, seeking to make him a grandfather surrogate. However, after initially telling her fairy tales as her grandfather had done, he had held her head and forced his phallus into her mouth.

The themes of Mrs. X's interactions with the chauffeur and of her behavior in front of her own son disappeared in the analysis. About three years after the recovery of this memory, when they did reappear, they could be interpreted as attempts to master by action her terror and feelings of dissolution when she had watched theretofore repressed sexual activities.

CONCLUSION

The borderline patient retains ego defects that result from psychological traumatization that occurs during or before the rapprochement phase. In her attempt to cope, Mrs. X continued to use primitive defenses, especially introjective and projective mechanisms and splitting, in addition to more mature defense mechanisms. Success in her therapy depended on replacing immature ego and superego functions with less archaic and self-punitive ones. Such rectification must take place before lasting successful treatment of neurotic problems can transpire.

Psychoanalytic treatment of the borderline patient is made possible when the therapist can provide a milieu in which regression to and reliving of the periods representative of the original traumas can transpire and be understood and rectified through the mutual effects of interpretation and developing object relations. Such treatment will differ from that of neurotics and is most easily understood in this case if one thinks in terms of the patient's use of splitting and projective identification in her attempts to cope. Such problems are likely to be more intense that those encountered in the therapy of neurotics.

References

Anthony, E. J. (1970). The influence of maternal psychosis on children—*folie à deux*. In *Parenthood. Its Psychology and its Psychopathology*, ed. E. J. Anthony and T. Benedek, pp. 571–598. Boston: Little, Brown.

Atkins, N. B. (1967). Comments on severe psychotic regressions in psychoanalysis. *Journal of the American Psychoanalytic Association* 15:584–604.

Belfer, M. L. (1979). Postpartum issues in prevention. In *Basic Handbook of Child Psychiatry. Vol. IV. Prevention and Current Issues*, ed. I. N. Berlin and L. A. Stone, pp. 77–86. New York: Basic Books.

Bennett, S. L. (1976). Infant–caretaker interactions. In *Infant Psychiatry: A New Synthesis*, ed. E. N. Rexford, L. W. Sander, and T. Shapiro, pp. 79–90. New Haven/London: Yale University Press.

Blank, M. (1976). The mother's role in infant development: a review. In *Infant Psychiatry: A New Synthesis*, ed. E. N. Rexford, L. W. Sander, and T. Shapiro, pp. 91–103. New Haven/London: Yale University Press.

Boyer, L. B. (1960). A hypothesis concerning the time of appearance of the dream screen. *International Journal of Psycho-Analysis* 41:114–122.

——— (1961). Provisional evaluation of psycho-analysis with few parameters in the treatment of schizophrenia. *International Journal of Psycho-Analysis* 42:389–403.

——— (1966). Office treatment of schizophrenics by psychoanalysis. *Psychoanalytic Forum* 1:337–356.

——— (1971). Psychoanalytic technique in the treatment of certain characterological and schizophrenic disorders. *International Journal of Psycho-Analysis* 52:67–86.

——— (1977). Working with a borderline patient. *Psychoanalytic Quarterly* 46:396–424.

——— (1979). Countertransference with severely regressed patients. In *Counter-*

transference: The Therapist's Contribution to the Therapeutic Situation, ed. L. Epstein and A. H. Feiner, pp. 347–374. New York: Jason Aronson.

———— (1980). Review of *Estructuras y Estados Fronterizos en Niños, Adolescentes y Adultos. I. Historia y Conceptualización* (1975). II. *Casuística y Consideraciones Teorias* (1976). III. *Investigación y Terapeútica* (1976). by C. A. Paz, M. Pelento, and T. Olmos de Paz. Buenos Aires: Nueva Visión. *Journal of Nervous Mental Diseases* 168:118–122.

———— (1981). On analytic experiences in working with regressed patients. In *Technical Factors in the Treatment of the Severely Disturbed Patient,* ed. L. Giovacchini and L. B. Boyer, pp. 65–106. New York: Jason Aronson.

Boyer, L. B., and Giovacchini, P. L. (1980). *Psychoanalytic Treatment of Schizophrenic, Borderline, and Characterological Disorders,* 2nd ed. New York: Jason Aronson.

Carter, L., and Rinsley, D. B. (1977). Vicissitudes of "empathy" in a borderline patient. *International Review of Psycho-Analysis* 4:317–326.

Ekstein, R. (1976). General treatment philosophy of acting out. In *Acting Out,* ed. L. Abt and S. L. Weissman, pp. 162–171. New York: Jason Aronson.

Fairbairn, W. R. D. (1952). *An Object Relations Theory of the Personality.* New York: Basic Books.

Federn, P. (1952). *Ego Psychology and the Psychoses.* New York: Basic Books.

Fenichel, O. (1945). *The Psychoanalytic Theory of Neurosis.* New York: W. W. Norton.

Fliess, R. (1953). Counter-transference and counter-identification. *Journal of the American Psychoanalytic Association* 1:268–284.

Frailberg, S. (1969). Libidinal object constancy and mental representation. *Psychoanalytic Study of the Child* 24:9–47. New York: International Universities Press.

Freud, S. (1915). The unconscious. *Standard Edition* 14:156–216.

Giovacchini, P. L. (1975). *Psychoanalysis of Character Disorders.* New York: Jason Aronson.

———— (1979). *Treatment of Primitive Mental States.* New York: Jason Aronson.

———— (1982). Structural progression and vicissitudes in the treatment of severely disturbed patients. In *Technical Factors in the Treatment of the Severely Disturbed Patient,* ed. P. L. Giovacchini and L. B. Boyer, pp. 3–64. New York: Jason Aronson.

Giovacchini, P. L., and Boyer, L. B. (1975). The psychoanalytic impasse. *International Journal of Psychoanalytic Psychotherapy* 4:25–47.

Greenacre, P. (1947). Vision, headache and the halo. *Psychoanalytic Quarterly* 16:177–194.

Gunderson, J. G. (1981). Formulations of borderline personality. University of California at Los Angeles Extension Division Conference: The Borderline Syndrome: Differential Diagnosis and Psychodynamic Treatment, March 13–15.

Hartmann, H. (1939). *Ego Psychology and the Problem of Adaptation.* New York: International Universities Press, 1958.

Isakower, O. (1938). A contribution to the pathopsychology of phenomena associated with falling asleep. *International Journal of Psycho-Analysis* 19:331–345.

Kernberg, O. F. (1975). *Borderline Conditions and Pathological Narcissism.* New York: Jason Aronson.

Lewin, B. D. (1946). Sleep, the mouth and the dream screen. *Psychoanalytic Quarterly* 15:419–434.

Lindon, J. A. (1981). Discussion of "Some aspects of separation and loss in psychoanalytic therapy with borderline patients," by H. F. Searles. University of California at Los Angeles Extension Division Conference: The Borderline Syndrome: Differential Diagnosis and Psychodynamic Treatment, March 13–15.

Loewald, H. (1960). On the therapeutic action of psycho-analysis. *International Journal of Psycho-Analysis* 41:16–33.

——— (1979). Reflections on the psychoanalytic process and its therapeutic potential. *Psychoanalytic Study of the Child* 34:155–167. New Haven, CT: Yale University Press.

Mack, J. E. (1975). *Borderline States in Psychiatry.* New York: Jason Aronson.

Mahler, M. S. (1972). A study of the separation-individuation process and its possible application to borderline phenomena in the psychoanalytic situation. *Psychoanalytic Study of the Child* 26:403–424. New Haven, CT: Yale University Press.

Mahler, M. S., Pine, F., and Bergman, A. (1975). *The Psychological Birth of the Human Infant.* New York: Basic Books.

Masterson, J. F. (1972). *Treatment of the Borderline Adolescent: A Developmental Approach.* New York: Wiley.

——— (1976). *Psychotherapy of the Borderline Adult: A Developmental Approach.* New York: Brunner/Mazel.

McCluskey, K. A., and Arco, C. M. B. (1979). Stimulation and infant development. In *Modern Perspectives in the Psychiatry of Infancy,* ed. J. G. Howells, pp. 45–73. New York: Brunner/Mazel.

McLaughlin, J. T. (1975). The sleepy analyst: some observations on states of consciousness in the analyst at work. *Journal of the American Psychoanalytic Association* 23:363–382.

Mester, R., Klein, H., and Lowenthal, U. (1975). Conjoint hospitalization of mother and baby in postpartum syndromes—why and how. *Israel Annals of Psychiatry and Related Disciplines* 13:124–136.

Modell, A. H. (1968). *Object Love and Reality: An Introduction to a Psychoanalytic Theory of Object Relations.* New York: International Universities Press.

Ogden, T. H. (1980). *Projective Identification and Psychotherapeutic Technique.* New York: Jason Aronson.

Ornstein, A., and Ornstein, P. (1975). On the interpretive process in schizophrenia. *International Journal of Psychoanalytic Psychotherapy* 4:219–271.

Paz, C. A., Pelento, M. L., and Olmos de Paz, T. (1975). *Estructuras y Estados Fronterizos en Niños, Adolescentes y Adultos.* I. *Historia y Conceptualizacion.* Buenos Aires: Nueva Visión.

Rosenfeld, H. A. (1966). Discussion of *Office Treatment of Schizophrenia* by L. B. Boyer. *Psychoanalytic Forum* 1:351–353.

Schafer, R. (1968). *Aspects of Internalization.* New York: International Universities Press.

Searles, H. F. (1979). *Countertransference and Related States: Selected Papers.* New York: International Universities Press.

Settlage, C. F. (1979). Clinical implications of advances in developmental theory. Presented at the 31st International Psycho-Analytic Congress, New York, August.

Shapiro, E. R., Zinner, J., Shapiro, R. L., and Berkowitz, D. A. (1975). The influence of family experience on borderline personality development. *International Review of Psycho-Analysis* 2:399–411.

Spiro, R. H., and Spiro, T. W. (1980). Transitional phenomena and developmental issues in borderline Rorschachs. In *Borderline Phenomena and the Rorschach Test*, ed. J. S. Kwawer, H. D. Lerner, P. M. Paul, and A. Sugarman, pp. 189–202. New York: International Universities Press.

Spitz, R. A. (1945). Diacritic and coenesthetic organization. *Psychoanalytic Review* 32:146–162.

——— (1970). The effect of personality disturbance in the mother on the well-being of her infant. In *Parenthood: Its Psychology and Psychopathology*, ed. E. J. Anthony and T. Benedek. Boston: Little, Brown.

Spitz, R. A., and Cobliner, W. G. (1966). *The First Year of Life: A Psychoanalytic Study of Normal and Deviant Development of Object Relations.* New York: International Universities Press.

Volkan, V. D. (1976). *Primitive Internalized Object Relations.* New York: International Universities Press.

——— (1981). A young woman's inability to say no to needy people, and her identification with the frustrator in the analytic situation. In *Technical Factors in the Treatment of the Severely Disturbed Patient*, ed. P. L. Giovacchini and L. B. Boyer, pp. 439–466. New York: Jason Aronson.

Weigert, E. (1954). Counter-transference and self-analysis. *International Journal of Psycho-Analysis* 35:242–246.

Wilson, C. P. (1968). Psychosomatic asthma and acting out: a case of bronchial asthma developed de novo in the terminal phase of analysis. *International Journal of Psycho-Analysis* 49:330–335.

Winnicott, D. W. (1953). Transitional objects and transitional phenomena: a study of the first not-me possession. *International Journal of Psycho-Analysis* 34:89–97.

———— (1965). *The Maturational Processes and the Facilitating Environment: Studies in the Theory of Emotional Development.* New York: International Universities Press.

Zinner, J., and Shapiro, E. R. (1975). Splitting in families of borderline adolescents. In *Borderline States in Psychiatry*, ed. J. E. Mack, pp. 103–122. New York: Grune & Stratton.

4

Christmas "Neurosis," Reconsidered

In "Christmas 'Neurosis,'" material from seventeen patients who suffered from severe characterological, borderline, or schizophrenic disorders and from four neurotics who had been treated either by psychoanalytically oriented psychotherapy or psychoanalysis revealed that all suffered from Yuletide depressions that stemmed from unresolved sibling rivalries (Boyer 1955). It was suggested tentatively that the birth of Christ, a fantasied rival against whom they were unable to compete, reawakened in them memories of earlier real or imagined failures to cope with siblings, thus causing the loss of self-esteem that regularly precedes depression (Abraham 1924, Fenichel 1945, Freud 1917, Garma and Rascovsky 1948, Jacobson 1971, Lewin 1950). Oral conflicts were stimulated and repressed cravings and frustrations were rearoused. In their attempts to undo the resultant narcissistic loss and to recover from their depression, those patients sought to obtain phalluses with which they could woo their mothers in order to give them the love that they felt had been unequally showered on their siblings.

Jekels (1936) suggested that Christmas had been introduced as a holiday in a culturally supported effort to deny inequalities between the Father and the Son, that is, in oedipal terms. My female patients, like those of Eisenbud (1941), sought to obtain penises with which they could influence their parents, but especially their mothers, to give them the love they desired. The male patients tried to obtain bigger, more effective penises. Some men viewed their competition with their fathers in terms of a triadic relationship. Others however, saw both brothers and fathers as siblings and imagined that owning a bigger and more potent phallus would enable them to sexually gratify their mothers, who would in turn eschew all others and permit their male children to symbolically nurse forever. One man fantasized a "perfect circle" consisting of his sucking endlessly on his mother's breast as her vagina nursed on his phallus. These patients' solutions to the problem only appeared to be oedipal in nature. Others also sought to recover from their depressions through an identification with Christ, attempting thereby to deny their own relative inferiority and to obtain the limitless favoritism accorded to Him. The issue of father's favoritism toward siblings arose rarely and then only with little emotional investment.

In the forty years that have intervened since the writing of "Christmas 'Neurosis,' " my practice has continued to involve, for the most part, those patients who have suffered from disorders near the psychotic end of the continuum of psychopathological states (Boyer 1961, 1976, 1983, Boyer and Giovacchini 1980, Giovacchini and Boyer 1982). For this reconsideration of the themes of the original paper, material is used from forty further seriously disturbed patients and ten more neurotic patients who have been analyzed or are now in analysis. Each patient has regressed at various times during the holiday season. Their reactions were almost always initially depressive in nature, but in some cases they deepened into blatant psychotic episodes that were confined almost totally to the consultation room. The Christmas "neuroses" of two patients began with hypomanic symptomatology. The great majority of the regressions were precipitated by reawakened, unresolved sibling rivalries. The means used by this series of patients in an attempt to recover were the same as those employed by the group I wrote of forty years earlier. Occasionally, depressive reactions were stimulated in other ways; for example, by monetary problems or the failure of a family reunion to establish harmony (E. Jones 1951). Two holiday regressions were anniversary reactions to early deaths of relatives (Hilgard 1953, 1969, Hilgard and Newman 1959).

Unexpectedly, those patients who focused on data pertaining to Christmas or Easter at other times of the year almost always did so while attempting to deal with unresolved sibling rivalry problems. In a similar fashion, their introduction of Christmas- or Easter-related material heralded such an attempt.

The clinical abstracts that follow show varieties of regression that were stimulated by unresolved sibling rivalry problems at Christmastime. Events in two of the case histories illustrate that actions and thoughts pertaining to Christmas or Easter at other periods of the year often occur while the patient seeks to deal with such problems.

CLINICAL MATERIAL

Mrs. A

Mrs. A was a 35-year-old architect, the mother of two unwanted sons, both of whom had been conceived in an effort to cleave her husband to her. She competed with them for his maternal concern. A lapsed Anglican, she had attended religious services from earliest childhood until she left home to attend college. Her wealthy, self-professed atheistic parents did not go to church or speak of religion; Mrs. A's churchgoing resulted from her mother's concern about the neighbors' opinions. An only child, she was accompanied during girlhood by a nursemaid and later went alone. She always enjoyed the pomp and the opportunity to exhibit her immense wardrobe but never listened to Sunday school lessons or sermons. From early on, she "spaced out" when her asocial parents talked of anything but her and in church she spent her time daydreaming of others' admiration of her or fantasizing that she was a lost princess who would eventually be found by her true parents.

Tremendously vain, she suffered from a severe narcissistic personality disorder with "as-if" qualities (Deutsch 1934, 1942, Kernberg 1975). She was a dependent, orally aggressive, exhibitionistic woman who manifested various hysterical and psychosomatic complaints. During the course of her analysis (when she achieved a capacity for meaningful object relations), she developed transient conversion symptoms: globus hystericus, tunnel vision, and clitoral anesthesia. In her preschool years she came to believe that her parents had previously lost a son and that she was supposed to replace him. She raised pigeons and rabbits and was intensely interested in their anatomy and sexual activities and the birth process. She dreamed then, and again during her analysis, that baby birds and rabbits turned into phalluses, which she acquired by eating them; in other dreams, as she stood erect, she became a huge, rigid phallus. Always believing herself to be unwanted except as a showpiece for her parents, she had ascribed her undesirability to being female. Physically beautiful and highly intelligent, she first became a professional model, unconsciously believing in the body-phallus equation (Lewin 1933), and later studied subjects usually especially interesting to men, believing that the acquisition of such knowledge would magically change her clitoris into a penis.

During the first two years of her analysis, her capacity for true object relations remained most tenuous. She was quite unable to believe that she was not the center of her parents', husband's, and analyst's thoughts, and she could not empathize with the needs of others. She did not manifest affectual reactions to the holidays, although her dreams included Christmas trees and ornaments in their manifest contents and she associated phalluses to them. In the third year she reacted to my Thanksgiving weekend absence with transient depression and a fear that I had been killed while enjoying the company of one of my sons. Following a dream of the "dream screen" variety (Boyer 1960, Lewin 1946, 1948, 1950, Rycroft 1951), she became depressed to a degree previously unexperienced. Her appetite flagged, she was insomniac, her movements were slowed, she could not concentrate, and her capacity to perceive brightness of colors diminished. A fortnight before Christmas she talked for the first time of her unhappiness during childhood Yuletides and remembered that she had always felt she had lost something that would be restored at her at Christmas. It became clear that she had wanted Santa Claus to bring her the missing penis. If I would somehow give her a penis, either by having intercourse with her or permitting fellatio, or by giving her a piece of jewelry in the shape of a Christmas tree, which she could then wear on the front of a sporran, she would deserve to be my only child. For the first time in her memory, she became preoccupied with religious thoughts, thinking that if she turned to religion and believed in the reality of God, He would give her a penis or He would restore her to her fantasied royal parents as their only child, a prince (Deutsch 1930, Ferreira 1963, Jacobson 1965, Kris 1956, Lehrman 1927). She said that if one couldn't *be* a Christchild, worshipped "by all mankind," one could "make it into a religion." She remembered that childhood family Christmases had seemed to her to be celebrations for her father. Just after Christmas, she dreamed that I brought her a magnificently wrapped package in which was a beautiful baby boy. She then was able for the first time to enjoy her sons' pleasure in using their Christmas toys and her anxious depression lifted.

Subsequent Yuletides stimulated depressions, each with the revival of unresolved rivalry with a baby boy who had died, as she believed, before her birth. The depressive episodes she experienced during the fourth and fifth Christmas seasons of her analysis were severe and lifted after she once again came to believe she was valuable to me both in my role of mother surrogate and as an actual love object (Loewald 1960). The sixth and last Yuletide depression was brief and mild. By then, dyadic relationship and pregenital aspects of her problems had been largely resolved, and her analysis had progressed to involving predominantly triadic relationship, oedipal material.

Mrs. A was one of approximately a dozen patients who spoke of Christmas or Easter while dealing with sibling rivalry problems at other times of the year. One day, about six weeks after Easter in the third year of her analysis, she began talking first of disappointing early Christmas experiences and then for the first time spoke of Easter and her confusion in childhood about its historical events and their meanings. She became depressed until she remembered that as a young girl she had come to believe that the alleged brother who had died before her birth had either been born, or died—perhaps both—on the May date when she had begun to think again of Christmas.

Mr. B

Mr. B was a childless junior business executive in his middle thirties, religiously inactive, although his childhood had been steeped in fundamentalist Protestantism (see also Boyer 1955, pp. 475–477). He suffered from a borderline disorder characterized by impulsivity, antisocial, obsessional, and paranoid traits, and psychosomatic problems. Initially he projected idealized, internalized good objects indiscriminately onto caregivers whom he then provoked to disappoint him and projected "unqualifiedly bad" parts of himself equally indiscriminately onto authority figures whom he induced to persecute him. During the first year of his analysis, he quickly came to view me uncritically as an idealized father figure whose traits, however, were predominantly nurturing (Shapiro 1978, Volkan 1976). As he did so, his initial severe free-floating anxiety, migraine, peptic ulcer symptoms, and intractable constipation were alleviated. He began to trust women enough to allow himself to have tenuous, fearful social relationships with them for the first time since his wife had left him three years previously. In order to maintain such an idyllic picture of me, he simultaneously pictured his business superior as totally hostile and persecutory and lived in constant fear that his veiled hatred of his superior (whom he had previously seen as totally benevolent) would lead to his termination. (See Boyer 1971 for a description of my earlier technical maneuver applied to a similar case.) During the period when these split transference relationships were unquestionably maintained by the patient, his initial troublesome symptomatology remained in abeyance.

His mother had wanted a girl to replace a sister she had lost in early childhood (Volkan 1982). From a reconstruction derived from data provided by Mr. B, it appears that the mother had held herself responsible for her sister's death and wanted to rid herself of guilt by being totally giving to a child of her own. She dressed Mr. B like a girl and kept his hair in long curls until he was 6 years old. Then his mother was required to dress him like a boy for his admission to grammar school. His mother rewarded him for "cute" or passively obedient behavior by cuddling and cooing, which often occurred when she took him to bed with her while his salesman father was "on the road" or carousing. She did not object to his neurosis while he slept in her arms. He especially enjoyed being held close to her as they knelt by the bedside during her impassioned nightly prayers in which she pleaded with God to punish her husband for his lewd, thieving, lying behavior and to keep Mr. B "saintly." He was ridiculed by his father throughout his childhood and when, in his latency years, he sought to be included on his father's fishing and hunting trips, he was rejected scornfully.

A sister was born when Mr. B was 7. Thereafter he was ignored or abused by his mother who now lavished her full loving attention on her daughter. An orphaned boy of S, a relative of the mother's, was adopted when Mr. B was 8 or 9. He was treated like a little prince by both of Mr. B's parents. His aggressive boyishness was overtly encouraged and his sexual curiosity was treated with laughing approval. Previously, Mr. B had been ashamed to have a penis and now he felt inferior because he compared his penis unfavorably to that of his foster brother. He no longer felt rivalry toward his sister, but found competition with his foster brother in masculine ways to be most frustrating. He later turned to various parental surrogates whom he sought, with transient success, to please through overt homosexual and criminal behavior.

During the first Christmas season of his analysis, while he still viewed me as totally benevolent, he hired a prostitute and entered a blissful trancelike state while they engaged in simultaneous fellatio and cunnilingus; he repressed the fantasies that accompanied the activity. He then dreamed that he was a baby in a crèche. He remained happy throughout the Yuletide.

During the ensuing years, inroads were made on his split transference and he sometimes viewed me as a hostile persecutor. While I had been the all-good father–mother, his recountings of sibling rivalry failures were recited with scant affect. As my transference aspects changed, his similar recollections included increasing anger and, at times, fury. Early in December, his initial symptomatology returned: anxiety, headaches, indigestion, and constipation. He quickly became depressed and the sibling rivalry data was accompanied by insomnia, anorexia, weight loss, and suicidal thoughts.

A week before the third Christmas he dreamed that as he slept, his flaccid penis grew into a magnificent, tall, decorated Christmas tree, its top surrounded by light. Although I conjecture that he had in very early childhood observed his father's erection and added to his observation a halo, no such memory was recovered during his analysis (Boyer 1971, Greenacre 1947). Many beautifully wrapped presents lay around its base, all for him. In the corner of the room appeared a crèche; the Christ child had Mr. B's early boyhood face. He now related for the first time having suffered Christmas depressions from childhood, dating their onset to his sister's birth. Following the addition of his foster brother to the family, Mr. B always felt the gifts and attention he received to be inferior to those accorded the new rival; he always wanted "something else." On that third Christmas Eve he suckled at his girlfriend's breasts and ejaculated without erection. In the interview following Christmas he recalled his childhood nocturnal wetting of his mother, but it was not until a year later that he came to understand that the action was his enactment of a fantasy that he could replace his father as his mother's sexual satisfier, with her vagina nursing on his penis as he suckled at her breast. Previously, he had imagined that his girlfriend was attracted to him solely because of his swashbuckling facade and sexual athletics. Now he found her to be pleased by his dependency and tenderness. On Christmas Day she told him she no longer wanted to see other men; his depression lifted almost immediately.

During each of the following two Yuletide periods, he reexperienced depression with diminished intensity; the content of his memories, dreams, and fantasies varied little. Some years after his analysis was successfully completed, he sent me a totem pole that looked very much like an erection, saying he "owed it" to me. In the accompanying letter he wrote he'd learned that I was interested in religious aspects of anthropology, that he'd been reading about phallic worship cults, that his new marriage was successful, and that he had a "fine, boyish son."

Mrs. C

Mrs. C was one of two manic patients who have been treated psychoanalytically by me. There was no record of mental disorder in her parental families nor any record of cyclic or other psychotic disorder in her extended family. A 45-year-old Jewish woman, she was the mother of several children, all of whom had done well. Before the sudden death thirteen years previously of her husband, a hyperactive, outgoing, somewhat paranoid, and immensely successful dealer in antiques, she had been a retiring, bookish woman, happily devoted to being a good wife and mother and to keeping a kosher household. She had studied the humanities in college and become knowledgeable in art history and art appreciation. When her husband died, she grieved for some weeks while simultaneously taking over his business, discovering previously unknown commercial capabilities. She gradually replaced the antiques with paintings and sculptures and within a year or so was almost as successful as her husband had been. Her identification with him was even more profound. She soon became aggressive, hyperactive, and suspicious. After a couple of years, she began to suffer from overt manic episodes that led to her brief hospitalization at least ten times during the ensuing years. She became very curious about the origins and mechanisms of her disorder and read much psychiatric and psychoanalytic literature. When she read "Mourning and Melancholia" (Freud 1917) and "Totem and Taboo" (Freud 1913), she believed she understood the dynamics of her personality change and was surprised that her intellectual understanding did not cure her. Her various psychiatrists tried unsuccessfully to keep her on a maintenance dose of lithium carbonate. She believed she should receive psychoanalytic treatment, but it was refused to her several times before analysis was begun with me on an experimental basis (Boyer 1961).

Her analysis began when she was emerging from an episode that had required hospitalization. She claimed she was taking a recommended dosage of lithium carbonate and agreed to continue to consult with her hospitalizing psychiatrist about her medication.

Mrs. C was the second youngest of many children of deeply religious Sephardim, her birth followed by that of a brother when she was 3 years old. Her immigrant parents settled in a ghetto in a large Eastern city when she was 5. She spoke no English until she was 6 and began attendance at a public school where the majority of her classmates were of African-American or Italian descent. After school, she attended classes with her brothers so that she could learn Hebrew to prepare for her bas mitzvah.

Unexpectedly, her analysis proceeded smoothly. Immediately upon its inception, her hypomanic tendencies diminished drastically. Although she spoke rapidly and denied connections between successive thoughts and was at all times hostilely vigilant, she nevertheless made every effort to be a "good patient." During the first seven months, she occasionally mentioned in passing that she had felt that her parents preferred their sons to their daughters. She said she had always been surprised that she had reacted blandly to the accidental death of her younger brother when she was 17, inasmuch as she had loved him very much and spent much time looking after him. During those months of treatment, the dominant theme was her handling of intense oral-sadistic hatred of her mother through denial and projection onto her mother and various maternal surrogates. Periodically, it was superposed by her tearful grieving for her beloved, all-good "nana," whom she had lost at 7, and her idealized father, who died when she was 10. She had read all of my writings, knew of my interest in anthropology, and viewed me as a totally benevolent omnipotent and omniscient shaman.

Chanukah preceded Christmas by about two weeks during the first year of her analysis. As had been the custom of her husband's family and then of her family with him, its celebration was both deeply religious and joyous. Every child received lavish gifts each night. At its end she suddenly became hyperactive and intensely paranoid and, for the first time, became critical of and directly hostile toward me. Previously comfortable on the couch, she now paced the room, shouted, and threatened to kill me by smashing my head with heavy books. Typical manic speech prevailed and its contents symbolized, among other things, her wish to destroy my brain and eat it. For her, brain power was equated with phallic power; my intelligence-masculinity made it possible for me to have become a shaman-rabbi. With infinite hatred she revealed her conviction that I was anti-Semitic and enamored of and favored by male patients, particularly admiring their intellectual capacities.

I finally learned that she had stopped taking lithium immediately after beginning her treatment with me despite her statements to the contrary. Following a tirade, she became expectantly silent and could listen to my interpretation that her regression was in the service of defending herself against anxiety engendered by cannibalistic fantasies. I also told her that she was now treating me as she had earlier stated she wished to treat her mother and was ascribing to me qualities she had stated previously belonged to her mother. Then she returned to the hospitalizing psychiatrist and resumed lithium treatment. Her gross hypomanic symptomatology disappeared within hours of her ingesting her first dose of lithium carbonate, long before its chemical effect would have been expected to cause such an amelioration.

The following day she brought me as a Christmas present a painting of an Easter egg. Although it is my policy to refuse gifts from patients, I chose to accept this one, believing that to refuse it would hurt her unnecessarily.

She did not mention the gift subsequently nor did I press for an understanding either of her giving it or my accepting it.

Immediately following her improvement, she revealed that just prior to her regression she had found herself to be very angry with one of her sons because he enjoyed his Chanukah presents. She was envious of his capacity to enjoy receiving. She unwittingly called him by the name of her dead younger brother. The night before, she dreamed that one twin crocodile fetus had eaten its sib while they were inside the egg. The dream had been succeeded by a transient flood of heavily cathected memories of her having been glad her younger brother had died and her guilty conviction that she had induced him to have taken the risk that had resulted in his having been killed. Those recollections had been concurrent with others pertaining to her childhood reactions to Jewish and Christian holidays.

For the first time, she revealed that her parents, especially her father, wanted their sons to become rabbis and, as she felt, belittled the intellectual capacities of women whose role it was to efface themselves, unstintingly support their husbands and children, and focus all of their activities and interests in the home. Now she said that the Jewish holidays were celebrated with great solemnity and comparative frugality by her childhood family. During the Feast of Lights, the children received Chanukah gelt but once and then only a small coin. In Iberia, she believed such an observance to be universal among Jews, and knew nothing of Christians except that there were colorful public performances during the holiday season. When she attended grammar school in this country, she was very envious of her classmates' reception of gifts at Christmastime, of their stated belief in Santa Claus, and of their having Christmas trees. She became interested in Christ and His teachings and composed prizewinning essays about the Yuletide and Easter in school competitions. Those writings and her envy of her classmates' Christmas experiences had been concealed from her family.

For some weeks she continued to deal with the vicissitudes of her unresolved rivalry with her younger brother. Periodically she returned to her wish that her family had celebrated Christmas and that she could have had a Christmas tree. It was clear that on one level she equated the tree with a penis and hoped that if she could magically obtain a penis, she would finally feel complete and be happy. Her envy of her son's pleasure at receiving a present resulted from her dissatisfaction with what she got at Chanukah. However, the reasons for the crocodile egg dream and the Easter egg Christmas present selection remained unexplained.

As Easter approached, she underwent another, milder, hypomanic episode. Once again, its onset was precipitate. Its content mirrored that of the regression that preceded Christmastime, and my similar statements were followed by her prompt improvement, this time without resumption of the lithium therapy, which had once again been abandoned secretly some weeks after her recovery from the pre-Christmas regression. Soon she talked of Easter and its symbolic meanings to her. Christ's death was an altruistic act aimed at making happy the lives of little children. He allowed His crucifixion to absolve Him of guilt from two sources. He was tormented because He lusted after his virgin mother who had been deprived by God and Joseph of sexual pleasures and He had oral sadistic wishes toward boys who were His peers because he envied the freedom of action that was forbidden to Him. Using the body-phallus equation, she viewed His crucifixion as both castration and execution. She thought of the cave within which He was interred as His mother's womb. The two women who awaited Him outside the cave, the virgin Mary and the reformed prostitute Magdalene, represented two aspects of one mother. Had He chosen to do so, He could have gratified Magdalene sexually for the privilege of having permanent infantile access to Mary. However, since, while in the cave, His good part had overcome His bad part, He was all good after His rebirth and could thereafter be with, care for, and be cared for by both Mary and Magdalene in a loving, guilt-free relationship.

Having spun this story, Mrs. C laughed, saying she had identified herself with Christ and ended up in a permanent fantasied relationship with two representatives of a totally good mother, a relationship exclusive of any male figure at all, whether father- or brother-surrogate. Then she recalled the dream in which the crocodile fetus had devoured its twin, now saying it later emerged as its mother's only child. Finally she talked of her thoughts about the Easter egg Christmas present she had made to me some years before. She said at the time she had actually believed herself to have been inside the egg and to have thought that she might emerge as the infant Christ.

A few patients who suffered from Christmas regressions had consciously or unconsciously identified themselves with Jesus earlier in their lives.

Mr. D

Mr. D, an unmarried man, held a professional position that enabled him to take care of young children. He perceived Christ to have been castrated and "feminine-masochistic." Like Lubin's (1959) patient, he preferred homosexual to heterosexual physical gratifications, and, like Van Gogh, who also identified himself with Christ (Lubin 1961), ambivalently enjoyed self-mutilation, partly in the service of revenge against his mother and as a bid for her exclusive love.

Mr. D's family called him "Jesus Baby" because of his religious preoccupation, his depicting himself as Christ in his drawings, and because, when he played "dress-up," he costumed himself alternately in Christ's or his mother's clothes. During much of his latency period, he chose to play in and around cemetery vaults, imagining that the corpses were alive and trapped in confining coffins as probable punishment for their murderous wishes toward their siblings. They could be released only after God or their parents had forgiven them. He simultaneously suffered intensely from nightmares in which he was similarly confined forever in a tight coffin, and could be solaced, when he awoke screaming, only by his mother's leaving "father's bed" to come to his.

Greatly interested from early childhood in esthetic phenomena and pageantry, Mr. D insisted on attending Catholic religious services although his parents, atheists who had been reared as Protestants, ridiculed him for that activity. He was preoccupied with Christ allowing His symbolic castration, which Mr. D believed was done to succeed in having His mother all to himself. From early boyhood Mr. D collected exotic Easter eggs, and from the age of 6 or 7 he constructed beautiful ones to give at Eastertime to almost everyone whose love he sought. They eventually evolved into artistic objects that could be opened and emptied like Fabergé's Easter eggs and then closed again, beautiful and undamaged. However, his Easter eggs were not filled with jewels or other valuables as additional gifts but with candy, which he identified as parts of himself or parts of Christ to be eaten in a kind of sacramental service.

During his analysis, his Christmas depressions were twice terminated when he dreamed that the confining coffin of his childhood nightmare turned into an Easter egg that was opened for him by a doting mother; he emerged as Christ whose "wounds-symbolic castrations" were healed, and thenceforth her exclusive favorite. They would have a "pure" relationship in which each would take care of the other and he, as Christ, would atone for childhood murderous wishes toward his siblings by devoting his life to the care of children. At other times his regressions would be lifted when he had fantasies in which I had eaten him and he had become an intrinsic part of my body so that we would live indistinguishably united forever.

In February of one year Mr. D became preoccupied with Easter themes; this was followed by depression and a return to the theme of his unsuccessful competition with his siblings. He awoke one night from a forgotten dream and found himself compelled to make Easter eggs although that holiday was two months away. He brought one to me the next morning, laughed, said he must be seeking to get inside me once again. Then, for the first time, he recalled his rage at the age of 4 when mother came home from the hospital with a new baby.

DISCUSSION

The holiday reactions of the current group of patients differed from those of the former group only because some of the regressions that occurred in the second sample progressed to deeper levels and then became transiently schizoaffective in nature. In two cases the holiday reaction began with hypomanic symptomatology. However, the major stimulus that precipitated the regressions, regardless of their nature, remained the same: reawakened conflicts related to unresolved sibling rivalries. In the earlier paper it was suggested tentatively that, "partly because the holiday celebrates the birth of a Child so favored that competition with Him is futile, earlier memories, especially of oral frustration, are rekindled" (Boyer 1955, p. 467). The present data strongly support that suggestion.

The means employed by both groups of my patients to undo the loss of self-esteem that set off their regressions were the same: either they sought to acquire penises with which they could court their mothers and give them permanent, exclusive union or they sought to identify with Christ, becoming the favorite child of all mankind, a maternal surrogate.

Eisenbud (1941) wrote of the regressive reactions of two women during their analyses. Each suffered from intense penis envy and a belief that she could not compete successfully with a brother for her mother's love. They were depressed at Christmastime because their renewed childhood hope that Santa Claus would bring them phalluses was once again dashed. All of my female patients who underwent Yuletide regressions also sought to obtain phalluses. While most similarly hoped to receive a penis as a gift, almost every woman also imagined obtaining it through aggressive, oral means, either through eating a man's penis with vaginal teeth or while performing fellatio. Others, as in the cases of Mrs. A and Mrs. C, imagined getting or becoming a phallus through ingesting symbolic sibling surrogates in the form of little animals or birds. The intensity of the hypomanic woman's oral aggression was represented by her choice of crocodiles as symbolic siblings.

Eisenbud did not spell out how his patients imagined they would use their newly acquired or reacquired penises. My female patients fantasized two means of becoming mother's favorite. When they imagined phalluses to have replaced their clitorides, they fantasized that they could satisfy their mothers sexually and make any male rival unnecessary to them. When they used the body-phallus equation, they had the same fantasy or imagined that they could get into their mothers' wombs and live in an idyllic, prebirth, symbiotic relationship. A very few alternately used the phallus-breast equation and thought of establishing a symbiotic union through imagining their mothers performing fellatio on them while they either did cunnilingus or suckled at their mothers' breasts. My male patients regularly sought to obtain bigger and better penises to be used in similar ways and to achieve similar ends. Their displacement of fathers and siblings for their mother's favoritism was in the service of dyadic, not triadic, relations.

Of the patients who supplied the data for the earlier paper, only three fantasized themselves to be in direct competition with Christ for maternal favoritism at Christmastime and no one had identified himself or herself with Jesus in childhood although some briefly imagined they were Christ at the Yuletide. Several patients in the latter series had believed with delusional intensity at different periods of time during their lives that they were Christ or could become Him. All of these patients included Easter in their Christmas fantasies or were preoccupied with Easter and Christ's rebirth at other times of the year.

However, we cannot assume that there is a high correlation between identification with Christ and Christmas "neurosis." The clinical experience of everyone who works with psychotics reveals that many psychotics delusionally identify themselves with Jesus, but the literature does not speak of their also undergoing Christmas "neurosis" (Lubin 1959). My informal survey of thirty-five psychiatrists and psychoanalysts who are aware of the "neurosis" as a clinical phenomenon indicates no significant statistical correlation.

Discussants of the first paper were surprised that Jewish as well as Christian patients suffered from Christmas "neurosis." My practice has involved more Jewish than Christian patients and all of the approximately fifty analysands discussed here underwent holiday regressions. However, all of the Jews were reared largely in areas in which Christianity was the dominant religion and Christians constituted a majority. We know from analyses of the cargo cults (LaBarre 1970) and the diffusion of folklore data (Boyer 1979) that members of the subordinate social groups tend to incorporate and use the religion and other expressive cultural elements of the dominant group in the service of the minority group and its individuals.

Various analysts who have practiced abroad present contradictory data regarding the incidence of Christmas "neurosis" in Europe. Siegfried Bernfeld (1953) found that his patients in Austria suffered less depression at the Yuletide than patients in America. Bernhard Berliner (1954), on the other hand, emphasized a sharp rise in the incidence of suicide in Germany on Christmas Eve. In Europe, religious aspects of Christmas are generally more important than in the United States. Thus one would think that since Christ's birth is an important stimulus for the revival of sibling rivalries, regressions would be observed more prominently in Europe. In the United States, however, Christmas has become associated more with gift giving in a family setting, and this probably leads to a focalizing of oral conflicts. The elements of favoritism probably become more important. Also, for many patients Santa Claus is a symbol for parents, and frustration resulting from his apportionment of presents plays an important role in the precipitation of regressive responses. We may remember at that point that Santa Claus is depicted as a woman in Italy despite his historical representation elsewhere as a man (C. W. Jones 1954, 1978, Lalanne 1847).

Clearly, Christmas "neurosis" is not a clinical entity. The regressive reactions that occur at this time of the year are phenomenologically and dynamically the same as those observed at other times. The cultural and emotional constellation surrounding Christmas makes it a more important holiday and a more powerful trigger for reactions in the predisposed. It is interesting to consider, nevertheless, the problem of whether there may be a phylogenetical vulnerability to regressive reactions at the period of the year when darkness predominates, as has been suggested to me by some Scandinavians. The celebrations and folklore of Western and Near Eastern worlds are replete with evidences of uneasy, manicoid reactions to the yearly threatened disappearance of the sun. Notwithstanding our psychologically deduced knowledge that darkness symbolizes separation from the mother and death, we know that darkness and cold produce physiological changes in animals and men (Berliner 1914).

Thirty years ago a research group composed of Drs. Philip Evans, Felix H. Ocko, Earl J. Simburg, and myself sought to determine the worldwide incidence and dynamics of Christmas regressions among psychoanalysands. Too few analysts answered our questionnaire to permit statistical confidence. However, we found a tendency toward a higher incidence of such regressions in countries in which Christianity predominated, regardless of climate. We also found that reawakened sibling rivalry problems were mentioned fairly regularly by those clinicians who had observed and analyzed holiday regressions. The northern Europeans who responded were more impressed with climatic causes of winter depressions and had not noticed regressive reactions to Christmas per se.

Jack (1936) surmised that the introduction of the festival of Christ's nativity indicated a growing tendency to regard the Son as coequal with the Father. He could see a wish, born of a "grandiose identification" with Jesus, that if the Son be the equal of the Father, there would be neither supremacy nor subordination, and therefore, because all was unity, equality, and harmony, guilt would cease to exist. He wondered whether this sort of psychological usefulness of Christmas partly led to its adoption as a major holiday.

Winter solstice celebrations have existed throughout recorded history. Men have always attributed the success of their crops to the existence of the sun. In widespread areas of the world they have feared that because of their misdeeds the sun would not reappear. Hence their crops would fail to grow again and they would starve. To assure themselves of a returning sun and a replenishment of food supplies, they have felt the necessity of atoning for their sins and pleading for divine forgiveness.

According to official Christian doctrine, Jesus had no earthly father and no siblings. Wherever Christianity has come to be accepted, and recent trends indicate it has begun to make significantly more inroads even in the Orient since World War II, the masses have chosen to believe that there must have been a son so fortunate as to have been the permanently primary object of his asexual mother's love. If we turn our attention briefly to artistic productions, we find that before the birth of Christ, the mother–child theme was very rarely portrayed in Western art (Bodkin 1949). Subsequently, however, that symbol of unity is a frequent theme in religious art (Belvianes 1951). The popularity of the Madonna paintings, which rarely include any suggestion of father or sibling, illustrates man's preoccupations with that dynamic idea.

The philosophical tenets of Mithraism and Christianity contain wide areas of agreement (Leach and Fried 1950, Reinach 1930, Taraporewala 1928, 1945). Although the development of the Christian religion out of Judaism has been traced from many standpoints (Fern 1951), one must wonder whether Christianity has succeeded in becoming the popular religion of at least the Western world partly because of the unconscious dream in all of us to retain the early belief in the unity of mother and child. This would supplement but not contradict Jekel's (1936) idea.

Christmas stemmed originally from festivals such as the Saturnalia (Goethe 1789) onto which Christian coloring was superposed. In recent centuries man has mastered the preservation of his crops and learned enough about the movements of celestial bodies that worries concerning the reappearance of the sun have been determined to be unrealistic. Nevertheless, his infantile anxieties about emotional and physical starvation persist. It would seem that the celebration of Christmas as a children's holiday is still an acceptable medium through which man can express those fears and seek to deny their existence. He is able to give his children food (gifts), and through his identification with them feel that he himself is fed by a beneficent mother. Perhaps this explains to some extent why it has been possible for Santa Claus to displace God temporarily as the figure to be worshipped.

Yet Christmas anxieties continue. In America, physicians in all specialties note a significant increase of all symptomatologies during the holiday season. Popular literature depicts the hostilities that appear at that season (Christie 1952). Families convene with the hope that old conflicts of various natures can be resolved (E. Jones 1951). The angers usually revolve around the theme of who will get the most and whether monetary sacrifices can be tolerated without harm to the givers. "It is more blessed to give than to receive" is an admonition necessary only because the wish to receive predominates over the wish to give.

THE USE OF CHRISTMAS "REGRESSIONS" IN TREATMENT

When I observed in the late 1940s and early 1950s that many of my patients underwent Christmas regressions and that the analyses of those reactions provided useful insights, it occurred to me that other patients might not experience similar regressions because the latter group were able to successfully use denial or isolation as a defense against dealing with material related to possible conflicts pertaining to the holiday season. Thus I began to put up simple Christmas decorations early in December: a holly wreath on the door to my consultation room, a lighted candle on a shelf in the room, perhaps a colorful Christmas tree ball hanging from a limb of one of the bonsai trees I customarily use for greenery. When patients ignored the decorations, I confronted them. At times the decorations have been more elaborate, but I have noted that the degree of complexity or specificity is unimportant.

I customarily use a technical device that helps patients to get in contact more rapidly with repressed material. Thinking about that which has been repressed follows regressed patterns; preverbal thinking employs visual images (Freud 1900). When patients make equivocal or otherwise indefinite statements, I sometimes ask them whether they have a mental picture that would illustrate what they mean. Frequently, when the patient remembers such a picture or conjures it, the imagery leads to a clearer exposition of a conflict, a significant memory, or both. Occasionally the device has helped patients recover conflicts and memories pertaining to Christmas.

Mrs. E

Mrs. E is a case in point. Although a lighted candle and Christmas ball had been displayed for three weeks, she mentioned neither them nor anything else pertaining to the holidays. Finally I commented that she had not spoken of Christmas and I wondered why. She could then tell me that she was very angry that I had so imposed my personal life on her, reminding her through the decorations that I was a patriarch who reveled in my grandchildren's adoration at Christmastime while I consigned the women in my "tribe" to "inferior, scut work roles." She could not elaborate until I inquired whether she had seen a mental picture. She was surprised to become aware that she saw me in Biblical garb, on a throne, with a chained woman washing my feet. This led to memories of how her mother complained on holidays that she got no help and had to do all the "scut work." For the first time, Mrs. E remembered that her mother had been incapable of permitting anyone to be happy on any holiday and always complained about the debased role of women. Eventually she recalled her childhood belief, long since proved erroneous, that a brother whom she believed to have been favored had stolen from her a prized Christmas present, a "magical" pen that could be used to write in three different colors, one of which matched the hue of my Christmas candle. The magical, beautiful candle and pen were both viewed as erect in her mind and led in another way (Arieti 1948, Von Domarus 1925) to fantasies within the framework of sibling rivalry that she had been born with a penis that had been subsequently stolen from her.

Much has been written about the necessary and beneficial role of periods of regression in normal processes of maturation and in psychoanalysis (Boyer 1983, Loewald 1960, 1982). Nevertheless, the majority of therapists who treat patients suffering from severe personality disorders and psychoses are reluctant to permit patients to experience transient psychotic episodes during treatment, even though such episodes may be limited to the consultation room. Along with Giovacchini (1979), Volkan (1976),

Winnicott (1971), and a growing number of others, it is my conviction that such regressions facilitate beneficial structural change. The surprisingly primary process-dominated associations that have been included here often occurred during periods of regression that I believe to have been deeper than most of my colleagues would have permitted. Thus, while they would have become aware of the depth of the patients' motivation by dyadic, not triadic, conflicts, they might not have permitted the emergence of fantasies and memories of fantasies involving such predicate-dominated logic. The fantasies that led to my patients' previously unconscious desires for "perfect circle" relationships led subsequently to Hermann's (1936) "dual-union" concept that has now become popularized as Mahler's (1968) "symbiosis."

SUMMARY

In "Christmas 'Neurosis'" (Boyer 1955), clinical data revealed that Yuletide depressions usually stem from unresolved sibling rivalries. It was tentatively suggested that the birth of Christ, a fantasized rival against whom patients were unable to compete, reawakened in them memories of earlier failures, real or imagined, to cope with siblings, and that oral conflicts were stimulated and repressed cravings and frustrations were rearoused. The depressions were alleviated when the patients imagined that they had found means of achieving their mother's unqualified favoritism, or the favoritism of their analyst as the mother-surrogate; their fantasies often involved the establishing of a variant of a symbiotic union with their mothers.

Review of case material obtained from fifty patients who have been analyzed during the intervening forty years affirms the observations and conclusions of the prior publication. Additionally, it was learned when patients become preoccupied with Christmas or Easter at times of the year other than the Yuletide or the Paschal seasons, they do so while attempting to deal with unresolved sibling rivalry problems.

References

Abraham, K. (1924). A short study of the development of the libido, viewed in the light of mental disorders. In *Selected Papers*, pp. 418–501. London: Hogarth.
Arieti, S. (1948). Special logic of schizophrenia and other types of autistic thought. *Psychiatry* 11:325–338.
Belvianes, M. (1951). *La Vierge par les Peintres*. Paris: Editions de Varenne.
Berliner, B. (1914). Der einfluss von klima, wetter und jahrzeit auf das nervenund

seelenleben auf physiologischer grundlage dargestellt. In *Grenzfragen des Nerven- und Seelenlebens.* Vol. 99. Wiesbaden: J. F. Bergman.

——— (1954). Discussion of "Christmas 'Neurosis'" by L. B. Boyer at the (Biannual) Meeting of the West Coast Psychoanalytic Societies, Coronado, California, October.

Bernfeld, S. (1953). Personal communication.

Bodkin, T. (1949). *The Virgin and Child.* New York: Pitman.

Boyer, L. B. (1955). Christmas "neurosis." *Journal of the American Psychoanalytic Association* 3:467–488.

——— (1960). A hypothesis concerning the time of appearance of the dream screen. *International Journal of Psycho-Analysis* 41:114–122.

——— (1961). Provisional evaluation of psycho-analysis with few parameters employed in the treatment of schizophrenia. *International Journal of Psycho-Analysis* 42:389–403.

——— (1971). Psychoanalytic technique in the treatment of certain characterological and schizophrenic disorders. *International Journal of Psycho-Analysis* 52:67–86.

——— (1976). *Die Psychoanalytische Behandlung Schizophrener.* Munich: Kindler Verlag.

——— (1979). *Childhood and Folklore. A Psychoanalytic Study of Apache Personality.* New York: Library of Psychological Anthropology.

——— (1983). *The Regressed Patient.* New York: Jason Aronson.

Boyer, L. B., and Giovacchini, P. L. (1980). *Psychoanalytic Treatment of Schizophrenic, Borderline, and Characterological Disorders.* 2nd ed. New York: Jason Aronson.

Christie, A. (1952). *A Holiday for Murder.* New York: Avon.

Deutsch, H. (1930). Zur genese des familienromans. *Internationale Zeitschrift für Artzliche Psychoanalyse* 16:249–253.

——— (1934). Uber einen typus des pseudoaffectivitat ("als ob"). *Internationale Zeitschrift für Psychoanalyse* 20:323–335.

——— (1942). Some forms of emotional disturbance and their relationship to schizophrenia. *Psychoanalytic Quarterly* 11:301–321.

Eisenbud, J. (1941). Negative reactions to Christmas. *Psychoanalytic Quarterly* 10:939–945.

Fenichel, O. (1945). *The Psychoanalytic Theory of Neurosis.* New York: W. W. Norton.

Ferm, V., ed. (1951). *Encyclopedia of Religion.* New York: Philosophical Library.

Ferreira, A. J. (1963). Family myth and homeostasis. *Archives of General Psychiatry* 9:457–463.

Freud, S. (1900). The interpretation of dreams. *Standard Edition* 4:549–553.

——— (1913). Totem and taboo. *Standard Edition* 13:100–161.

——— (1917). Mourning and melancholia. *Standard Edition* 14:237–258.

Garma, A., and Rascovsky, A. (1948). *Psicoanálisis de la Melancoliá.* Buenos Aires: Editorial "El Araneo."

Giovacchini, P. L. (1979). *Treatment of Primitive Mental States.* New York: Jason Aronson.

Giovacchini, P. L., and Boyer, L. B., eds. (1981). *Technical Factors in the Treatment of the Severely Disturbed Patient.* New York: Jason Aronson.

Goethe, J. W. von (1789). *Das Roemische Carneval.* Weimar: Carl Wilhelm Ettinger.

Greenacre, P. (1947). Vision, the headache and the halo. In *Trauma, Growth and Personality,* pp. 132–148. New York: W. W. Norton, 1952.

Hermann, I. (1936). Clinging—Going-in-Search. *Psychoanalytic Quarterly* 45:5–36.

Hilgard, J. R. (1953). Anniversary reactions in parents precipitated by children. *Psychiatry* 16:73–80.

——— (1969). Depressive and psychotic states as anniversaries to sibling death in childhood. In *Aspects of Depression,* ed. E. Shneidman and M. Ortega, pp. 197–212. Boston: Little, Brown.

Hilgard, J. R., and Newman, M. F. (1959). Anniversaries in Mental Illness. *Psychiatry* 22:113–122.

Jacobson, E. (1965). The return of the lost parent. In *Drives, Affects and Behavior. Essays in Honor of Marie Bonaparte,* vol. 2, ed. M. Schur, pp. 193–211. New York: International Universities Press.

——— (1971). *Depression.* New York: International Universities Press.

Jekels, L. (1936). The psychology of the festival of Christmas. In *Selected Papers,* pp. 142–158. New York: International Universities Press, 1952.

Jones, C. W. (1954). Knickerbocker Santa Claus. *The New York Historical Society Quarterly* 38:357–384.

——— (1978). *Saint Nicholas of Myra, Bari and Manhattan. Biography of a Legend.* Chicago: University of Chicago Press.

Jones, E. (1951). The significance of Christmas. *Essays in Applied Psycho-Analysis* 2:212–224. London: Hogarth.

Kernberg, O. F. (1975). *Borderline Conditions and Pathological Narcissism.* New York: Jason Aronson.

Kris, E. (1956). The personal myth: a problem in psychoanalytic technique. *Journal of the American Psychoanalytic Association* 4:654–681.

LaBarre, W. (1970). *The Ghost Dance. The Origins of Religion.* New York: Dell.

Lalanne, L. (1847). *Curiosites des Traditions, des Moeurs et des Legendes.* Paris.

Leach, M., and Fried, J., eds. (1950). *Standard Dictionary of Folklore, Mythology and Legend.* 2 vols. New York: Funk and Wagnalls.

Lehrman, R. P. (1927). The fantasy of not belonging to one's family. *Archives of Neurology and Psychiatry* 18:1015–1023.

Lewin, B. D. (1933). The body as phallus. *Psychoanalytic Quarterly* 2:24–47.

———— (1946). Sleep, the mouth and the dream screen. *Psychoanalytic Quarterly* 15:419–434.

———— (1948). Inferences from the dream screen. *Psychoanalytic Quarterly* 29:234–241.

———— (1950). *The Psychoanalysis of Elation*. New York: W. W. Norton.

Loewald, H. (1960). On the therapeutic action of psychoanalysis. *International Journal of Psycho-Analysis* 41:16–33.

———— (1982). Regression: some general considerations. In *Technical Factors in the Treatment of the Severely Disturbed Patient*, ed. P. L. Giovacchini and L. B. Boyer, pp. 107–130. New York: Jason Aronson.

Lubin, A. J. (1959). A boy's view of Jesus. *Psychoanalytic Study of the Child* 14:155–168. New York: International Universities Press.

———— (1961). Vincent Van Gogh's ear. *Psychoanalytic Quarterly* 30:351–384.

Mahler, M. S. (1968). *On Human Symbiosis and the Vicissitudes of Individuation*. New York: International Universities Press.

Reinach, S. (1930). *Orpheus*. New York: Liveright.

Rycroft, C. (1951). A contribution to the study of the dream screen. *International Journal of Psycho-Analysis* 32:178–184.

Shapiro, E. R. (1978). The psychodynamics and developmental psychology of the borderline patient: a review of the literature. *American Journal of Psychiatry* 135:1305–1315.

Taraporewala, I. (1928). Some aspects of the history of Zoroastrianism. *Journal of the K. R. Cama Oriental Institute*, no. 2. Bombay.

———— (1945). Mithraism. In *Forgotten Religions*, ed. V. Ferm, pp. 205–214. New York: Philosophical Library.

Volkan, V. D. (1976). *Primitive Internalized Object Relations. A Clinical Study of Schizophrenic, Borderline and Narcissistic Patients*. New York: International Universities Press.

———— (1982). A young woman's inability to say no to needy people and her identification with the frustrator in the analytic situation. In *Technical Factors in the Treatment of the Severely Disturbed Patient*, ed. P. L. Giovacchini and L. B. Boyer, pp. 439–466. New York: Jason Aronson.

Von Domarus, E. (1925). The specific laws of logic and schizophrenia. In *Language and Thought in Schizophrenia*, ed. J. Kasanin, pp. 104–114. Berkeley: University of California Press.

Winnicott, D. W. (1971). *Playing and Reality*. New York: Tavistock, 1982.

5

On Man's Need to Have Enemies

INTRODUCTION

The history of instinct theory began in early philosophical thought, but modern research on instincts dates from Darwin's theory of evolution (Fletcher 1968). Early psychologists ascribed long lists of kinds of human behavior to individual instincts, a strange admixture of universal qualities and specific, socially conditioned character traits including such diverse phenomena as kleptomania, pugnacity, fear, curiosity, and jealousy (James 1890, McDermott 1967, McDougall 1923). In the eighteenth century Lichtenberg (1959, 1967) hypothesized multiple combined motivations for war, including a "lust for aggression" and destruction; shortly thereafter, Hegel (Kojeve 1969) wrote of man's animalism and hypothesized a social and psychological development through enslavement to empathic civilized maturity, in which he saw other men as equals.

Freud (1915–1916) elegantly unified the multiple so-called "instincts" about which earlier psychologists had written into the sexual and self-preservative instincts, including aggression as a "component instinct" of the sexual instinct (Freud 1905). In 1908 Adler suggested that the aggressive instinct might be primary and this led to a severance of relationships with Freud in 1911 (Ekstein 1984, Jones 1955) after Freud (1909), in the Little Hans paper, explicitly renounced the notion of a primary aggressive instinct. Yet the subject of man's aggressivity continued to plague Freud, as was obvious in his "Thoughts for the Times on War and Death" and "Instincts and Their Vicissitudes," each published in 1915. There he thought of destructiveness both as a component of the sexual instinct and also as an independent force.

From the 1920s Freud's views changed radically; then he postulated a new dichotomy of instincts, those of Eros and Thanatos (Freud 1923). He believed there to be a biologically determined death instinct that was aimed at the destruction of the being but could be directed outward. In "Civilization and Its Discontents," written in 1930, he wondered how he could have overlooked earlier the ubiquity of nonerotic destructiveness. From the time that Freud introduced his new concept, most psychoanalysts have been skeptical, holding with biologists (Lorenz 1963, 1965, Tinbergen 1953, 1968) that animal aggression is indeed innate but that its being directed toward self-destruction is psychopathological.

The notion that man had an instinct that impelled him to be destructive was so repugnant to some psychoanalysts, neo-Freudians and/or Marxists (Fromm 1873, Fromm and Maccoby 1971, Torres 1960), that they aligned themselves with those psychologists, anthropologists, and political scientists who idealistically sought to prove that aggressivity is solely the product of frustration due either to societal deficiencies or faulty socialization practices (Boyer 1977, 1978, Skinner 1953). All but a very few of those psychoanalysts are now deceased and their ideas have largely disappeared (although see Maccoby 1972 and Millan and Maccoby 1975).

Psychoanalysts gather the information from which they extrapolate their ideas from various sources: their patients, longitudinal observations of psychosocial development, and the studies of other social disciplines, such as anthropology, sociology, and political science. As Freud responded to Einstein's query, "Why War?" in 1933, psychoanalysts can make more understandable the effects on behavior of unconscious thinking and motivations, but are in no position to offer any but the most general of recommendations to be implemented by others.

Given the presence of a destructive instinct, it follows that man must find means to circumvent its ultimate potential effects for survival of society and himself. This has become terrifyingly obvious in the light of the technological advance in armaments. One of Freud's great contributions was his demonstration that instincts are partially deflected and tamed during ego development and that resolution of the Oedipus conflicts results in superego formation and a partial turning inward of the aggressive drive. This chapter will speak of man's need to have enemies upon whom to externalize or project his aggression, to preserve the sense of self and the social group.

THE PROTECTION AND REGULATION OF THE SENSE OF SELF THROUGH THE DEVELOPMENT OF TARGETS OF EXTERNALIZATION[1]

"The sense of self, put simply, is the impression one carries of how his emotional, intellectual and physical components combine in response to the world around him" (Volkan 1985, p. 231). Various psychoanalytic authors have investigated the means by which an individual's sense of self is intertwined with his sense of ethnicity and nationality and rises and falls as do his nation's fortunes (Kohut 1977, Mack 1983). People are more stubbornly ethnistic when stressed by political or military crises (Volkan 1979).

What Volkan calls *suitable targets of externalization* have much to do with how the individual begins to become part of the group, beyond the influence of internalized parental and social values. Those "targets" play a part in the genesis of ethnicity and nationality and are the foundation for building up concepts of enemies and allies.

Modern psychoanalysts have been particularly interested in how our images of ourselves and others develop in early life (Jacobson 1964, Kernberg 1976, Mahler et al. 1975, Volkan 1976, Winnicott 1958, 1965). From child developmental observation and from greatly regressed patients we find that an early task for the infant is to learn to differentiate himself from his mothering figure(s). The baby develops images of the self and the other in a bipolar way; a later task of his growing ego will be to integrate the opposing images.

The bipolarity results from the early ego's capacity to distinguish pleasure from displeasure and its inability to integrate contrary experiences and their accompanying feeling states. The vast number of enjoyable and disagreeable stimuli that impinge on the infant leave "memory islands" (Mahler 1968) that become saturated with loving drives or aggression. The

---

1. The author is heavily indebted to Volkan's Presidential Address at the Seventh Annual Meeting of the International Society of Political Psychology, University College, Toronto, June 27, 1984 (Volkan 1985; see also Stein 1985, 1986).

hungry baby has a dawning awareness of his unpleasant, angry, bad, needy self, but after feeding has a good image of himself; he cannot integrate the two images. Similarly, he is unable to integrate the bipolar images of the good (that is, the need-satisfying) mother and the bad, depriving mother who has waited too long to gratify him. The memory islands of the "good" and "bad" mothers, invested with love and hate, are of two separate people. The infant begins to integrate the images of himself and his mother at about 8 months but the process is incomplete until about the age of 3 years. By then the intensity of his drives has been somewhat blunted and he can tolerate ambivalence, that is, love and hate the same person or himself, from time to time.

However, the integration is never complete and some images remain intact unconsciously and invested with primitive feeling states of love or hate that are accompanied by unmodified, primary-process-dominated, irrational thinking. The child avoids anxiety by conceptualizing those images to exist in "reservoirs" in the outer world, thus investing real circumstances with a magic that represents aspects of the child's unconscious mentation, saturated with his own primitive feeling states (Volkan 1979). Those reservoirs constitute Volkan's suitable targets of externalization. We seek throughout life to protect and regulate our sense of self and self-approval. Such targets of externalization assist us in doing so. They are, of course, part of a spectrum, on one end of which are psychobiological methods and, at the other, creative, flexible, adaptive, and sublimated ego mechanisms (Hartmann 1944).

During the first weeks of life, the infant's self is a psychobiological unity that he regulates with psychobiological mechanisms (Jacobson 1964), one of which is the ability to filter external stimuli (Freud 1920). Thus, for example, he may sleep through loud noises. The baby is less a passive recipient than was thought formerly. Almost from the outset, he seeks human stimulation and titrates its intensity (Stern 1983). At the same time the child's psychobiological self is also protected and regulated by the mothering person (Boyer 1956, Winnicott 1965). Likewise, he uses his innate autonomous ego functions (Hartmann 1939) and his mouth and hands as tools to discover the outside world (Hoffer 1949) and eventually to achieve a "psychological birth" with differentiated self-images. Throughout this process the mothering figure is called upon to contribute a particularly large portion of symbiotic help toward the maintenance of the infant's homeostasis. Otherwise, the neurological patterning processes are thrown out of kilter (Mahler 1968).

During this process, we see also the child's first purely psychological way of protecting and regulating his developing sense of self, his active use of what Winnicott (1953) called a "transitional object." Frequently, some object such as a teddy bear or blanket is chosen that is treated at times as if it were more important than the mother. Instead of soft objects, some children become "addicted" to transitional phenomena, such as a tune or a favorite bedtime story (Greenacre 1969, Grolnick et al. 1978). The capacity to develop a transitional object depends on the child's having received adequate care from a mother to whom he can transfer his affection from the object. Autistic children are attracted to hard, angular objects from which they cannot detach their emotional ties (Tustin 1984). Winnicott wrote: "I am not specifically studying the first object of object-relationships. I am concerned with the intermediate area between the subjective and that which is objectively perceived" (1953, p. 90).

The transitional object creates an illusion of there being an external reality corresponding to the child's capacity to create, and lies in an ill-defined psychological space between the child and the external world (Ogden 1985a,b). Under normal conditions the magical qualities of a transitional object gradually disappear although memory of it may persist. When he is about 3, the child plays another game with inanimate objects, imposing unintegrated aspects of himself and perceived others onto "suitable targets." While some of them may have been chosen by himself, external teaching and/or reinforcement will determine what they are. His own "badness" will thus be ascribed to cultural bogies or people who are considered to be outside the group. This process involves at various stages of psychological development the primitive defense mechanisms known as *externalization* (Novick and Kelly 1970), *projective identification*, or *projection* (Kernberg 1975). At the same time the child externalizes pleasant self fragments for safekeeping onto familiar attributes of home, such as foods, movements, and sounds, and they serve as the bases for more complex symbols of the expanded "family" that constitute the ethnic group, such as flags and songs. The importance of figures supplied by folklore and religion as substitute good and bad object representations can scarcely be overestimated, quite apart from their implicit and explicit behavioral recommendations (Bascom 1954, Boyer 1979).

It must be stressed that environmental parts that are used as repositories as parts of the self are invested largely by raw feelings of love and hate directed by early infantile concepts of "mother–me." They are extensions of the self and the important other and those invested with pleasant, loving feelings will support the cohesion of the sense of self, while those invested with aggression will threaten it. Paradoxically, however, they will enhance the self's cohesion when used for comparison with good units kept inside or at a safe distance (Volkan 1985).

While the transitional object protects and regulates the primitive self, the reservoirs of group-specific externalizations tie children together. At this point in their preoedipal development the suitable targets bridge the distance between individual and group psychology.[2] Later, as Erikson (1966) discussed, the aggressive and sexual instincts will be used to mold each group into a "pseudo-species" with a distinct sense of identity and a conviction that outsiders were "extra-specific and inimical to 'genuine' human endeavor" (p. 606). Pinderhughes (1982) also concluded that discrimination and the paranoid process are universal and wrote in a series of articles (1970, 1974, 1979) of group bonding through directed aggression, comparing human group activities with those Lorenz (1963) had described for animals.

Membership in the subspecies does not crystallize until the individual traverses the adolescent passage. Although the person may have as suitable targets of externalization only concrete objects such as a national flag, a mascot, or suitable architecture as examples, later he comes to have a surge of emotions for such abstractions as nationality or ethnicity, although during periods of stress he may revert to the use of inanimate or nonhuman objects in connection with his magic, returning to his childhood method of protecting his sense of self. What sociologists (Shils 1957) and anthropologists (Geertz 1973) call *primordial alliances* can be seen as suitable targets for externalization, sometimes the products of centuries of gradual crystallization. However, historical realities can invalidate the potency of a formerly magical symbol. Thus, since Ataturk banned the wearing of the fez, once a traditional sign of Turkish manhood, donning it does not bolster the modern Turk's sense of self (Volkan 1981, Volkan and Itzkowitz 1984). At the same time, his forbidding the long established use of the woman's veil might well have enhanced her sense of self. The influences of deculturation and enculturation have drastically reduced the utility of cultural bogies by the Apaches as suitable externalizations.

Freud's views about the resolution of the Oedipus conflict and the formation of the superego are too well known to require detailed discussion here; other psychoanalysts' views about earlier superego roots or the development of the superego in the female must be omitted. For our present

---

2. For a relevant discussion of psychoanalytic ideas about group psychology, including Bion's (1961) contributions, see Volkan 1985, pp. 226–231.

purposes, it is enough to say that Freud saw the 3- to 5-year-old boy as considering his father to be his main rival for his mother and conceptualized the enmity to rest on genital sexual grounds. By this time, given normal ego development, his instinctual drive derivatives had been deflected and tamed considerably and their urgency had been diminished. Being dependent upon his father, the boy repressed his wish to castrate his father and then, using the *lex talionis* that is a part of primary-process-dominated thinking, feared castration by his father. That fear led to identification with his father, his father's moral aspects, his "thou shalls" and "thou shalt nots" being taken into the boy's superego. His relatively tamed aggressive drive would now be directed toward himself in the form of guilt. Superego gratification demanded self-punishment.

In almost all cultural groups formal education of children begins at the age of 5 or 6. It would appear that with the resolution of the Oedipus conflict the child's sexual concerns are diminished and his attention can be more easily directed toward prescribed learning. At the same time, he develops the capacity to actively fantasize privately and partially solve his conflicts through personal, but more usually culturally supplied, symbolic figures and actions (Sarnoff 1976). Among the aforementioned Apaches, latency children began to learn more systematically the group's mythology with its targets for externalization.

For our purposes, little more need be said concerning the development of the self. As the ego matures and with the resolution of the Oedipus conflict, its defense mechanisms become more advanced and include repression, sublimation, regression in the service of the ego, denial in the service of protecting a psychological perception that one's mental images really fit characters in the world, and so forth. Suitable targets for externalization answer or have the potential to answer the normal need for enemies and allies. Usually the ego controls the psychological distance between them and the self in order to protect and regulate the self.

During adolescence, ties to infantile object and self representations are loosened and there is a regression of both ego and superego that is phase specific (A. Freud 1958), in the service of development (Blos 1968). Blos holds that the child has only traits before character crystallization takes place during the adolescent passage. The loosening of ties from internalized infantile objects, images, and representations makes it possible for the teenager to find external, extrafamilial love- and hate-objects. New identifications take over superego functions; the "family myth" is corrected and continuity of the ego is preserved. Sexual, as contrasted with gender, identity is established.

All of these formulations deal with what happens within the character or ego identity. During the adolescent second individuation, insofar as the suitable targets of externalization are concerned, they become modified further by the group ethos, and solidified. Now the individual will die for his "good" suitable targets and such action will be labeled patriotism with its protection of the symbolic extended family. The self-concept and concepts of the suitable targets are intertwined (Erikson 1956). Identification with the beloved and respected leader, the father and/or mother surrogate, includes taking over his ethics and prejudices in the service of self-love as well as group cohesion. In sum, characterological solutions for the good and bad internal representations of self and other are accompanied by a progressive sharing of ethnically determined good and bad targets.

THE CREATION AND USE OF ENEMIES AS A MEANS OF ACHIEVING SOCIAL SOLIDARITY

Each society must handle the aggression that is both innate in man and engendered through inevitable frustrations during socialization, in manners that maintain social solidarity (Freud 1930, Boyer 1970). This section briefly discusses how externalization and the creation of enemies has assisted the Apache Indians in handling their massive aggression and in supporting group cohesion and persistence. The material here is taken from the closely related Chiricahua and Mescalero Apaches, with whom my wife and I worked collaboratively for some forty years. During the early years, the principal focus of my wife, Dr. Ruth Boyer, was an intensive and extensive socialization study (R. M. Boyer 1962, 1964, Boyer and Layton 1992). My main task was office psychotherapy that was mostly limited to the interpretation of resistance and transference (Boyer 1964a, 1979, Boyer and Boyer 1967a, 1972, 1976).[3] For twenty-odd years we studied expressive culture and its interactions with personality configurations (Boyer 1964b, 1975, Boyer and Boyer 1967b, 1968–71, 1977, R. M. Boyer 1972). (For the purposes of this discussion, the data obtained from the Chiricahuas and Mescaleros are generalizable to other Apaches. Space does not

---

3. My wife and I were engaged in continuous fieldwork among the Apaches of the Mescalero Indian reservation beginning in 1957, making field trips at least yearly, lasting from a week to a maximum of fourteen-plus months. The research was partially supported by NIMH Grants M-2013 and M-3088 and Faculty Grants from the University of California, Berkeley.

permit a discussion of Apache social structure beyond aspects of religio-medical practices and related folklore [Basehart 1959, 1960, Opler 1941, 1969].)

Despite immense hardships in a very hostile environment, the Apaches remained free and terrorized the inhabitants of thousands of square miles of land for a period of at least 400 years until they were overwhelmed by the sheer number of emigrating white men in the nineteenth century.[4] The Apaches were known for their savagery and mercilessness; they were ferocious and proud. One observer wrote, "In point of intellect, in cunning and duplicity, in tenacity of purpose and wondrous powers of endurance [they] have no equals among the Indians existing in North America" (Cremony 1868, p. 203). It was said that only on their sufferance did the governments of the United States and Mexico exist in the Great Southwest over a period of some two centuries (Chittenden 1902).

Historically, beginning perhaps a millennium ago, groups of Athabascan language-speaking people (Hoijer 1938a), each numbering probably no more than forty or so people, migrated southward from northwest Canada and maybe Alaska. Those who reached the Great Southwest of the United States and northern Mexico divided into two groups, those who were heavily influenced by the resident Pueblo Indians becoming the sedentary Navajos and those who chose to continue their nomadic hunting, gathering, and raiding lifestyle becoming the Apaches who separated into seven tribes, each dominating an area of many hundreds of square miles of desert and mountainous land (Gunnarson 1956, Hall 1944, Huscher and Huscher 1942, Mails 1974, Schroeder 1974, Worcester 1979). The tribes probably never numbered more than a thousand each. Being closely interbred over the centuries, we suppose that their innate aggressive drive was selectively enhanced.

Over time, these Apaches evolved child-rearing patterns that produced people with personality configurations that were adaptive to their aboriginal lifestyle. Those configurations included a high degree of aggressivity, stoicism, endurance, suggestibility, and the capacity to withstand the loss of kith and kin through death or desertion without developing debilitating depressive reactions. This latter was important because of the ever-

---

4. Ball 1970, 1980, Bourke 1891, Calhoun and Twitchell 1912, Chavez 1939, 1944, Debo 1976, Diccionario 1964, Forbes 1960, Haley 1981, Hall 1944, Lummis 1966, Ochoa 1949, Ogle 1940, Romero 1944, Spicer 1962, Stout 1974, Terrazas 1905, Terrell 1974, Thomas 1959a,b,c, Thrapp 1967, 1974, Wellman 1934, Woodward 1961.

present threat of death due to hardship or the actions of actual enemies. It is probable that the infant mortality was over 50 percent.

In the past, the rearing of children was one of the adults' most serious preoccupations (Opler 1941, 1969). Consciously treasuring their young, parents have always had to cope with *unconscious* hostility toward them. Although the Rascovskys (1980) have postulated the existence of a filicidal drive, clinical work and extrapolations from Apache customs, rituals, and folklore indicate that their destructive wishes toward their children are based primarily on the adults' envy of the idealized fantasized symbiotic state. Their anger toward their young is implicit in their performing many ceremonies as the child grew, to protect him from the hostile wishes that were ascribed to supernatural forces, witches, ghosts, and cultural bogies. Their variants of evil-eye practices obviously revealed the presence of externalized envy (Maloney 1976, Roheim 1952, Tourney and Plazak 1954, Vereecken 1968).

Today Apache neglect and abuse of their children is reflected in the presence of subdural hematomata in some 30 percent of infants of 6 months of age and younger (Clements and Mohr 1961). Dramatic evidence of their unconscious hostility toward children can be inferred from a practice the Apaches call "throwing the child away." Over time, the vast majority of nuclear families have given one or more children away, often with scant overt reason for doing so, and without subsequent remorse. The past incidence of the practice is undeterminable but to obtain reliable census data is very difficult because so many relatives had forgotten about the existence of children who had been "thrown away."

The unconscious hostility was especially intense toward babies and young children. When twins were born, one of them was permitted to die or was killed in cruel fashion. There are accounts that the younger or less strong, or the female of the two, was placed on an anthill in the desert sun, its eyes smeared with honey, to die while being eaten. The externalization of infantile oral aggression could scarcely be more apparent. Overtly, children were not considered to be human beings until they could talk and were thought to be soulless until they were of early adolescent age. Not only is the former thought verbalized, but the concept can be deduced from ghost sickness practices. When an Apache dies, his relatives have acute anxiety attacks based on fear of the ghost of the dead. Without shamanic intervention, the lonely or angry soul can drive a loved one mad and can lead him to kill himself. However, no ghost-chasing ceremony is required if a child or adolescent dies.

The Apache baby is the pampered, idolized ruler of the family until the birth of the next sibling. The mother may spend hours in tenderly bathing and anointing the infant and, even in a roomful of talking and laughing people, may enter into a dreamy state lasting for many minutes while holding her baby and looking into its eyes or contemplating its face. At such times her wish to achieve fantasized infantile symbiosis is most obvious. Yet the same mother may within hours leave the baby, with or without a caregiver of any age, for hours or even days while she pursues narcissistic pleasures, particularly drinking and carousing. Four houses of one family were burned down when children of 4 years of age and younger were left unattended for days at a time (Boyer et al. 1983). Desertions of infants and children have been commonplace historically. Formerly, with the matrilocal presence of sisters, were the mother to leave the camp or band, her baby would have a caregiver.

Inconsistency is the most striking characteristic of Apaches' attitude toward their young. The seeds of shallow object relations are sown early in the child's life and a sense of basic trust has little chance of developing (Erikson 1950). It is small wonder that Apaches become suspicious. The good and bad self- and mother images that develop in all babies are not corrected by actual experience. As we know, small children blame themselves for traumatic experiences that are imposed on them. An Apache custom reinforces the prolongation of the good-mother, bad-mother split, namely, that when the child has grandmotherly care, it is likely that that care will be much more consistently loving, considerate, and dependable. The grandmother then may become a good-mother surrogate while the mother's bad image may become more fixed, at least unconsciously.

The baby is the family idol within the limits of the parents' capacities to relate to him. His slightest evidence of discomfort may bring immediate tender concern. He sleeps with his mother, or with both parents should the father be at home. But dethronement is immediate and drastic with the birth of the next baby when the former king is about 2 years old. Then his cries and temper tantrums are ignored or ridiculed or, if he is too insistent, he may be shoved away from his mother as she attends the new rival, even, it has been observed, by a kick in the face. Aggression toward the younger sib is prohibited thenceforth, although, even during later years, the older child's or adolescent's property may be destroyed with utter impunity by the younger sib. The immense hostility engendered by these experiences is turned inward in part and, ideally, results in Apache endurance and stoicism, in addition to finding its outlet through externalization, as noted below.

Clear evidence of stoicism is observable by the time the child is 3 to 4 years old. He has learned that temper tantrums gain no positive reward; he tries to cry silently if at all, knowing his mother may reward him somehow for not "bothering" her. While mother tends the younger sib, the next older child starts to become angry. His neck and face flush, his arms and legs become tense, and his fists clench. But suddenly he becomes pale, his legs relax, his arms hang at his sides, and his hands open. Rather than casting himself to the floor screaming, he has now learned muscular and emotional control.

When the aboriginal child reached the age of 5 or 6, increasingly rigorous physical training was undertaken to make him develop stamina and endurance and to further his stoicism. By the time he was preadolescent, he would be expected to arise before the morning star emerged, to patrol the camp carrying the bow and arrows and spear he had learned to make to fight off enemies, and to swim in an icy pool. Later in the day he would run several miles to the top of a neighboring mountain and back without swallowing any of the water he was carrying in his mouth. In his early teens he would accompany the men on hunting and raiding expeditions that might cover a thousand miles, either afoot or on horseback. Much aggression was thus turned inward and resulted in pride and stature.

But let us return to the externalization of aggression. Apache children are very rarely disciplined physically. Rather, they are systematically trained to use culturally provided targets for their aggression. The disobedient toddler will be terrified with the threat that the whippoorwill, a tiny, seed-eating bird that is seen and heard especially in the evening, will carry him from his bed during the night and eat him. People in their eighties will say, with mild embarrassment, "I'm still afraid of that pretty little bird." Or the annoyed mother will say, "Ah shee," meaning "the ghost is coming." The Apache countryside abounds in bogies. Witches prevail. Owls herald one's death, saying, "I'm going to drink your blood." All canines are dangerous, even the most helpless little puppy, and may be tortured without fear of disapproval. The bêtes noires, ghosts, and witches become bad self- and parental imagos upon whom to externalize aggression.

Further frustration and aggression is produced in children by Apache sexual practices. When sober, they are by and large gentle, considerate, humorous, and decorous people. In preservation times the women were frequently referred to as "chaste" by United States military men. When intoxicated, they often become incredibly lewd and violent. A jealous drunken man may perforate his wife's vagina by jamming a stick into it or may hold his best friend's arm in a campfire to the degree that the member will require amputation. A frustrated brother may fracture his favorite sister's skull with a rock and then disfigure her face for life, raking it with his spurs. When participants are intoxicated, sexual practices are sometimes public, obscene, and accompanied by much physical aggression. Until comparatively recently, Apaches lived in crowded dwellings and the sexual activities of the adults took place in the same room where several children of varying ages might be asleep. Even in the presence of gentle, loving sexual activities, the very young child imagines one parent is hurting the other and can interpret the actions only in the light of his stage of psychosexual development. He is frightened and angry. He is also excited and wants to be included, but is frustrated and lonely. In clinical practice with borderline and psychotic non-Apache patients, one often observes that their having been subjected to repeated primal scene traumata while young contributed heavily to their immature character structure, including their heightened aggression (Boyer 1983).

While drunkenness was sporadic aboriginally, occurring only at times of celebration when the Apaches made and drank a relatively mild beer called *tiswin*, the same pattern prevailed. Disapproved activities sometimes resulted in feuds that would require one family to leave the band for self- and group preservation. The military forces kept careful watch that pre-reservation Apaches being held captive in various forts did not ferment some of their favorite brew.

Apache religion provides vehicles for externalization. The universe is flooded by vague, undefined, diffuse supernatural power (Opler 1947), which, to become effective, must "work through" mankind. It inhabits animate and inanimate objects, appears to an Apache in a personified guise, and offers him supernatural help and the choice of becoming a shaman. However, this benevolent power, when affronted, is also an implacable enemy, and may demand the death of a person who insults it by some transgression. The sinner can be saved or cured only by shamanic intervention. The shaman and supernatural power itself serve as good-mother, bad-mother surrogates. If an Apache accepts the power that is offered to him and becomes a shaman, he can use it for group or individual benefit or witchcraft purposes as he chooses. That is, he can use it to intervene with the affronted supernatural being and cure a suffering client, or he can use his power to act in the role of a witch who can, for example, kill people, bring floods or famines, or change a person into any animate or inanimate object. But the shaman may also unwittingly use his power for evil purposes, resulting in damage to himself or others (Boyer et al. 1982, Boyer et al. 1985). Thus the shaman is to be greatly feared, because he also practices witchcraft passively. As mentioned, the affronted power demands someone's death. Should the shaman effect a cure, he must permit the power to take his life or that of a loved one.

Aboriginally, indoctrination into Apachean philosophies, morals, aspirations, accepted and admired behavior, and beliefs in general was conveyed in great part through nightly narrations of folklore and frequent observations of religiomedical ceremonies, which were numerous. Small rites would be observed every day, as when before a tree was felled to make a tipi pole, its supernatural power was assuaged by an orison, or a woman prayed to each plant she gathered for food or medicinal purposes. The spirit of the stars, the sun, the moon, the breeze—all required obeisance in the form of daily or nightly rituals. Then there were the larger ceremonies, the dramatic shamanic cures, the celebration of the girl's reaching puberty or the young man's first successful raid, the eerie and forceful dancing around the huge bonfire late at night of the menacingly costumed representatives of underground gods, and the repetitive drumming and singing of songs that themselves carried educational messages. The mythology and folklore involved primarily the exploits of animals (Boyer 1979, Boyer and Boyer 1967a,b, 1968–71, R. M. Boyer and Boyer 1981, Hoijer 1938b, Opler 1938, 1940, 1942). It can surely be no coincidence that the major figure in Apache folklore is the coyote, that representative of all admirable and despicable human traits, and that canines across the board are cultural bogies.

Thus far we have spoken only of culturally provided, imaginary objects used for the externalization of hostility onto operational enemies. Aboriginally, when Apaches did not question the veracity of their world view, such folklore, and religious figures, combined with cultural bogies, effectively served their purposes (Bascom 1954). Today, with growing contact with the rest of the world, faith in such veracity is badly eroded and aggression is more and more often turned toward the self in unhealthy ways. The overt hostility of individuals toward relatives and other members of the group, family surrogates, results in tribal erosion. The efficacy of culturally provided enemies has diminished greatly and tribal cohesion suffers, as does the mental health of individuals.

Obviously, throughout the existence of these Athabascan-speaking Indians, their nomadic, warring lifestyle and existence in the wilderness made inevitable the eternal presence of actual human and animal enemies. Like the people of all other groups, they considered themselves to be *indeh*, the people, and all others to be *indah*, the enemy. Outsiders were inferior beings, to be treated more or less like dangerous animals and, ultimately, like things. An unknown Indian would have to prove his kinship relatedness or friendship or he would be treated like an enemy; whites and Mexicans were automatically assumed to be enemies. The Apaches, to replenish their numbers and obtain slaves, made kidnapping forays, especially among the Mexicans, to capture women and children. The offspring of Mexican captives who have been official tribal members for generations are still looked upon as inferiors, even as "things." On such raids the men were killed.

In order to rationalize their immeasurable cruelty toward defeated males, the Apaches ascribed to them intense sadistic desires and treachery. They may have served more convincingly as bad-parent surrogates than did dangerous wild animals, which were simply killed and not tortured.

CONCLUSION

Man's aggression must be dealt with in ways that enable him to function effectively as a prideful citizen and to permit his continued existence in an evermore dangerous world. Man needs external objects, real or imaginary, that he defines as bad, or as enemies, upon which to externalize his inner bad self- and other representations in order to maintain a favorable self-image and peace in his group. The data pertaining to Chiricahua and Mescalero Apache Indians demonstrate their use of externalization of aggression as an effective adjunct to the maintenance of group solidarity and continuity. Their religion and folklore are shown to be most important in the presentation of culturally prescribed figures upon which to externalize aggression.

References

Adler, A. (1908). Der Aggressionstrieb im Leben und in der Neurosen. *Fortschrift Der Medizin*, Vol. 19.
Ball, E. (1970). *In the Days of Victorio*. Tucson: University of Arizona Press.
——— (1980). *An Apache Odyssey. Indeh*. Provo, UT: Brigham Young University Press.
Bascom, W. (1954). Four functions of folklore. *Journal of American Folklore* 66:333–349.
Basehart, H. W. (1959). *Chiricahua Apache Subsistence and Socio-Political Organization*. University of New Mexico Mescalero-Chiricahua Land Claims Project, mimeographed.
——— (1960). *Mescalero Apache Subsistence Patterns and Socio-Political Organi-*

zation. University of New Mexico Mescalero-Chiricahua Land Claims Project, mimeographed.

Bion, W. R. (1961). *Experience in Groups.* New York: Basic Books.

Blos, P. (1968). Character formation in adolescence. In *The Adolescent Passage*, pp. 171–191. New York: International Universities Press, 1979.

Bourke, J. G. (1891). *On the Border with Crook.* Chicago: Rio Grande Press, 1962.

Boyer, L. B. (1956). On maternal overstimulation and ego defects. *Psychoanalytic Study of the Child* 11:236–256. New York: International Universities Press.

———— (1964a). Psychological problems of a group of Apaches: alcoholic hallucinosis and latent homosexuality. *Psychoanalytic Study of Society* 3:203–277. New York: International Universities Press.

———— (1964b). An example of legend distortion from the Apaches of the Mescalero Indian reservation. *Journal of American Folklore* 77:118–142.

———— (1970). La guerra interpretada como una institución social que promueve la solidaridad del grupo. In *El Psicoanálisis Frente A La Guerra*, ed. R. Alonso. Buenos Aires: Editorial Rodolfo Alonso.

———— (1975). The man who turned into a water monster. A psychoanalytic contribution to folklore. *Psychoanalytic Study of Society* 6:100–133. New York: International Universities Press.

———— (1977). Anthropology and psychoanalysis. *International Encyclopedia of Neurology, Psychiatry, Psychoanalysis and Psychology*, vol. 2, ed. B. B. Wolman, pp. 56–62. New York: Van Nostrand Reinhold/Aesculapius.

———— (1978). On aspects of the mutual influences of anthropology and psychoanalysis. *Journal of Psychoanalytic Anthropology* 1:265–296.

———— (1979). *Childhood and Folklore. A Psychoanalytic Study of Apache Personality.* New York: Library of Psychological Anthropology.

———— (1983). *The Regressed Patient.* New York: Jason Aronson.

Boyer, L. B., and Boyer, R. M. (1967a). Some influences of acculturation on the personality traits of the old people of the Mescalero and Chiricahua Apaches. *Psychoanalytic Study of Society* 4:170–184. New York: International Universities Press.

———— (1967b). A combined anthropological and psychoanalytic contribution to folklore. *Psychopathologie Africaine* 3:333–372.

———— (1968–1971). Un aporte mixto, antropologic y psicoanalítico, al folklore. *Cuadernos Del Instituto Nacional De Antropología* (Buenos Aires) 7:111–138.

———— (1972). Effects of acculturation on the vicissitudes of the aggressive drive among the Apaches of the Mescalero Indian reservation. *Psychoanalytic Study of Society* 5:40–82. New York: International Universities Press.

———— (1976). Prolonged adolescence and early identification: cross-cultural study. *Psychoanalytic Study of Society* 7:95–106. New York: International Universities Press.

———— (1977). Understanding the patient through folklore. *Contemporary Psychoanalysis* 13:30–51.

Boyer, L. B., Boyer, R. M., and De Vos, G. A. (1982). An Apache woman's account of her recent acquisition of the shamanistic status. *Journal of Psychoanalytic Anthropology* 5:299–331.

Boyer, L. B., De Vos, G. A., and Boyer, R. M. (1983). A longitudinal study of three Apache brothers as reflected in their Rorschach protocols. *Journal of Psychoanalytic Anthropology* 6:125–161.

——— (1985). Crisis and continuity in the life of an Apache shaman. *Psychoanalytic Study of Society* 11:63–113. Hillsdale, NJ: Analytic Press.

Boyer, R. M. (1962). *Social structure and socialization among the Apache of the Mescalero Indian reservation.* Unpublished doctoral dissertation, University of California, Berkeley.

——— (1964). The matrifocal family among the Mescalero; additional data. *American Anthropologist* 66:593–602.

——— (1972). A Mescalero Apache tale: the bat and the flood. *Western Folklore* 31:189–197.

Boyer, R. M., and Boyer, L. B. (1981). Apache lore of the bat. *Psychoanalytic Study of Society* 9:257–262. New York: Psychohistory Press.

Boyer, R. M., and Layton, N. D. (1992). *Apache Mothers and Daughters.* Norman, OK and London: University of Oklahoma Press.

Calhoun, J. S., and Twitchell, R. E. (1912). *The Leading Facts of New Mexican History,* 5 Vols. Cedar Rapids: Torch Press.

Chavez, J. C. (1939). Extinctión de los Apaches. *Boletin de la Sociedad Chihuahuense de Estudios Históricos* 1:336–377.

——— (1944). El indio "Victorio." *Boletin de la Sociedad Chihuahuense de Estudios Historicos* 5:509–513.

Chittenden, H. M. (1902). *A History of the American Fur Trade of the Far West.* Vol. 2. Stanford, CA: Academic Reprints, 1954.

Clements, W. W., and Mohr, D. V. (1961). *Chronic subdural hematomas in infants.* Paper presented at the Annual U.S. Public Health Service National Clinical Meeting, Lexington, KY, April.

Cremony, John G. (1868). *Life among the Apaches.* Tucson: University of Arizona Press, 1954.

Debo, A. (1976). *Geronimo. The Man, His Life, His Place.* Norman: University of Oklahoma Press.

Diccionario Porrua Historia, Biografía y Ceografut de Mexico (1964). Mexico City: Editorial Porrua.

Einstein, A., and Freud, S. (1933). Why war? *Standard Edition* 22:199–218.

Ekstein, R. (1984). Freud and Adler. *Bulletin of the Southern California Psychoanalytic Institute and Society* No. 68, pp. 7–10.

Erikson, E. H. (1950). *Childhood and Society.* New York: Norton.

——— (1956). The problem of identity. *Journal of the American Psychoanalytic Association* 4:56–121.

——— (1966). Ontogeny of ritualization. In *Psychoanalysis—A General Psy-*

chology. Essays in Honor of Heinz Hartmann, ed. R. M. Loewenstein, L. M. Newman, M. Schur, and A. J. Solnit, pp. 601–621. New York: International Universities Press.

Fletcher, R. (1968). *Instinct in Man in the Light of Recent Work in Comparative Psychology.* New York: International Universities Press.

Forbes, J. D. (1960). *Apache, Navaho, and Spaniard.* Norman: University of Oklahoma Press.

Freud, A. (1958). Adolescence. *Psychoanalytic Study of the Child* 13:225–278. New York: International Universities Press.

Freud, S. (1905). Three essays on the theory of sexuality. *Standard Edition* 7:130–243.

——— (1909). Analysis of a phobia in a five-year-old boy. *Standard Edition* 10:5–152.

——— (1915a). Thoughts for the times on war and death. *Standard Edition* 14:273–302.

——— (1915b). Instincts and their vicissitudes. *Standard Edition* 14:109–140.

——— (1915–1916). Introductory lectures on psychoanalysis. *Standard Edition* 15.

——— (1920). Beyond the pleasure principle. *Standard Edition* 18:7–66.

——— (1923). The ego and the id. *Standard Edition* 19:12–68.

——— (1930). Civilization and its discontents. *Standard Edition* 21:64–148.

Fromm, E. (1973). *The Anatomy of Human Destructiveness.* New York: Holt, Rinehart and Winston.

Fromm, E., and Maccoby, M. (1971). *Social Character in a Mexican Village: A Sociopsychoanalytic Study.* New York: Prentice-Hall.

Geertz, C. (1973). *The Interpretation of Culture.* New York: Basic Books.

Greenacre, P. (1969). The fetish and the transitional object. In *Emotional Growth,* vol. 1. New York: International Universities Press, 1971.

Grolnick, S. A., Barkin, L., and Muensterberger, W. (1978). *Fantasy and Reality. Transitional Objects and Phenomena.* New York: Jason Aronson.

Gunnarson, D. A. (1956). *The Southern Athapascans: Their Arrival in the Southwest.* Santa Fe: Museum of New Mexico.

Haley, J. L. (1981). *Apaches: A History and Culture Portrait.* Garden City, NY: Doubleday.

Hall, E. T., Jr. (1944). Recent clues to Athabascan prehistory in the Southwest. *American Anthropologist* 46:98–106.

Hartmann, H. (1939). *Ego Psychology and the Problem of Adaptation.* New York: International Universities Press, 1958.

——— (1944). Psychoanalysis and sociology. In *Essays on Ego Psychology. Selected Papers in Psychoanalytic Theory,* Chapter 2. New York: International Universities Press, 1964.

Hoffer, W. (1949). Mouth, hand and ego-integration. *Psychoanalytic Study of the Child* 3/4:49–56. New York: International Universities Press.

Hoijer, H. J. (1938a). The Southern Athabascan language. *American Anthropologist* 40:74–87.

——— (1938b). *Chiricahua and Mescalero Texts*. Chicago: University of Chicago Press.

Huscher, H. A., and Huscher, B. H. (1942). Athabaskan migration via the intermontane region. *American Antiquity* 8:80–88.

Jacobson, E. (1964). *The Self and the Object World*. New York: International Universities Press.

James, W. (1890). *Principles of Psychology*. New York: Holt, Rinehart and Winston.

Jones, E. (1955). *The Life and Work of Sigmund Freud. 1901–1919. Years of Maturity*, Chapter 3. New York: Basic Books.

Kernberg, O. F. (1975). *Borderline Personality and Pathological Narcissism*. New York: Jason Aronson.

——— (1976). *Object Relations Theory and Clinical Psychoanalysis*. New York: Jason Aronson.

Kohut, H. (1977). *The Restoration of the Self*. New York: International Universities Press.

Kojeve, A. (1969). *Introduction to the Reading of Hegel*. New York: Basic Books.

Lichtenberg, G. C. (1959). *The Lichtenberg Reader. Selected Writings*, trans. H. Mautner and H. Hatfield. Boston: Beacon.

——— (1967). *Werke in Einem Band*. Hamburg: Hoffman und Campe Verlag.

Lorenz, K. (1963). *On Aggression*. New York: Harcourt, Brace & World, 1966.

——— (1965). *Evolution and Modification of Behavior*. Chicago: University of Chicago Press.

Lummis, C. F. (1966). *General Crook and the Apache Wars*. Flagstaff, AZ: Northland.

Maccoby, M. (1972). *Technology, Work and Character*. Cambridge: Harvard University Press.

Mack, J. E. (1983). Nationalism and the self. *Psychohistory Review* 2:47–69.

Mahler, M. S. (1968). *On Human Symbiosis and the Vicissitudes of Individuation*. New York: International Universities Press.

Mahler, M. S., Pine, F., and Bergman, A. (1975). *The Psychological Birth of the Human Infant*. New York: Basic Books.

Mails, T. E. (1974). *The People Called Apache*. Englewood Cliffs, NJ: Prentice-Hall.

Maloney, C., ed. (1976). *The Evil Eye*. New York: Columbia University Press.

McDermott, J. J., ed. (1967). *The Writing of William James*. New York: Random House.

McDougall, W. (1923). *An Outline of Psychology*. London: Methuen.

Millan, I., and Maccoby, M. (1975). Que es el sociopsicoanálisis? *Revista Mexicana de Sociología* 37:393–423.

Novick, J., and Kelly, K. (1970). Projection and externalization. *Psychoanalytic Study of the Child* 25:69–95. New York: International Universities Press.

Ochoa, H. E. (1949). *Integración y Desintegración de Nuestra Frontera Norte.* Mexico City: Universidad Nacional.

Ogden, T. H. (1985a). On potential space. *International Journal of Psycho-Analysis* 66:129–142.

——— (1985b). *The Matrix of the Mind.* New York: Jason Aronson.

Ogle, R. H. (1940). *Federal Control of the Western Apaches: 1848–1886.* Albuquerque: University of New Mexico Press.

Opler, M. E. (1938). Myths and tales of the Jicarilla Apaches. *Memoirs of the American Folklore Society,* vol. 31. New York: Augustin.

——— (1940). Myths and legends of the Lipan Apaches. *Memoirs of the American Folklore Society,* vol. 36. New York: Augustin.

——— (1941). *An Apache Life-Way.* Chicago: University of Chicago Press.

——— (1942). Myths and tales of the Chiricahua Apaches. *Memoirs of the American Folklore Society,* vol. 37. New York: Augustin.

——— (1947). Notes on Chiricahua Apache culture. 1. Supernatural power and the shaman. *Primitive Man* 2:1–14.

——— (1969). *Apache Odyssey. A Journey between Two Worlds.* New York: Holt, Rinehart and Winston.

Pinderhughes, C. A. (1970). The universal resolution of ambivalence by paranoia with an example of black and white. *American Journal of Psychotherapy* 24:597–610.

——— (1974). Ego development and cultural differences. *American Journal of Psychiatry* 131:171–175.

——— (1979). Differential bonding: toward a psycho-physiological theory of stereotyping. *American Journal of Psychiatry* 136:33–37.

——— (1982). Paired differential bonding in biological, psychological and social systems. *American Journal of Social Psychiatry* 2:5–14.

Rascovsky, A., and Rascovsky, M. W. de (1980). La matanza de los hijos. In *La Matanza de Los Hijos y Otros Ensayos,* ed. A. Rascovsky, pp. 9–38. Buenos Aires: Kargieman.

Roheim, G. (1952). The evil eye. *American Imago* 9:351–363.

Romero, M. (1944). Victor el Apache que creo mi madre era hijo del gran jefe de los Apaches "Victorio." *Boletin de la Sociedad Chihuahuense de Estudios Históricos* 6:509–513.

Sarnoff, C. (1976). *Latency.* New York: Jason Aronson.

Schroeder, A. H. (1974). *Study of the Apache Indians.* 2 vols. New York: Garland.

Shils, E. (1957). Primordial, personal, sacred and civil ties. *British Journal of Sociology* 8:130–145.

Skinner, B. F. (1953). *Science and Human Behavior.* New York: Macmillan.

Spicer, E. H. (1962). *Cycles of Conquest: The Impact of Spain, Mexico and the United States on the Indians of the Southwest.* Tucson: University of Arizona Press.

Stein, H. F. (1985). Psychological complementarity in Soviet-American relations. *Political Psychology* 6:249–261.

———— (1986). To find a good enough enemy: the psychological "fit" between the United States and Soviet Union. In *Slaying Mankind's Most Pernicious Dragon: Basic Human Aggression*. New York: Human Sciences Press.

Stern, D. N. (1983). Implications of infancy research for clinical theory and practice. *Dialogue* 6:9–20.

Stout, J. A. (1974). *Apache Lightning. The Last Great Battles of the Ojo Calientes*. New York: Oxford University Press.

Terrazas, D. J. (1905). *Memorias*. Juarez: Imprinta de "El Agricultor Mexicano" Escobar Hnos.

Terrell, J. U. (1974). *Apache Chronicle. The Story of the People*. New York: Crowell.

Thomas, A. B. (1959a). *The Mescalero Apache, 1653–1874*. University of New Mexico Mescalero-Chiricahua Land Claims Project, mimeographed.

———— (1959b). *The Lipan Apache, 1718–1856*. University of New Mexico Mescalero-Chiricahua Land Claims Project, mimeographed.

———— (1959c). *The Chiricahua Apache, 1695–1876*. University of New Mexico Mescalero-Chiricahua Land Claims Project, mimeographed.

Thrapp, D. L. (1967). *The Conquest of Apacheria*. Norman: University of Oklahoma Press.

———— (1974). *Victorio and the Mimbres Apaches*. Norman: University of Oklahoma Press.

Tinbergen, N. (1953). *Social Behavior in Animals, with Special Reference to Vertebrates*. New York: Wiley.

———— (1968). Of war and peace in animals and men, an ethologist's approach to the biology of aggression. *Science* 160:1411–1418.

Torres, M. (1960). *El Irracionalismo en Erich Fromm*. Mexico City: Editorial Paz Mexico.

Tourney, G., and Plazak, D. J. (1954). Evil eye in myth and schizophrenia. *Psychiatric Quarterly* 28:478–495.

Tustin, F. (1984). Autistic shapes. *International Review of Psychoanalysis* 11:279–290.

Vereecken, J. L. T. (1968). A propos du mauvais oeil. *Hygiene Mentale* 57:25–38.

Volkan, V. D. (1976). *Primitive Internalized Object Relations*. New York: International Universities Press.

———— (1979). *Cyprus — War and Adaptation*. Charlottesville: University Press of Virginia.

———— (1981). "Immortal" Ataturk. Narcissism and creativity in a revolutionary leader. *Psychoanalytic Study of Society* 9:221–255. New York: Psychohistory Press.

———— (1985). The need to have enemies and allies: a developmental approach. *Political Psychology* 6:219–247.

Volkan, V. D., and Itzkowitz, N. (1984). *The Immortal Ataturk. A Psychobiography*. Chicago: University of Chicago Press.

Wellman, P. I. (1934). *The Indian Wars of the West*. Garden City, NY: Doubleday.

Winnicott, D. W. (1953). Transitional objects and transitional phenomena. *International Journal of Psycho-Analysis* 34:89–97.

——— (1958). *Collected Papers. Through Paediatrics to Psycho-Analysis.* New York: Basic Books.

——— (1965). *The Maturational Process and the Facilitating Environment.* New York: International Universities Press.

Woodward, A. H. (1961). Side lights on fifty years of Apache warfare. *Arizoniana* 2:3–14.

Worcester, D. E. (1979). *The Apaches. Eagles of the Southwest.* Norman: University of Oklahoma Press.

6

Approaching Cross-Cultural Psychotherapy

INTRODUCTION

Psychotherapeusis is most challenging with two groups of patients: those who have primitive personality disorders and those whose cultural backgrounds differ significantly from that of the therapist. Specialized education enhances the therapist's effectiveness with each group (Boyer 1964a, 1982). A major impediment to successful clinical work with the individual from either group is the therapist's incapacity to understand and respond significantly to the patient's communications. The verbal and nonverbal messages of the regressed patient are confusing largely because of idiosyncratic distortions while those of the transcultural patient are baffling additionally because of the communication style and ethnic expectations that become automatic for him due to his socialization experiences. Unless the therapist is aware of some of those cultural expectations and can frame his actions according to that awareness, therapy is almost bound to fail.

This brief chapter will deal only with a discrepancy between the patient's and the therapist's therapeutic goals. Such a discrepancy appears most often in the Americas and Western Europe in the treatment of individuals who stem from ethnic minorities that have fostered the development and retention of religiomedical philosophies that are consistent with the practice of shamanism, including *curanderismo, espiritismo,* voodoo, *obeah,* rootwork, *candomble,* and other forms of faith healing (Bastide 1961, Bird and Canino 1981, Comas-Diáz 1981, de Rio 1976, Freyre 1936, Garrison 1977, Golden 1977, Gonzalez-Wippler 1982, Herskovits 1976, Hillard 1982, Hillard and Rockwell 1978, Kiev 1968, Leininger 1973, Moerman 1979, Ribeiro 1952, Rodrigues 1900, Snow 1974, Tinling 1967, Trotter and Chavira 1981, Williams 1932, Wintrob 1973, Wohlcke 1970, 1972). Clearly, the treatment problem will be especially complicated when the patient's expectations of such supernatural cure is repressed.

SHAMANISTIC PHILOSOPHIES

During my 50 years of practice in an urban area populated predominantly by ethnic minorities I have treated patients whose expectations of psychotherapy were colored by all but one of the varieties of faith healing mentioned above. Nevertheless, I shall deal here solely with Apache shamanism. I know this variety best because I did combined psychoanalytic and anthropological research among some Apaches for forty years, during two of which my principal investigative mode was the practice of psychotherapy in which I practically limited my activities to the interpretation of resistance to therapy and to personal growth, and the transference (Boyer 1979). The underlying philosophies of Apache shamanism are shared by all of the just-named kinds of faith healing, although manifest variations occur in all other cultures and subcultures.

Apache religion and medical practices are inextricably related. Almost the gamut of their mythology and folklore is an extension of their religiomedical practices and serves both to indoctrinate aboriginal beliefs into children and to support those same beliefs. Discussion here is limited to the essence of shamanistic philosophies and practices.

In the aboriginal Apache conceptualization, all disease and misfortune is caused by the actions of affronted "powers"—witches and ghosts—and shamanistic intervention is required to negate those actions (Boyer 1964b, 1979, Opler 1941). This belief appears to exist in all of today's Apaches on some level of consciousness despite more than 100 years of westernization and the graduation of some individuals from universities.

The Apaches conceptualize supernatural power to be universal and to inhabit all natural phenomena. The site of residence of power determines its name. To make contact with a person, snake power, bear power, lightning power, or yucca power, as examples, appears to him and offers him its use and the songs and ceremonies that make its application effective. The man or woman who accepts the power must agree to assume its implicit awesome responsibilities and the potential dangers involved in its use. He may receive various powers in subsequent visitations. Typically, two fundamental steps are involved in an individual's acquisition of sha-manistic status. He must accept as his possession supernatural power that has appeared to him in a "power dream," ordinarily in an altered ego state, more rarely during a vision quest (Benedict 1922). Subsequently, his claim that he has come into possession of supernatural power must be credited by his culture mates (Boyer et al. 1964).

Once a person has accepted supernatural power as his own, be it snake, bear, or some other power, he may use it for good, that is, shamanistic, or bad, that is, witchcraft purposes as he chooses. Thus he may serve as a good or bad maternal part-object projection which is culturally supported. The shamanistic practices of most of the North American Indians, including the Apaches, seldom include the entrance of the curer into a trance or ecstatic state as is required of shamans in most parts of the world and of other faith healers as well (Backman and Hultkrantz 1978, Best 1922, Devereux 1956, Ducey 1976, Edsman 1967, Eliade 1951, Kim 1972, Lommel 1967, Luckert 1979, Nadel 1946, Parin et al. 1963, Roheim 1951, 1954, Shirokogoroff 1924, Vajda 1964). In Apache shamanistic cure, the laying on of hands, the administration of herbs, and the use of prestidigi-tation and the like serve essentially to enhance the patient's belief in the curer's omnipotence. In many cultures hallucinogens and consciousness-altering drugs are used for that purpose and to reduce the patient's capacity to think logically (Boyer et al. 1973, Furst 1972, La Barre 1980).

In the past, specific powers were thought to be effective against specific illnesses but some powers might be used indiscriminately. Today identical powers are used to counteract all misfortunes, and shamanistic cure is sought primarily for the treatment of "ghost sickness," which is attributed to the actions of lonely or vengeful spirits of dead loved ones.

SOME POINTS OF COMPARISON BETWEEN FAITH HEALING AND INSIGHT-ORIENTED PSYCHOTHERAPY

In faith healing, diagnosis is fundamentally irrelevant and recovery depends on supernatural forces. Its therapeusis uses exhortation and mobilizes religious and personal fervor, often in an effort to induce altered levels of consciousness to diminish the patient's use of rational thought. The role of suggestion is paramount and the patient's submission is obligatory. The therapist's effort is to remove immediately a symptom or symptom complex and the duration of relief is not crucial since the curer aims to maintain his emotional hold over the patient, that is, to exploit transference and subjugate the patient to continuing dependency. In faith healing, reliance on evidence is in itself irreligious.

Western psychiatry holds with the attitude that diagnosis is essential and treatments are ideally specific. For the insight-oriented psychotherapist, belief is no substitute for evidence; his hypotheses are to be tested against emerging data and the therapeutic alliance (Greenson 1965, Meissner 1982, Schafer 1959, Zetzel 1956) is vitally important. He invites his patient to retain an observing part of the ego and interprets regression as defense and/or resistance. He sees the patient's wish to view him as omnipotent as a part of transference phenomena and his aim is to free the patient both of transference distortions and of his relationship with the therapist. He knows that abrupt symptom removal frequently disguises underlying psychopathology. He views suggestion therapy to be not infrequently a manifestation of countertransference problems (Cesio 1973, Grinberg 1979, Little 1951, Marcondes 1966, Orr 1954, Prado Galvao 1966, Racker 1968).

DISCUSSION

The practice of good insight-oriented psychotherapy with patients with primitive personality organizations requires specialized training. A main obstacle to successful treatment is the therapist's inability to understand and respond beneficially to the client's distorted verbal and nonverbal communications. Such inability may be the product of his not having learned adequately to comprehend the effects of regression on those communications or his being unable to avoid damaging countertransference involvement (Boyer 1982, Giovacchini 1979, Giovacchini et al. 1975, Searles 1979). It is rare that the second problem can be alleviated without personal psychoanalysis.

Additional knowledge is required for good psychotherapy of whatever genre with the transcultural patient. The style, content, and implications of his verbal and nonverbal communications will be both idiosyncratic and determined by his specific background. Clearly, if the therapist and his client cannot converse in the same tongue, treatment will be impeded (Mason 1981). The therapist's capacity to understand and communicate effectively with the cross-cultural patient will be enhanced if he has learned enough about the patient's specific cultural or subcultural social structure and child-rearing processes to reduce his seeing the material of the interviews in terms of his own ethnocentric expectations (Boyer and Boyer 1977). Stated otherwise, he must know enough about his client's background and about himself to be able to put aside perceptions distorted by stereotyped thinking that is based on the ignorance and prejudices that result from his own unconscious conflicts.

A major problem in psychotherapy with some transcultural patients is a discrepancy between the therapist's and the client's expectations of treatment. This is particularly true when the patient hopes for cure through faith healing. In cultures in which such expectations are generated, religio-medical practices are bound inextricably with mythology and other forms of folklore and much of which is taught to growing children through story telling. In those cultures, everyday verbal and nonverbal communications include frequent allusions to mythological and legendary events that reinforce belief in indigenous, shamanistically oriented religiomedical philosophies (Bascom 1954). In order for the therapist to understand his patient's messages, he must know not only the principles of shamanistic philosophies and practices but also the details of the specific brand of faith healing that has constituted a highly emotionally charged part of the patient's background.

The discrepancy between the patient's and the therapist's expectations of treatment need not constitute an overwhelming obstacle to ongoing and successful insight-oriented psychotherapy. Many authors have reported favorable outcomes of such treatment. My interpretative treatment of Apaches in the field successfully removed phobias, psychosomatic symptomology, and episodes of "ghost sickness" and strengthened individuals' ego structures so that they could ameliorate sadomasochistic entanglements and renounce drunkenness for varying lengths of time.

A special and fascinating problem exists when the transcultural patient's expectations of faith healing has been repressed, as often occurs with the highly acculturated individual. The therapist's thorough knowledge of the mythology, folklore, and religiomedical philosophies and practices of the patient's culture or subculture will help him understand allusions to such material of which the patient is unaware. An example will suffice.

The analysis of a black university professor whose early years had been spent in a rural community in the Deep South had reached an impasse. I suspected that progress was impeded because of an unconscious expectation of faith healing connected with repressed memories associated with rootwork. My more detailed inquiries about his childhood experiences led to changes in his manifest dream content. First appeared teeth with their roots, then underwater plants that reminded him of "animated roots," and finally a tree with its exposed roots. Further inquiries and interpretations led to his recovery of repressed childhood experiences and their inculcation within him of the unconscious expectation of faith healing. This significant knowledge alleviated the impasse and proved to be a turning point in his analysis.

SUMMARY

Optimal psychotherapy requires mutual understanding of verbal and non-verbal messages by the therapist and the patient. Transcultural patients have culturally determined as well as idiosyncratic ways of expressing themselves. In cultures in which the expectation of faith healing is indoctrinated, everyday language includes allusions to the mythology and folklore through which shamanistic religiomedical philosophies and practices are communicated to the growing person and support them. The therapist should know the specific religiomedical philosophies and practices and relevant folklore of his cross-cultural patient. Such knowledge will make it easier for him to detect the patient's expectation of cure through faith healing and to take that expectation into account in designing a treatment program.

References

Backman, L., and Hultkrantz, A. (1978). *Studies in Lapp Shamanism*. Acta Universitatis Stockholmiensis. Stockholm Studies in Comparative Religion, No. 16. Stockholm: Almqvist & Wiksell.

Bascom, W. (1954). Four functions of folklore. *Journal of American Folklore* 67:333–349.

Bastide, R. (1961). *The African Religions of Brazil*. Baltimore: Johns Hopkins University Press, 1978.

Benedict, R. (1922). The vision quest in Plains Indian culture. *American Anthropology* 24:1–23.

Best, E. (1922). *Spiritual and Mental Concepts of the Maori*. Wellington, NZ: Government Printer.

Bird, H. R., and Canino, I. (1981). The sociopsychiatry of Espiritismo. Findings of a study in psychiatric populations of Puerto Rican and other Hispanic children. *Journal of American Academy of Child Psychiatry* 20:725–740.

Boyer, L. B. (1964a). Psychoanalytic insights in working with ethnic minorities. *Social Casework* 45:519–526.

———— (1964b). Folk psychiatry of the Apaches of the Mescalero Indian reservation. In *Magic, Faith and Healing. Studies in Primitive Psychiatry Today*, ed. A. Kiev, pp. 348–419. Glencoe, IL: Free Press.

———— (1979). *Childhood and Folklore. A Psychoanalytic Study of Apache Personality*. New York: Library of Psychological Anthropology.

———— (1982). On analytic experience in working with regressed patients. In *Technical Factors in the Treatment of the Severely Disturbed Patient*, ed. P. L. Giovacchini and L. B. Boyer, pp. 65–106. New York: Jason Aronson.

Boyer, L. B., and Boyer, R. M. (1977). Understanding the patient through folklore. *Contemporary Psychoanalysis* 13:30–51.

Boyer, L. B., Boyer, R. M., and Basehart, H. W. (1973). Shamanism and peyote use among the Apaches of the Mescalero Indian reservation. In *Hallucinogens and Shamanism*, ed. M. Harner, pp. 52–66. New York: Oxford University Press.

Boyer, L. B., Klopfer, B., Brawer, F. B., and Kawai, H . (1964). Comparisons of the shamans and pseudoshamans of the Apaches of the Mescalao Indian reservation. *Journal of Protective Techniques and Personality Assessment* 28:173–180.

Cesio, F. R. (1973). Los fundamentales de la contratransfaencia. El yo ideal y las identificaciones directas. *Revista de Psicoanalysis* 30:5–16.

Comas-Diás, L. (1981). Puerto Rico *Espiritismo* and psychotherapy. *American Journal of Orthopsychiatry* 51:636–644.

de Rio, J. (1976). *As Religoes No Rio*. Rio de Janeiro: Nova Aguilar.

Devereux, G. (1956). Normal and abnormal; the key problem of psychiatric anthropology. In *Some Uses of Anthropology, Theoretical and Applied*, pp. 23–48. Washington, DC: Anthropological Society of Washington.

Ducey, C. (1976). The life history and creative psychopathology of the shaman: ethnopsychoanalytic perspectives. *Psychoanalytic Study of Society* 7:173–230. New Haven, CT: Yale University Press.

Edsman, C. M., ed. (1967). *Studies in Shamanism*. Scripta Instituti Donneriani Aboensis. Stockholm: Almqvist & Wiksell.

Eliade, M. (1951). *Shamanism: Archaic Techniques of Ecstasy*. New York: Bollingen Foundation, 1964.

Freyre, G. (1936). *Sobrados e Macumbas*. São Paulo: Nacional.

Furst, P. S., ed. (1972). *Flesh of the Gods: The Ritual Use of Hallucinogens*. London: George Allen & Unwin.

Garrison, V. (1977). The "Puerto Rican syndrome" in psychiatry and *espiritismo*. In *Case Studies in Spirit Possession*, ed. V. Crapanzano and V. Garrison, pp. 383–449. New York: Wiley.

Giovacchini, P. L. (1979). Countertransference with primitive mental states. In *Countertransference: The Therapist's Contribution to the Therapeutic Situation*, ed. L. Epstein and A. H. Feina, pp. 235–265. New York: Jason Aronson.

Giovacchini, P. L., Flarsheim, A., and Boyer, L. B., eds. (1975). *Tactics and Techniques in Psychoanalytic Therapy*. Vol. II: *Countertransference*. New York: Jason Aronson.

Golden, K. M. (1977). Voodoo in Africa and the United States. *American Journal of Psychiatry* 134:1425–1427.

Gonzales-Wippler, M. (1982). *The Santería Experience*. Englewood Cliffs, NJ: Prentice-Hall.

Greenson, R. R. (1965). The working alliance and the transference neurosis. *Psychoanalytic Quarterly* 34:155–181.

Grinberg, L. (1979). Countertransference and projective identification. *Contemporary Psychoanalysis* 15:226–247.

Herskovits, M. (1976). The social organization of the Candomble. *Anais XXXVI Congresso de Americanistas*. Nendeln, Lichtenstein: Kraus Reprints.

Hillard, J. R. (1982). Diagnosis and treatment of the rootwork victim. *Psychiatric Annals* 12:705–714.

Hillard, J. R., and Rockwell, W. J. K. (1978). Dysesthesia, witchcraft and conversion reaction: a case treated successfully with psychotherapy. *Journal of the American Medical Association* 240:1742–1744.

Kiev, A. (1968). *Curanderismo: Mexican-American Folk Psychiatry*. New York: Free Press.

Kim, K. (1972). Psychoanalytic consideration of Korean shamanism. *Journal of the Korean Psychoanalytic Association* 1:121–129.

La Barre, W. (1980). Anthropological perspectives on hallucination, hallucinogens and the shamanic origins of religion. In *Culture in Context*, pp. 37–92. Durham, NC: Duke University Press.

Leininger, M. (1973). Witchcraft practices and psychocultural therapy with urban United States families. *Human Organization* 32:73–83.

Little, M. (1951). Counter-transference and the patient's response to it. *International Journal of Psycho-Analysis* 32:3240.

Lommel, A. (1967). *Shamanism: The Beginnings of Art*. New York: McGraw-Hill.

Luckert, K. W. (1979). *Coyoteway: A Navaho Holyway Ceremonial*, p. 12. Tucson: University of Arizona Press.

Marcondes, D. (1966). A regressão na contratransferencia. *Revista Brasileira de Psicanálisis* 2:11–21.

Mason, J. C. (1981). Ethnicity and clinical care: Indians. *Hospital Physician* 10:112–125.

Meissner, W. W. (1982). Psychotherapy of the paranoid patient. In *Technical Factors in the Treatment of the Severely Disturbed Patient*, ed. P. L. Giovacchini and L. B. Boyer, pp. 111–123. New York: Jason Aronson.

Moerman, D. E. (1979). Anthropology of symbolic healing. *Current Anthropology* 20:59–80.

Nadel, S. F. (1946). A study of shamanism in the Nuba mountains. *Journal of the Royal Anthropological Institute* 7:25–37.

Opler, M. E. (1941). *An Apache Life-Way.* Chicago: University of Chicago Press.

Orr, D. W. (1954). Transference and countertransference. A historical survey. *Journal of the American Psychoanalytic Association* 2:621–670.

Parin, P., Morganthaler, F., and Parin-Matthey, G. (1963). Die Weissen Denken Zuviel. Psychoanalytischen Untersuchungen bei den Dogon in Westafrika. Zurich: Atlantis.

Prado Galvão, L. de A. (1966). Contratransferencia frente a regressão. *Revista Brasileira De Psicanâlise* 2:22–34.

Racker, H. (1968). *Transference and Countertransference.* New York: International Universities Press.

Ribeiro, R. (1952). *Cultos Afro-Brasileiros de Recife: Um Estudo de Adjustamento Social.* Recife: Boletim do Instituto Joaquim Nabuco de Pesquisa Social.

Rodrigues, N. (1900). *O Animismo Fetichista dos Negros Bahianos.* Rio de Janeiro: Civilizacao Brasileira, 1935.

Roheim, H. (1951). Hungarian shamanism. *Psychoanalysis and the Social Sciences* 3:131–169. New York: International Universities Press.

—— (1954). Hungarian and Vogul mythology. *Monographs of the American Ethnological Society* No. 23. Locust Valley: NY: J.J. Augustin.

Schafer, R. (1959). Generative empathy in the treatment situation. *Psychoanalytic Quarterly* 28:342–373.

Searles, H. F. (1979). *Countertransference and Related Subjects. Selected Papers.* New York: International Universities Press.

Shirokogoroff, S. M. (1924). *Psychomental Complex of the Tungus.* London: Kegan Paul, Trench, Trubner.

Snow, L. F. (1974). Folk beliefs and their implications for the care of patients. A review based on studies among Black Americans. *Annals of Internal Medicine* 81:82–96.

Tinling, D. C. (1967). Voodoo, rootwork and medicine. *Psychosomatic Medicine* 29:483–490.

Trotter, R. T., and Chavira, J. A. (1981). *Curanderismo, Mexican American Folk Healing.* Athens, GA: University of Georgia Press.

Vajda, L. (1964). Zur Phaseologischen Stellung des Schamanismus. In *Religionsethnologie*, ed. C. A. Schmitz, pp. 265–295. Frankfurt am Main.

Williams, J. J. (1932). *Voodoos and Obeahs: Phases of West India Witchcraft.* New York: L. MacVeagh, Dial Press.

Wintrob, R. (1973). The influence of others: witchcraft and rootwork as explanation of behavior disturbances. *Journal of Nervous and Mental Diseases* 156:318–326.

Wohlcke, M. (1970). Macumba und Umbanda in Lichte der Marginalität. Hamburg.

——— (1972). Macumba und Umbanda: Religiose auf die Gesellschaftliche-unterprivilerte Antworten Situation. *Zeitschrift für Kulturaustaustausch* 22:10–13.

Zetzel, E. R. (1956). Current concepts of transference. *International Journal of Psycho-Analysis* 37:369–376.

7

Psychoanalysis with Few Parameters in the Treatment of Regressed Patients, Reconsidered

Although I never had the privilege of studying under Frieda Fromm-Reichmann personally, she and her work inspired me and contributed substantially to my decision to work psychoanalytically with so-called primitive patients. I have two special memories of her that periodically delight me, pertaining to the presentation of a paper in a panel devoted to the difference between psychoanalysis and psychotherapy at a meeting of the American Psychoanalytic Association. Her contribution was, as it seemed to me, treated with smug contempt by two leading figures in the association. She was imperturbable in her quiet rebuttal that made them both look somewhat foolish. That evening, at a social gathering, someone asked her what she did when psychotic male patients wanted to have sexual relations with her. With a quiet smile she replied, "The last time that happened, I told the man I would have no objection to making love with him, but I did not believe it would be in the best interests of his treatment."

In this chapter I shall review briefly my experience in working with regressed patients, present some rough statistics pertaining to the efficacy of treatment, and give clinical material demonstrating the utility of the therapist's making interpretations on the basis of his reactions to material presented by the patient.

For fifty years my practice has consisted largely of patients who have suffered from disorders now included under the broadly defined category borderline syndrome, frequently a primitive and psychosis-prone variety. During the past forty years, all patients have been seen privately in my consultation room.

After having spent some years in treating such patients in traditionally recommended ways and studying the writings of therapists who, like Frieda Fromm-Reichmann (1950), were gifted in understanding and working with primitive patients, I concluded that Freud's belief that such patients were incapable of developing therapeutically useful transference relationships was incorrect. I knew that soon after the introduction of the structural theory with its profound influence on goals and technique, a few therapists had suggested that relatively unmodified psychoanalysis might be applicable to the treatment of patients who had "narcissistic neuroses" (Brunswick 1928, Garma 1931, LaForgue 1935, Landauer 1924, Waelder 1924) and that many case histories written by respected mid-century analysts showed that they maintained an orthodox analytic stance when their patients underwent serious regressions (Balint 1959, Jacobson 1954, Lewin 1946, 1950, H. A. Rosenfeld 1952a). Accordingly, I attempted psychoanalysis with few parameters as the experimental treatment mode for regressed patients. In 1961 I suggested that such therapy might be the treatment of choice for some primitive patients and ventured the then highly unpopular opinion that a principal impediment to the successful outcome of their therapy was to be found in unresolved countertransference problems. That position now receives considerable support (Ekstein 1966, Giovacchini 1979, Grinberg 1962, Kernberg 1975a,b, Maltsberger and Buie 1974, McDougall 1979, Milner 1969, Racker 1968, Volkan 1982, Wilson 1983, Winnicott 1960). Later, with many others, I became aware that the therapist's reactions to the patient can be used to the great enhancement of therapy (Cohen 1952, Gill 1982, Hann-Kende 1933, Little 1981, Searles 1979, Szalita-Pemow 1955, Volkan 1984).

My subsequent experience affirms my conjecture that psychoanalysis is the treatment of choice for many of such patients and is based on the following statistics.

I have treated 112 such patients; fifty were seen in face-to-face psychotherapy, once or twice weekly; the remainder received psychoanalysis, four or five, rarely three, times weekly. The choice of treatment was determined almost exclusively by finances and geography. Of the fifty patients seen in psychotherapy, thirteen improved and one was much improved. These individuals were principally from lower economic strata and had a long record of social irresponsibility; the vast majority terminated their therapy after only a few interviews. Of the psychoanalytic patients, nine stopped during the first year—one was improved; eighteen left in less than two years—fifteen were somewhat and one was much improved; twenty-nine continued to planned termination—three were improved and twenty-six were much improved. Treatment lasted seven to twelve years with patients whose pathologies included severe narcissistic disorders, long-term, fixed fetishism, and/or antisocial trends, as contrasted with four to seven years spent with other patients.

Marked impulsivity was a common trait, but no patient was addicted to hard drugs. No immoderate user of marijuana or alcohol did well in treatment until the practice was renounced. The patients ranged in age from 17 to 60 when treatment began (17–20, 1 percent; 21–30, 38 percent; 31–40, 32 percent; 41–50, 16 percent; 51–63, 13 percent). A few patients had not received previous treatment, but the great remainder had undergone therapy of various kinds for from three to twenty years.

All of the figures cited concerning the incidence of improvement result from the patients' and my subjective assessments. Even if they are roseate, they are far more encouraging than the figures given by others for treatment by means other than psychoanalysis (Carpenter et al. 1975, Stanton et al. 1984). Most writers provide no figures. Recent studies indicate that psychoanalysis is being used more frequently than formerly for the treatment of the so-called high-level patient and that others who function less well receive classical analysis following earlier psychotherapy with modifications (Adler 1985).

Those who have reviewed my work have been impressed with two primary qualities that emerge from my approach (Meissner 1985). The first pertains to my "capacity to tolerate the patient's regressive manifestations and to maintain the therapeutic contact with such patients through the course of the regression, thus maintaining the basic structure of the therapeutic situation and keeping the therapeutic alliance within reach" (p. 90). From boyhood I had an unusual capacity to understand primary-process-dominated thinking and early in my psychiatric training it became clear that patients' regressive manifestations provoked less anxiety in me than in most of my peers (Boyer 1983). In working with patients during periods of psychotic regression, I am ordinarily able to hold the analytic position calmly, both tolerating and dealing with the patient's behavior.

The second quality pertains to the structuring of the therapeutic context. I believe the most important element of the successful outcome of such treatment to be the provision and maintenance of a consistent, optimistic, empathic environment in which indirect ego and superego support is given. In structuring the setting, the prospective analysand is given details having to do with the specifics of running the therapy, such as appointment times, fees, arrangements for payments, being charged for missed appointments, and other details to be mentioned later, many having to do with the patient's responsibility within the therapy. The therapist's role and function are similarly carefully delineated. Treatment is carried out in a manner that constantly reinforces and never undermines the supposition that the patient carries much responsibility for his own growth and development of self-knowledge.

Social relationships of any degree are discouraged and telephone contacts are exceedingly rare. Searles has commented that I am more abstemious and employ fewer parameters in my treatment of primitive patients than he does with neurotics. Obviously this stance gives the patient the correct idea that I deem him to be less helpless and more capable of growth than he had thought himself to be.

On empirical grounds, some thirty years ago I discovered that the appearance early in the treatment of regressed patients of strongly cathected triadic relationship material regularly served to defend against the patient's dealing with dyadic conflicts (see also Volkan 1976). When such material was interpreted from its aggressive and defensive aspects, early serious impasses were avoided. Today, with our advanced understanding of the development of object relations, it is commonplace knowledge that the development of dyadic conflicts in the transference and their mutative interpretation usually must precede the analysis of oedipal data.

Fully cognizant of the regressed patient's preoccupation with separation and abandonment and also of the fact that I frequently absent myself from my practice for varying periods, I let my patients know from the outset that I shall be away four or five times yearly for from one to four or more weeks and I shall inform them of the dates of my proposed absences as soon as I know them myself. I have found that the patient's continuing background awareness of coming separations has kept active issues pertaining to abandonment and its causes, and facilitated their analysis. Patients who are being reanalyzed after treatment by others have often opined that their previous analysts' anxiety about separations had frightened them and made them more dependent. My attitude that patients can tolerate separations is quickly internalized by them.

The use of intellectualization as a stubborn defense is often troublesome, particularly with some patients who are schizoid, highly narcissistic, or have anal characters. Its resolution depends in large part on the patient's developing the capacity to cathect his thoughts affectually. Traditionally, analysts instruct their patients to try to disclose their thoughts during the session. I ask them to make a sincere effort to disclose also whatever emotion, physical sensation, or urge of which they become aware. It is my impression that this maneuver, with the patient's being reminded of it from time to time, may shorten the period taken before he begins to look for an emotional accompaniment to his thinking and to get to the generic material that led to separation of affect and thought.

It is clear that the nature of the transference of the regressed patient differs significantly from that of the person who suffers from a transference neurosis. The type of material projected by primitive patients is determined by the immature nature of their mental operations, including the selectively deficient modulation of their drives. Many therapists have noted the central position of conflicts related to the presence of untamed aggression (Fromm-Reichmann 1958, Hartmann 1953, Lidz and Lidz 1952). When the infantile nature of the transference is in full flower, the analyst is reacted to tenaciously as though he were representative of the infantile mother. Although Giovacchini (Boyer and Giovacchini 1980) believes that the psychopathology of borderline patients may be rooted in earlier periods of development, most observers think that it lies in patients' failure to traverse successfully the rapprochement subphase (Mahler 1972, Masterson 1972).

My belief in the importance of the unfolding transference–countertransference situation has led me to view automatically each session as if it were a dream, the most likely day residue determinant of which is to be found in an unresolved transference conflict of the last interview or series of interviews. That day residue will energize and be energized by a relevant unconscious infantile conflict or combination of conflicts. I regard the content of the interview as though it were the product of the dream work and, of course, attempt to influence that work. As do Greenacre (1975) and others, I keep copious process notes that make review dependable when I remain confused following a session or series of sessions, review that reduces the number of analytic impasses. This viewpoint has enabled me to be more objective while simultaneously empathetic. Its assumption has been particularly helpful to those of my supervisees who have overestimated the degree to which the patient responds realistically to the therapist. I think most analysts in essence treat interviews as though they were dreams, probably without labeling their behavior as such, but perhaps without focusing so specifically on the unresolved transference issue as the day residue of the "dream."

Previous writings have delineated technical changes over time (Boyer 1971, 1977), and this chapter, too, will focus on alterations in technique. Partly they have resulted from my growing conviction that a too-passive stance on the part of the therapist at best lengthens and at worst stultifies analytic progress with primitive patients. Partly, they have come about because of my increasing understanding of the contributions of British object relations theorists, particularly Winnicott, and synthesis of their views with those of ego psychological theorists, especially Jacobson and Mahler. In what follows I present background data and then clinical examples.

BACKGROUND DATA

Since the advent of the structural theory, we have come to understand better the interaction between the individual's environment and the formation, development, and integrity of the psychic apparatus. Attention has been focused more and more on the nature of ever-earlier aspects of the interactions of mother and child and of the importance of a "facilitating" (Winnicott 1965) or "holding environment" (Modell 1976) for healthy psychological growth. At first the most influential elements of that surround will be the mothering figure whose capacities will determine her ability to enhance or retard the baby's psychic differentiation. The *Anlagen* of psychic structure that are established then materially influence all subsequent relationships (Loewald 1979) and the ability to handle optimally the potential traumas of later family interactions (Boven 1921).

The goal of therapy now is to establish structural changes in the patient's personality, that is, to resume ego development (Loewald 1960), and to progressively recapture self-alienated personal experience, that he may become more fully alive as a subjective, historical being (Ogden 1985). This resumption and recapturing depend on his relationship with a new object, the analyst. Probably the more the patient is regressed, the greater is the importance of environmental facilitation in his treatment and of the capacities of the analyst to interact comfortably with the individual whose drives are urgent and untamed, whose superego is archaically sadistic, and whose communication techniques are confusing and determined (as is much of his perception and behavior) by his use of primitive psychical mechanisms.

THE WORKING ALLIANCE

It is generally conceded that the development of a cooperative relationship with such patients may be difficult to achieve. Fenichel (1941) named that relationship the "rational transference" and Stone (1961) wrote of the "mature transference." Today the relationship is commonly called the "therapeutic" (Zetzel 1956) or "working alliance" (Greenson 1965). Its accomplishment depends on the patient's developing the capacity to form a special variety of object relationship in which he can simultaneously experience and observe with adequate neutrality. Its presence will enable the borderline patient to listen and effectively use the analyst's or his own interventions to recover from primitive reactions and reestablish the secondary process, to split off a relatively reasonable object relationship to the analyst (Greenson 1965), and devote himself to work. In my experience, the regressed patient in analysis is much more likely to achieve such an alliance than one who is in psychotherapy. The establishment of the cooperative alliance depends on the interactions of the various factors discussed below. Perhaps the most important of these factors is the establishment of the holding or facilitating environment.

THE HOLDING OR FACILITATING ENVIRONMENT

If there is a premature rupture of the facilitating environment in infancy, the baby soon becomes a reactive creature, developing hypertrophied, rigid defensive structures (Ogden 1985, Winnicott 1965). The latter characterizes structurally defective patients. On the other hand, if the environment is too permissive for too long, the infant is prevented from experiencing dosed frustration, tolerable anxiety, desire, and conflict, and will not develop internal differentiation and the capacity to traverse dyadic relationships satisfactorily.

The mutual influences of transference and changing object relationships in analysis have been discussed masterfully (Loewald 1960) and will not be dealt with here. Suffice it to say that internalization is not, of course, with reality, but of an interpersonal experience. The child identifies first with his mother's and later with others' experiences of reality. In Winnicott's terms (1971), "the behavior of the environment is part of the individual's own personal development" (p. 53). Primitive patients retain a fundamental disturbance in the early development of object relationships (Blatt et al. 1975). In analysis, especially, the regressed patient internalizes his analyst's experience of reality. Among the qualities any analyst possesses is that of giving emotionally tamed, sublimated, and appropriately delayed responses. My consistent, indirectly supportive, and investigative stance and therapeutic optimism are readily available to the patient and are generally internalized. A most unusual but demonstrative case fragment comes to mind.

> A brilliant research scientist, a woman of 45, had suffered for twenty years from depression during which she was unable to work for about six months of the year. During the other semester she was hypomanic, often requiring brief hospitalization, but worked so effectively that she was world renowned for her contributions. Her four years of treatment were occupied principally with analysis of her oral aggression and fears of its magical effects. Although she improved steadily from the outset, each interpretation I made during the first three-odd years was greeted with scorn and conscious rejection, often remarkably vitriolic and obscene. During the fourth year she had brief periods of mild elation and scant depression; to my surprise, no regression preceded her planned termination date. To the end of her work with me, she never wholeheartedly agreed with any interpretation I made. Bemused, I asked her why she had improved so obviously, since she had disagreed with everything I had said. She looked surprised, and scornfully said, "I fell in love with you and you wanted me to get well."

ANALYTIC TOLERANCE AND REGRESSIVE BEHAVIOR

Oscillation between regression and progression is a necessary aspect of psychological development (A. Freud 1965, Khan 1960). Regression and ego disorganization are crucial steps in the progressive consolidation of the personality (Loewald 1960). In analysis, through interpretation within the holding environment, the primitive parts of the psyche that emerge through regressive experiences acquire structure and meaning (Loewald 1982). As noted earlier, I have given examples previously of my handling of dramatic regressive episodes of acting-out (or acting-in) patients during treatment (Boyer 1971, 1977, 1982); I shall not repeat them here.

Borderline and other regressed patients regularly use two primitive defensive mechanisms, splitting and projective identification, as do some other analytic patients when undergoing regressive episodes (Grotstein 1981, Ogden 1982, Shapiro 1978). The use of splitting involves reversion to an omnipotent fantasy that unwanted parts of the personality or internal objects can be split, projected into an external object, and controlled. (For dissenting views see Gunderson and Singer 1975, Mack 1975, Pruyser 1975, Robbins 1976.) In their transference these patients split the love and hate associated with internalized relationships to avoid the anxiety that would result if they were experienced simultaneously (Kernberg 1975a, 1976, Volkan 1976). During treatment, the patient's use of splitting is generally fairly obvious, and causes the experienced analyst who works with regressed patients little anxiety and thus results in few countertransference-caused impasses. Projective identification is quite another matter.

An ever-growing number of analysts turn to the concept of projective identification to understand their responses to primitive patients (Bion 1962, Flarsheim 1972, Garma 1962, Grinberg 1962, Kernberg 1975a, 1976, Paz et al. 1975–1976, Racker 1968, D. Rosenfeld and Mordo 1973, H. A. Rosenfeld 1952b, 1965, 1975, Searles 1963). The patient unconsciously fantasizes that he has gotten rid of an unwanted part of his own personality by projecting it into the therapist. Such unwanted parts usually have to do with aggression and its potential magical aspects, but regressed patients sometimes project love they deem to be destructive (Fairbairn 1941, Giovacchini 1975, Klein 1946, Searles 1958) and even sanity (Bion 1962). The patient remains an unconscious connection with the analyst by means of the projection he believes to have become a trait of the therapist.

The therapist is used as a "container" (Bion 1956) that will help process the projection (Grotstein 1981, Ogden 1982). One of my patients said that her projection had been "detoxified." Speaking of it late in her analysis, she said that until she had been in treatment for two or three years, she had been aware only of anxiety, fears, and obsessions, and believed she had never had an angry thought or feeling. Now she knew that she had treasured her anger as a child, believing it gave her power. She had kept it secret from herself and others, however, because she feared that her thoughts and feelings had resulted in deaths and abandonment. Speaking of her relationship with me, she said that the first time I had gone away for longer than a weekend, she had spent her days and nights kneeling on street corners, praying that God would keep me alive. She went on, "I know now that for years I've tried to hurt you with my thoughts, words, and actions, although I thought for a long time that it was you who were trying to hurt me with yours. Now I know that my anger is not dangerous like I thought before."

Sometimes the patient's behavior induces the analyst to believe that the ascribed trait is in fact his own (Racker 1968). It has long been known

that countertransferences are determined largely by the analyst's introjection of qualities of the patient that come into contact with the therapist's
unresolved infantile conflicts (Federn 1952, Fenichel 1945, Fliess 1953).
The therapist's unconscious assumption of the patient's projection may
lead to serious impasses and even termination of treatment (Giovacchini
1979). I have written previously of therapeutic fiascos of my own, due to
this phenomenon (Boyer 1977, 1982).

In primitive patients traumatic infantile relationships have been split
off from the main psychic current and continue to exert their pathological
effects on the patient's mental equilibrium and external adaptations. Such
early "islands" of trauma pathologically influence emotional and structural
development, resulting in constriction, arrest, and distortion of the innate
drive toward maturation. The split-off infantile relationships regularly
cause such patients to develop psychotic transference reactions (Hoedemaker 1967, Little 1958, H. A. Rosenfeld 1965, Searles 1963). If the
holding environment and the working alliance have been well established,
such psychotic reactions will be confined almost exclusively to the consultation room. The analyst and patient must be able to tolerate them, learn
from them, and use them for therapeutic ends. The analyst's comprehension of the extent to which projection and projective identification are
involved will help him preserve his objectivity.

TECHNICAL MODIFICATIONS

Earlier I noted that I expect my patient to pay especial attention to his
emotional and physical experiences during the interview, in addition to
his thoughts. The first of my relatively recent technical modifications
consists of my turning more of my attention to my own emotional and
physical reactions to the patient's productions. To my awareness, this
approach has not been specifically recommended by others, although many
analysts, past and present, especially some Latin American followers of the
British object relations theorists, infer similar activity. The second modification is that I am now selectively more aggressive in the pursuit of
information.

Jaffe (1986) wrote, "The psychological perceptiveness of psychoanalysts depends on their ability to regress and thereby to utilize their own
unconscious processes. This provides an effective base upon which a
cognitive elaboration can then build a more comprehensive understanding

than is otherwise possible of the emotional life of patients as well as of one's own" (p. 239).

Although much of my thinking during analytic sessions with regressed patients continues to be directed and secondary-process dominated, I have become progressively more able to let my attention wander simultaneously, to permit the development of a split-off, slightly altered ego state, and then to become aware of more of the nuances and symbolism implied by the patient's manifest productions, to "listen with the third ear" (Reik 1949). To achieve such free-floating attention is easier with neurotic patients with their slower orientational shifts. Obviously, we are all attentive not only to the content of the patient's utterances but to the qualities of their deliverance, and attempt to remain aware simultaneously of gestures, however slight, and signs of physiological changes. I have come to pay increasing attention to my own emotional shifts and physical sensations, however, and consistently to analyze privately the fantasies I have during my altered ego states and the rare related dream that subsequently occurs when I am still confused about the meaning of the patient's productions or behavior. I assume that my emotional, physical, or mental experience reflects the patient's hidden message, perhaps on the basis of my transitory concordant and complementary identifications (Kernberg 1984), and subsequently interpret on the basis of my extrapolation from my experience. I am able to relax and achieve free-floating attention almost solely while patients are reclining. As is clear from the above, my apperception is influenced varyingly by different combinations of primary and secondary process thinking during the session, as will be illustrated by the clinical material.

CLINICAL MATERIAL

First I shall speak of a use of my personal experience in the treatment of these patients. Analysts respond differently to even ordinary behavior. Patients' silence, having been discussed from the standpoint of resistance, transference, and countertransference, is a case in point (Atkins 1968, Bergler 1938, Flarsheim 1972, Levy 1958, Loomie 1961, Waldhorn 1959). The patient's words have been viewed as nutriment for the therapist (Racker 1957), who, feeling deprived or frustrated by his inability to comprehend the meanings of the patient's inability or refusal to talk, and to influence the analysand to change his behavior, may be retributively hostile (Zeligs 1960). Some analysts are incapable of tolerating the intimacy of silence (Searles 1976) and some refuse to treat silent patients (Erikson, personal communication).

In what follows I discuss my reactions to and interventions during a patient's being silent for long periods while her body was rigid and immobile. Her analysis was begun immediately following a hospitalization for an acute psychotic reaction characterized by confusion, terror associated with persecutory delusions, and a conviction that during her sleep or while driving her car she had murdered a mother surrogate and forgotten the act. Highly successful in the business world although in her mid-twenties, she had had to stop working to spend her days checking gas jets and door locks and seeking to find corpses in areas where she might have walked in her sleep or driven her car.

She had docilely conformed to the demands of her perfectionist, manipulative, aggressive mother, achieving excellent grades, advancing rapidly professionally, and being an active organizer in activities supporting Zionism. She conformed also to her sexually inhibited mother's covert demand that she be promiscuous with men of lower social strata and regale her mother with disguised recountings of her thrilling activities. Her seduction and discarding of men was apparently ego-syntonic and met with maternal approval. It reflected symbolically the mother's historical behavior with her passive, easygoing husband.

When the patient reached high school, she had begun to be somewhat aware that she resented her mother's different behavioral requirements for two younger siblings, a boy and a girl, whose irresponsibility and peccadillos received overt approval. Unaware of the involvement of the vengeful aspect of her action, she fell madly in love with an antisocial, promiscuous gentile athlete who was totally uninterested in education or being successful in any practical way. She unconsciously identified him with her father. Although her lover continued his sexual relations with a number of other women, the patient successfully excluded the obvious evidence from her awareness. She felt no anxiety while she focused her attention on a quest for perfection through self-starvation and on her torrid affair, and continued to feed her mother with recountings of her conformation to the two sets of approved activities. Finally, when she had become almost skeletal, her lover abandoned her. Then she became anxious, ridden with the obsessions and fears mentioned previously, and sought psychotherapy.

Thus far in her analysis, three unconscious motivations for her development of anorexia have been uncovered. In addition to the achieved resolution of the incestuous conflict posed by her affair, she imagined she could make her mother feel guilty for having nursed the two younger siblings, while symbolically starving her with bottle feedings performed by hired help, and also conquer a dangerous oral impulse to cannibalize her mother.

In her supportive, noninterpretational psychotherapy, she made of her male therapist a mother surrogate. While she believed herself to be his favorite patient, she regained her weight. Her therapist, obviously alarmed by her deepening emotional involvement with him and apparently unaware of its transference aspects, eventually defended himself by telling her of his adulterous affairs and emotional involvement with other patients. Then she became terrified that she had unwittingly murdered him, and was hospitalized.

During that psychotherapy she had become increasingly angry with her mother and sought vengeance through frustrating that woman's need to be fed words. From the beginning of her analysis, she was predominantly silent. Knowing something of the functions both of her talking and muteness with her mother, I felt I understood some of the reasons for her silence and did not feel frustrated. For a few weeks I limited my remarks about her preferring not to talk to its obvious defensive functions. Her response to my mentioning her fear that if she spoke she might become emotionally involved once again was a scornful sniff. She was sarcastic when I suggested that she feared that saying words aloud would make her fears more believable and lead to rehospitalization. She told me that she had no need for me to tell her what she already knew, and resumed her customary silence and watchful rigidity. She responded similarly when I told her that she sought to protect me as a mother surrogate from her fear that she would harm me if she verbalized her anger and disappointment in me, saying that unreported dreams had given her *that* knowledge.

Eventually, during a silent period, I become somewhat drowsy, although I had had ample sleep and her session came very early in the morning. During the altered ego state I saw myself as a small child, playing by my own choice in a room adjoining one in which my mother was reading. Then I recalled themes from Winnicott's *Playing and Reality* (1971) and said that perhaps during her silence she was permitting herself to be alone in my presence and to play with her own thoughts. Her response was dramatic. Obviously grateful, she physically relaxed for the first time and tentatively and briefly touched the blanket that lay alongside her. Also for the first time, she cried aloud, and the next few hours were flooded with spoken memories of her rapturous daydreams and imagined games, which clearly involved themes from favorite fairy tales during silent periods when she was with her lover.

Then, following a recounted dream that obviously indicated, along with her associations to it, the development of erotic conflicts pertaining to me as a mixed father and mother surrogate and her fear that she would hurt me by ridiculing my obesity as mother derided father's lack of competitive elan, silence ensued for several interviews. My rare queries and statements, related to defensive functions of her silence, were just ignored.

Finally I became aware of a pattern, namely, that she appeared to be willing or able to speak a few words only after I had made some noise, commented, or asked a question. While musing about this phenomenon, I became aware that I felt hungry, although I had just eaten. Then I thought of Racker's (1968) work and that I had empathized with a need of hers. I suggested that she could not talk until she had felt fed by my words. Again, she was highly gratified that I had finally understood something and released much affectively charged related material for a couple of weeks.

Earlier I spoke of another patient having talked of her handling aggression in her therapy by means of projective identification. I shall now speak of how she became aware during analysis of the existence of anger and hatred within her.

This physically attractive virgin in her late thirties had graduated from a prestigious university with high honors in a scientific field and had been encouraged by her faculty to become an academician. Unconsciously fearing that her comparative success would devastate her three older sisters and kill her father, a medical school professor whose skills and reputation had declined following a brain injury, she had become instead a skilled technician. She had been relatively schizoid during much of her life, and had undergone minimally helpful lengthy psychotherapy during her latency and teens for a very severe obsessive-compulsive disorder. She had begun to date occasionally two years earlier and was being pressured to have intercourse. Her fears of pregnancy and that her father, actually happily married, would be devastated if he learned that she had had intercourse, conflicted with her wish to get married and have children, and caused her great anxiety to which she reacted by spending many hours daily checking the safety of her home. At work she rechecked chemicals endlessly lest an error result in the deaths of experimental animals.

So far as she could recall, she had never had an angry thought or impulse. Her intense unconscious hostility was manifested in fears, obsessions, and compulsive behavior. She had always been concerned about her health, dieting carefully and exercising extensively. She claimed her athletic activities—running, hiking, and swimming—had always been solitary. During the first years of her analysis, she remained unaware of anger. She lay motionless, usually rigid, on the couch, with her arms at her sides, and either spoke monotonously or cried as she endlessly recounted her fears and worries. My careful interpretations directed toward helping her become aware of her anger were without effect. Eventually I noted that she occasionally pronated her left arm slightly, but I discerned no connection with spoken subject matter. She was unaware of her arm movement and, when I called it to her attention, indifferent. The activity became more frequent over a period of some months, remaining ununderstood. Finally I found myself imitating her movement, but to no avail. Then I recalled that while she was left-handed, I was not, and imitated it with my right arm. As I did so, I remembered having similarly pronated my arm while serving at tennis as a youth. I asked my patient whether she had ever played tennis; her answer was a flat no.

She soon began to have dreams in which she was watching competitive athletics and two weeks later dreamed that she herself was engaged in a tennis game. This led to her amazed recollection that when she was 8 or 9 she had been playing tennis with her next older sister with whom she had been highly rivalrous for parental favoritism. On one occasion she had intentionally smashed a ball into her sister's face and had been both delighted and terrified. As she recalled the incident, she became aware of rage. This event proved to be the most significant turning point of her lengthy and highly successful analysis.

I turn now to instances of my having become selectively more aggressive in the pursuit of information.

Thinking about that which has been repressed follows regressed patterns. Preverbal thinking often employs visual imagery (Arieti 1948, Freud 1900). When a patient becomes silent even for a short time and then shifts the subject matter in such a manner that I cannot follow the latent linking idea, I may ask him to return to the silent period and recall the omitted thought. If the patient states he had none, I inquire whether he had become aware of a sensory experience then, or while remembering the intermediary silence. If the analysand recalls such an experience, the sensory mode will usually entail vision, and the recollected visual perception may stimulate the recovery of a significant memory or provide analyzable symbology. The same will be true of other sensory experiences, but I shall recount here only an instance of the recovery of a visual image during a silence.

A physician who was sincerely dedicated to doing the very best for his patients had been involved in a series of malpractice suits resulting from his having forgotten to perform obviously necessary medical and surgical procedures while treating patients. He was depressed and bewildered. Early in his analysis it became quite clear to me that he had identified with his mother, a woman devoted to taking care of children but so insecure that if she felt unappreciated, she cried, took to her bed, and slept for many hours, sometimes failing to prepare dinner or perform other necessary routine tasks. My patient was unaware of anger and vengeful impulses when he considered his efforts to have been unappreciated, knowing only of his feeling hurt.

Several months into analysis he opened a session wondering in passing whether I knew how hard it was for him to arrange his schedule to permit his treatment. That was the first time he had hinted that he felt himself to be unappreciated by me. Then he found himself anxious while talking of a patient's having complained about his bill. He became silent for a few seconds and then talked of something totally unrelated in emotional or topical theme. When I interrupted him to inquire, he denied recalling a thought during the interim but remembered a fleeting vision of a child in a forest. This led during the same session to memories of childhood involvements with fairy tales and especially with Hansel and Gretel, a story that has been interpreted to deal with conflicts pertaining to oral sadism and wishes for reunion with the mother (Lorenz 1931, Róheim 1953). At the end of the hour he recalled the "absurd" thought that he might want to bite me. During following hours he began to get into contact with the oral-sadistic urges that had been hidden by his feeling hurt and being forgetful.

Eventually his forgetfulness with his patients was understood as a repetition of his mother's withdrawals into sleep. It kept unconscious his urges to devour them as maternal surrogates to attain fantasized fusion with her. Simultaneously it resulted in their being deprived and damaged as he had considered himself to be by his mother's actions.

In play therapy for children, the therapist may choose to suggest games or other make-believe situations as a means of access to threatening material. At times I use a similar device, one in which I ask the patient to imagine a situation.

A patient who suffered a primitive borderline personality disorder had been severely traumatized as a child in various ways, one of which was her having been frequently subjected to the observation of sadomasochistic primal-scene activities (Boyer 1977). She became an alcoholic and a promiscuous masochistic victim who repressed her sexual experiences. During her analysis, when she finally could remember having engaged in sex with men whom she had picked up in bars, and her occasional masturbation, it became clear that her attention during any sexual activity was focused exclusively on physical sensations and the achievement of orgasm. After some months during which her sexual fantasies continued to remain hidden, following a reported episode of masturbation, I asked her to visualize what she might have fantasized if she could shift her attention from the physical experience and her fear that either she would not have an orgasm or, if she did, it might damage her. She closed her eyes and saw angular geometric forms about which she became curious (Tustin 1980). During subsequent interviews the forms became rounded and eventually unified into a hand and an arm, tearing at her perineum as she now revealed she did in fact during her sleep. She was sure she continued to have pinworms from childhood. When stool examinations were negative, she could enter into an examination of her fusion of clitoral, vaginal, urethral, and anal sensations and the meanings of her having failed to differentiate them. Parental sexual activities had frightened and excited her. She had sought to interrupt them by noisy bathroom activities, while simultaneously discharging her perineal excitement through urination and/or defecation.

I limit myself to one further example of my heightened clinical activity in an effort to speed the return of the repressed. I have learned that when a patient is dealing actively with a conflict and suddenly stops doing so, he may have undertaken unreported acting out of the transference. After a long period of sexual abstinence, a woman became aware of wishes and fantasies that I enter into sexual activities with her; she adamantly rejected the idea that transference was involved (Boyer 1971). The subject preoccupied and frustrated her for some weeks and was abruptly discontinued, being replaced by old and little-cathected conflicts. Finally I said I did not understand why the subject had been discontinued in the absence of any resolution and asked whether she was engaged in some unreported activity. She could then tell me that she had begun a torrid affair with a man of my age. When to her surprise she became cognizant that he looked like and resembled her father in other ways, she became aware of some degree of her viewing me as a father surrogate and stopped the affair.

DISCUSSION

It is commonly held that the effectiveness of psychoanalysis as a therapeutic mode depends on properly timed interpretation as the effective mutative agent. In my view, this principle holds as well in the treatment of regressed patients and those who suffer from the transference neuroses. In working with either group of patients, the provision of a setting within which a working alliance can be established is mandatory, since without such an alliance interpretations are usually ineffective in achieving structural change, our true therapeutic goal. In a sense, every analysand must be trained to be a patient, and this is truer of the disturbed person, whose drive-derivative urges are less controlled and whose infantile transference projections often make him perceive the analyst as a grossly distorted early maternal surrogate, an actual caregiver, one who will gratify his wishes promptly. Obviously, not all regressed patients are so transparently clamorous and many are simultaneously closer to their need to have the therapist help them learn to view reality as do others around them, and also to be able to communicate in manners that will be understood and not be provocative. But beyond our need to train the analysand to be a patient, ultimately our goal is to help him or her to become a constructive person who can use his or her innate capacities to the fullest and enjoy doing so while at the same time being empathic to the needs of others, a potential caregiver. Loewald (1960) has brilliantly discussed the ways in which transference and real object-relationship changes are interactive in the analytic setting; the analysand learns to be a patient, and ultimately, it is hoped, an empathic adult, through a complex process that includes identification with attributes of the analyst and the setting, using the word *setting* in its broadest sense.

I have found that the traditional analytic environment and the exclusion of the use of parameters achieves these goals in a high percentage of patients who continue to planned termination. During the past thirty-five years or so, this has been particularly true. This change coincides with my growing awareness of the nature of the development of early object relationships and the degree to which the primitively functioning patient distortedly perceives the therapist. While the ego psychologists contributed much to my comprehension, especially Mahler, Jacobson, and Erikson, I was made more consciously aware of the facilitating nature of the therapeutic environment for these patients through increased understanding of the British object relations therapists, especially Winnicott, as discussed earlier in this volume. Study of their views also gave me more understanding of primitive defenses. I have spoken here particularly of projective identification. It is easier for me to comprehend the all-important transference–countertransference interactions in the treatment of regressed patients when I use this concept, although I am aware that others find it unnecessary.

This chapter delineated changes in my ever-progressing technique in working with primitive patients. What I have stressed is my having become selectively more aggressive in treatment, in addition to my having come to pay especial attention to my own reactions to the patient and his productions, verbal or nonverbal. As illustrated, I have found that sometimes reactions that occur when I am in a slightly altered ego state while listening prove to be especially illuminating and helpful. I have concluded that two reasons contribute to my preference to treat disturbed patients while they are on the couch: I am more comfortable and less inappropriately and defensively active when the patient is not scrutinizing me and automatically changing what he might have produced on the basis of hints resulting from observations of my reactions or spontaneous physical contributions to the interchange. Second, it is evident to me that the patient's remaining on the couch helps him to establish distance between urge and action and to learn that delay is possible and even an accomplishment.

It will have become clear from this discussion that I believe the active pursuit of fantasies, whether they are expressed verbally or perceived nonverbally by the patient, assists in making the unconscious conscious in ways that permit analysis of defenses and resistances. I refer here to my asking the patient to give information he or she consciously or unconsciously prefers to conceal, rather than waiting for its subsequent emergence, either spontaneous or as the result of interpretation.

CONCLUSION

The provision of a facilitating environment is all-important in the treatment of the regressed patient. A significant aspect of that environment is a clear understanding of the degree to which the disturbed patient perceives the therapist to be a distorted version of his infantile caregiver(s). The comprehension of the nature of the transference–countertransference interaction is mandatory.

In this chapter I have described how I have come to include a study of my own reactions to the patient's behavior and verbal productions, be those reactions mental, emotional, or physical, and to make interpretations at times on the basis of my eventual understanding of those reactions. In addition, I have spoken of ways of more aggressively pursuing suppressed or repressed information.

References

Adler, G. (1985). *Borderline Psychopathology and Its Treatment*. New York: Jason Aronson.

Arieti, S. (1948). Special logic of schizophrenia and other types of autistic thought. *Psychiatry* 11:325–338.

Atkins, N. B. (1968). Acting out and psychosomatic illness as related to regressive trends. *International Journal of Psycho-Analysis* 49:221–223.

Balint, M. (1959). *Thrills and Regressions.* New York: International Universities Press.

Bergler, E. (1938). On a resistance situation: the patient is silent. *Psychoanalytic Review* 25:170–176.

Bion, W. R. (1956). Development of schizophrenic thought. *International Journal of Psycho-Analysis* 37:344–346.

——— (1962). *Learning from Experience.* London: Heinemann.

Blatt, S. J., Wild, C. M., and Ritzler, B. A. (1975). Disturbances of object relations in schizophrenia. *Psychoanalysis & Contemporary Science* 4:235–288.

Boven, W. (1921). Études sur les conditions du developpement au sein des familles, de la schizophrenie et de la folie maniaque. *Archives Suisses de Neurologie and Psychologie* 8:89–116.

Boyer, L. B. (1971). Psychoanalytic technique in the treatment of certain characterological and schizophrenic disorders. In *The Regressed Patient*, pp. 89–120. New York: Jason Aronson.

——— (1977). Working with a borderline patient. In *The Regressed Patient*, pp. 137–166. New York: Jason Aronson, 1983.

——— (1982). On analytic experiences in working with regressed patients. In *Technical Factors in the Treatment of the Severely Disturbed Patient*, ed. P. L. Giovacchini and L. B. Boyer, pp. 65–106. New York: Jason Aronson.

——— (1983). *The Regressed Patient.* New York: Jason Aronson.

——— (1985). Christmas "neurosis" reconsidered. In *Depressive States and Their Treatment*, ed. V. D. Volkan, pp. 297–316. New York: Jason Aronson.

Boyer, L. B., and Giovacchini, P. L. (1980). *Psychoanalytic Treatment of Schizophrenic, Borderline, and Characterological Disorders*, 2nd ed. New York: Jason Aronson.

Brunswick, R. M. (1928). A supplement to Freud's "A History of an Infantile Neurosis." *International Journal of Psycho-Analysis* 9:439–476.

Carpenter, W. T., Gunderson, J. T., and Strauss, J. S. (1975). Considerations of the borderline syndrome: a longitudinal comparative study of borderline and schizophrenic patients. In *Borderline Personality Disorders*, ed. P. Hartocollis, pp. 231–253. New York: International Universities Press.

Cohen, M. B. (1952). Countertransference and anxiety. *Psychiatry* 15:231–243.

Ekstein, R. (1966). *Children of Time and Space, of Action and Impulse. Treatment of Severely Disturbed Children.* New York: Appleton-Century Crofts.

Fairbairn, W. R. D. (1941). A revised psychopathology of the psychoses and psychoneuroses. *International Journal of Psycho-Analysis* 22:250–279.

Federn, P. (1952). *Ego Psychology and the Psychoses.* New York: Basic Books.

Fenichel, O. (1941). *Problems of Psychoanalytic Technique.* New York: Psycho-
analytic Quarterly.
—— (1945). *The Psychoanalytic Theory of Neurosis.* New York: W. W. Norton.
Flarsheim, A. (1972). Treatability. In *Tactics and Techniques in Psychoanalytic
Therapy*, ed. P. L. Giovacchini, pp. 113–134. New York: Jason Aronson.
Fliess, R. (1953). Counter-transference and counter-identification. *Journal of the
American Psychoanalytic Association* 1:268–284.
Freud, A. (1965). *Normality and Pathology in Childhood.* New York: International
Universities Press.
Freud, S. (1900). The interpretation of dreams. *Standard Edition* 4/5:1–626.
Fromm-Reichmann, F. (1950). *Principles of Intensive Psychotherapy.* Chicago:
University of Chicago Press.
—— (1958). Basic problems in the psychotherapy of schizophrenia. *Psychiatry*
21:1–6.
Garma, A. (1931). La realidad exterior y los instinctos en la esquizofrenia. *Revista
de Psicoanálisis* 2:56–82.
—— (1962). *El Psicoanálisis*, 3rd ed., Buenos Aires: Paidos, 1978.
Gill, M. M. (1982). *Analysis of Transference*, I. Psychological Issues, Monograph
53. New York: International Universities Press.
Giovacchini, P. L. (1975). *Psychoanalysis of Character Disorders.* New York: Jason
Aronson.
—— (1979). *Treatment of Primitive Mental States.* New York: Jason Aronson.
Greenacre, P. (1975). On reconstruction. *Journal of the American Psychoanalytic
Association* 23:693–712.
Greenson, R. R. (1965). The working alliance and the transference neurosis.
Psychoanalytic Quarterly 34:155–181.
Grinberg, L. (1962). On a specific aspect of countertransference due to the
patient's projective identification. *International Journal of Psycho-Analysis*
43:430–436.
Grotstein, J. S. (1981). *Splitting and Projective Identification.* New York: Jason
Aronson.
Gunderson, J. T., and Singer, M. T. (1975). Defining borderline patients. *American
Journal of Psychiatry* 132:1–10.
Hann-Kende, F. (1933). On the role of transference and countertransference
in psychoanalysis. In *Psychoanalysis and the Occult*, ed. G. Devereux, pp.
158–167. New York: International Universities Press, 1953.
Hartmann, H. (1953). Contribution to the metapsychology of schizophrenia.
Psychoanalytic Study of the Child 8:177–198. New York: International Uni-
versities Press.
Hoedemaker, E. D. (1967). The psychotic identifications in schizophrenia. The
technical problem. In *Psychoanalytic Treatment of Schizophrenic and Characterological Disorders*, ed. L. B. Boyer and P. L. Giovacchini, pp. 189–207.
New York: Science House.

Jacobson, E. (1954). Contribution to the metapsychology of psychotic identifications. *Journal of the American Psychoanalytic Association* 2:239–262.

Jaffe, D. (1986). Empathy, counteridentification, countertransference. *Psychoanalytic Quarterly* 55:215–243.

Kernberg, O. F. (1975a). *Borderline Conditions and Pathological Narcissism.* New York: Jason Aronson.

——— (1975b). Transference and countertransference in the treatment of borderline patients. Strecker Monograph Series, No. XII. Philadelphia: Institute of Pennsylvania Hospital.

——— (1976). *Object Relations Theory and Clinical Psychoanalysis.* New York: Jason Aronson.

——— (1984). Projection and projective identification. Presentation at the First Conference of the Sigmund Freud Center of the Hebrew University of Jerusalem, May 27–29.

Khan, M. M. R. (1960). Regression and integration in the analytic setting. *International Journal of Psycho-Analysis* 41:130–146.

Klein, M. (1946). Notes on some schizoid mechanisms. *International Journal of Psycho-Analysis* 27:99–110.

LaForgue, R. (1935). Contribution a l'étude de la schizophrenie. *Évolution Psychiatrique* 3:81–96.

Landauer, K. (1924). "Passive" Technik. *Internationale Zeitschrift für Ärztliche Psychoanalisis* 10:415–422.

Levy, K. (1958). Silence in the analytic session. *International Journal of Psycho-Analysis* 39:50–58.

Lewin, B. D. (1946). Sleep, the mouth, and the dream screen. *Psychoanalytic Quarterly* 15:419–434.

——— (1950). *The Psychoanalysis of Elation.* New York: W. W. Norton.

Lidz, R. W., and Lidz, T. (1952). Therapeutic considerations arising from the intense symbiotic needs of schizophrenic patients. In *Psychotherapy with Schizophrenics*, ed. E. B. Brody and F. C. Redlich, pp. 168–178. New York: International Universities Press.

Little, M. (1958). On delusional transference (transference psychosis). In *Transference Neurosis and Transference Psychosis*, pp. 81–92. New York: Jason Aronson, 1981.

——— (1981). *Transference Neurosis and Transference Psychosis.* New York: Jason Aronson.

Loewald, H. W. (1960). On the therapeutic action of psychoanalysis. *International Journal of Psycho-Analysis* 41:16–33.

——— (1979). The waning of the Oedipus complex. *Journal of the American Psychoanalytic Association* 27:751–776.

——— (1982). Regression. Some general considerations. In *Technical Factors in the Treatment of the Severely Disturbed Patient*, ed. P. L. Giovacchini and L. B. Boyer, pp. 107–130. New York: Jason Aronson.

Loomie, L. S. (1961). Some ego considerations in the silent patient. *Journal of the American Psychoanalytic Association* 9:56–78.

Lorenz, E. F. (1931). Hänsel and Gretel. *Imago* 17:119–125.

Mack, J. E., ed. (1975). *Borderline States in Psychiatry.* New York: Grune & Stratton.

Mahler, M. S. (1972). A study of the separation-individuation phase and its possible application to borderline phenomena in the psychoanalytic situation. *Psychoanalytic Study of the Child* 26:403–424. New Haven, CT: Yale University Press.

Maltsberger, J. T., and Buie, D. H. (1974). Countertransference hate in the treatment of suicidal patients. *Archives of General Psychiatry* 30:645–653.

Masterson, J. F. (1972). *Treatment of the Borderline Adolescent. A Developmental Approach.* New York: Wiley.

McDougall, J. (1979). Primitive communication and the use of countertransference. In *Countertransference: The Therapist's Contribution to the Therapeutic Situation,* ed. L. Epstein and A. H. Feiner, pp. 267–304. New York: Jason Aronson.

Meissner, W. M. (1985). Review of *The Regressed Patient* by L. Bryce Boyer. *Psychoanalytic Quarterly* 54:89–91.

Milner, M. (1969). *The Hands of the Living God—An Account of a Psychoanalytic Treatment.* New York: International Universities Press.

Modell, A. H. (1976). "The holding environment" and the therapeutic action of psychoanalysis. *Journal of the American Psychoanalytic Association* 24:285–308.

Ogden, T. H. (1982). *Projective Identification and Psychotherapeutic Technique.* New York: Jason Aronson.

——— (1985). *The Matrix of the Mind. Aspects of Object Relations Theory.* New York: Jason Aronson.

Paz, C. A., Pelento, M. L., and Olmos de Paz, T. (1975–1976). *Estructuras y Estados Fronterizos en Niños, Adolescentes y Adultos,* 3 vols. Buenos Aires: Nueva Visión.

Pruyser, P. W. (1975). What splits in "splitting"? *Bulletin of the Menninger Clinic* 39:1–46.

Racker, E. (1957). The meanings and uses of countertransference. *Psychoanalytic Quarterly* 26:303–357.

——— (1968). *Transference and Countertransference.* New York: International Universities Press.

Reik, T. (1949). *Listening with the Third Ear: The Inner Experiences of a Psychoanalyst.* New York: Farrar, Straus.

Robbins, M. D. (1976). Borderline personality organization: the need for a new theory. *Journal of the American Psychoanalytic Association* 24:831–853.

Róheim, G. (1953). Hansel and Gretel. *Bulletin of the Menninger Clinic* 17:90–92.

Rosenfeld, D., and Mordo, E. (1973). Fusión, confusión, simbiosis e identificación proyectiva. *Revisita de Psicoanálisis* 30:413–422.

Rosenfeld, H. A. (1952a). Transference-phenomena and transference-analysis in an acute catatonic schizophrenic patient. *International Journal of Psycho-Analysis* 33:457–464.

——— (1952b). Notes on the psycho-analysis of the superego conflict of an acute schizophrenic patient. *International Journal of Psycho-Analysis* 33:111–131.

——— (1965). *Psychotic States: A Psycho-Analytical Approach.* London: Hogarth.

——— (1966). Discussion of *Office Treatment of Schizophrenia*, by L. B. Boyer. *Psychoanalytic Forum* 1:351–353.

——— (1975). Negative therapeutic reaction. In *Tactics and Techniques in Psychoanalytic Therapy*, II, ed. P. L. Giovacchini, A. Flarsheim, and L. B. Boyer, pp. 217–228. New York: Jason Aronson.

Searles, H. F. (1958). Positive feelings in the relationships between the schizophrenic and his mother. In *Collected Papers on Schiozphrenia and Related Subjects*, pp. 216–253. New York: International Universities Press, 1965.

——— (1963). Transference psychosis in the treatment of chronic schizophrenia. In *Collected Papers on Schiozphrenia and Related Subjects*, pp. 626–653. New York: International Universities Press.

——— (1976). Transitional phenomena and therapeutic symbiosis. In *Countertransference and Related Subjects*, pp. 503–576. New York: International Universities Press, 1979.

——— (1979). *Countertransference and Related Subjects.* New York: International Universities Press.

Shapiro, E. R. (1978). The psychodynamics and developmental psychology of the borderline patient. A review of the literature. *American Journal of Psychiatry* 135:1305–1315.

Stanton, A. H., Gunderson, J. G., Knapp, P. H., et al. (1984). Effects of psychotherapy in schizophrenia: I. *Schizophrenia Bulletin* 10:520–563.

Stone, L. (1961). *The Psychoanalytic Situation.* New York: International Universities Press.

Szalita-Pemow, A. B. (1955). The "intuitive process" and its relation to work with schizophrenics. *Journal of the American Psychoanalytic Association* 3:7–18.

Tustin, F. (1980). Autistic objects. *International Review of Psychoanalysis* 7:27–39.

Volkan, V. D. (1976). *Primitive Internalized Object Relations: A Clinical Study of Schizophrenic, Borderline and Narcissistic Patients.* New York: International Universities Press.

——— (1982). A young woman's inability to say no to needy people and her identification with the frustrator in the analytic situation. In *Technical Factors in the Treatment of the Severely Disturbed Patient*, ed. P. L. Giovacchini and L. B. Boyer, pp. 439–466. New York: Jason Aronson.

——— (1984). *What Do You Get When You Cross a Dandelion with a Rose? The True Story of a Psychoanalysis.* New York: Jason Aronson.

Waelder, R. (1924). The psychoses: their mechanisms and accessibility to treatment. *International Journal of Psycho-Analysis* 6:259–281.

Waldhorn, H. F., reporter (1959). The silent patient. Panel discussion. *Journal of the American Psychoanalytic Association* 7:548–560.

Wilson, C. P. (1983). Contrasts in the analysis of bulimic and abstaining anorexics. In *Fear of Being Fat, The Treatment of Anorexia Nervosa and Bulimia*, ed. C. P. Wilson, C. C. Hogan, and I. L. Mintz, pp. 169–193. New York: Jason Aronson.

Winnicott, D. W. (1960). Counter-transference. In *The Maturational Processes and the Facilitating Environment*, pp. 158–165. New York: International Universities Press, 1965.

——— (1965). *The Maturational Processes and the Facilitating Environment.* New York: International Universities Press.

——— (1971). *Playing and Reality.* London: Tavistock.

Zeligs, M. A. (1960). The role of silence in transference, countertransference and the psychoanalytic process. *International Journal of Psycho-Analysis* 41:407–412.

Zetzel, E. R. (1956). The concept of transference. In *The Capacity for Emotional Growth*, pp. 168–181. New York: International Universities Press, 1970.

8

Thinking of the Interview
As If It Were a Dream

Thinking of the interview as if it were a dream has facilitated my work, particularly with regressed patients. This brief chapter focuses especially on two topics: (1) the clinical utility of assuming that the day residue of the imaginary dream, the interview, arises from the major unresolved transference issue of the previous interview or interviews; and (2) a function of the dream that is served at times by the interview—the discharge of affects and mental contents.

Genetically, the analytic hour is an altered hypnotic situation (Jones 1953, Lewin 1955a) and patients equate the hypnotic state with being asleep (Freud 1886). Lewin (1954) noted that the wish in the hypnotic situation of the patient to be put to sleep was supplemented by the wish to associate freely in the analytic situation. He came to regard what happens on the couch as being both like a neurosis and like the dream (1955b). Lewin's (1932, 1946, 1950, 1953a,b) seminal studies of the dream and some regressed patients influenced heavily the development of my earlier therapeutic techniques (Boyer 1983).

Freud (1900) found intrinsic connections between the structure of the dream and psychoses, analogies pointing to their being essentially akin, and applied the topographical hypothesis to the phenomenon of regression in both instances. Countless observers have discussed the similarities and differences in the structures of dreams and psychoses and psychic processes facilitating the merging of dream and psychosis (Bion 1962a, Freud 1907, Frosch 1976, Meltzer 1983). That hallucinations and delusions can be interpreted as though they were dreams is commonplace knowledge.

Early in my analytic work with regressed patients I became aware of finding myself in an altered ego state while listening to the dreamlike quality of their associations.[1] At those times my thinking sometimes became dominated by the primary process and I regained my equilibrium by directed thinking of the possible symbology of their productions or their wish-fulfilling and resistance aspects. Others have had similar experiences (M'Uzan 1976).

Many analysts have assumed the similarity of the interview to the dream without focusing directly on the transference–countertransference interplay as a determinant in their comprehension of the interview. Kern (1987) found the interactional features of a transference neurosis to be the waking equivalents of a manifest dream and wrote of technical innovations he considered to be required of the analyst (see also Zusman 1974).

Some thirty-five years ago, as I have discussed earlier in this volume, I came to assume that the day residue of the imaginary dream, the interview, arose from the unresolved transference issue of the previous session or sessions. Of course, that day residue repeated an infantile situation. This approach has improved my therapeutic effectiveness and that of my supervisees, especially those who had been insufficiently aware of the degree to which their patients' reactions to them constituted transference phenomena. Examples follow.

A borderline patient became anxious whenever I announced a forthcoming separation; her fantasies usually hovered around the possibil-

---

1. Not infrequently, I experienced simultaneously kinesthetic or tactile sensations while in the altered ego state (Boyer 1986). Today I would explain these phenomena through using the concept of projective identification, although I am well aware of the effectiveness of the analyst's discerning subliminal cues, both consciously and unconsciously. It is of interest that the Norwegian philosopher Vold (1910–1912) studied extensively the effects of muscular and cutaneous stimulations on dreams and that, based in part on his studies, Rorschach concluded that repressed kinesthetic perceptions reappear in sleep and furnish the most important material in dreams (Ellenberger 1954). Rorschach's thoughts about the antagonism between kinesthetic perceptions and movements led to significant conclusions regarding the meanings of movement responses on his projective test.

ity that I was ill and that she had caused my sickness. I told her that I would be away on a Friday, three weeks thence. During the ensuing interval, she did not refer to the forthcoming separation. Three days before the Friday, she opened the hour saying she had seen and wanted to take care of a sick old man en route to the office. My understanding her communication as a transference statement easily enabled me to help her understand her repression of the absence to be the product of her apparently new frightening phantasy that her disordered thinking had given me cancer and that I had canceled the interview to get medical care. Additionally, new material emerged from the past, namely that she had held herself responsible as a child of 5 for the death of her beloved grandfather.

A schizophrenic woman opened a session speaking of having the illusion that she had seen the bloody carcass of a dog in the street outside my office. When she trusted me and herself, she imagined that either she resided in me, protected and enclosed by my skin, or her skin contained me inside her body. We were then continuous fluids. When she was engrossed with fears that her hostility destroyed our relationship, she hallucinated our bleeding since we had lost our skin and our capacity to contain one another and preserve our loving continuity, mutual trust, and the working relationship. My understanding the initial communication in transference terms enabled me to focus quickly on my having forgotten a hint during two previous interviews that I had treated too cavalierly a symbolic expression of anxiety lest we were angry with one another.

Now I discuss a function of the dream that is served also by the interview, namely, the discharge of affects and mental contents. Understanding this function of the interview facilitates work with that group of patients who use their sessions as milieus within which they hope to be able to empty themselves of tensions and their associated mental contents, deposit them into the therapist (Boyer 1989), and effect a magical cure.

Freud (1900) found that the dream preserves sleep. A compromise between repressive and repressed forces permits a forbidden infantile wish to find gratification in a disguised form, thus enabling the dreamer to rid himself of its attendant affectual stress. Klein (1932, 1946), Lewin (1955a,b), and Segal (1981) found the dream to serve also the psychic task of working through, binding affectual tension. Bion (1962a) found the capacity to dream to protect the individual from experiencing a psychotic state and postulated an apparatus for dreaming that enables a person to process his sensorial impressions into dream elements. When mental components are inappropriate for thinking, dreaming, and remembering, they are evacuated through projective identification and/or acting out.[2] Both acting out and somatization are regressive means of reestablishing presymbolic thought. Klein (1946) wrote of the evacuation functions of splitting and projective identification; then, after Bion introduced the communicative functions of projective identification (Grotstein 1987), discussed the evacuation of mental contents into either a container or into space (Klein 1955). Grinberg and colleagues (1967) emphasized the evacuation functions of dreams. Here I stress the use during the regressions undergone by some patients of the evacuation function of the interview as a more primitive use of projective identification than its true communicative function that is employed at other times.

The apparatus for dreaming dreams is formed gradually in the child's mind, giving it the capacity to think, through the internalization of repeated experiences of its relationship with a mother who has a capacity for reverie, and has served as a container for the child's unbearable affects, returning them to the child later in what Winnicott (1965) referred to as an attenuated form that one of my patients called "detoxified" (Boyer 1986). Similarly, in analysis, the analyst with a capacity for reverie assumes and metabolizes the patient's projections and returns them through timely interpretive activity. Bion (1956, 1962b) postulated that the baby's projective identification enlists his sympathetic mother to experience for him and later feed him metabolized material. At times patients overtly acknowledge their awareness of this transaction. Some years following her successful analysis, a previously hypomanic scientist called for a further interview, saying, "I need to empty my mind into yours again and have you feed me back more useful understanding." Another patient, one who had never read psychological literature, said, following a regression early in treatment, "You can help me best by being a container for my craziness until I understand it and can make it a part of myself again."

Isakower (1938) found breast symbols to be experienced as swallowing the individual as he or she falls asleep, and various observers have noted patients' fantasies of entering their mothers either by being swallowed or by gnawing their way inside (Fenichel 1929, Klein 1928), at times with the

---

2. According to Ogden (personal communication), evacuation results when there is no containment of a projective identification and is a reexperiencing of the mother's earlier failure to contain the baby's projection.

fantasy that once inside the mother, the invader sleeps and is fed (Lewin 1935).

Lewin (1946) initially found the dream screen to represent the breast, flattened after nursing, and his observation stimulated great interest. Eventually Lewin (1950, 1953a) understood the function of the "breast" symbolized by the dream screen to be its sleep-giving power and he saw the screen's representing both breast and sleep at the breast to predicate a triad of oral wishes: the wish to eat, the wish to be eaten, and the wish to sleep; others' clinical data confirm his hypotheses. Garma found the light of the luminous dream screen onto which the dream contents are projected to constitute a primordial hallucination coming from a reactivation of the repressed memory of the "dazzling vision of light which was received at the moment of birth" (Garma 1969, p. 494).

The similarities between the interview and the dream are made quite explicit at times. A number of mental health professionals, conversant with the literature, have called me, as a representative of the interview, their "dream screen" onto whom they projected their fantasies to be fed to them in new forms. A more startling observation makes one wonder whether Garma's postulation has merit. At the end of an interview during which he had become aware that he had projected images onto me "as if you were a movie screen," a patient who was totally unacquainted with psychological literature said that when he had entered the consultation room, he had thought me to be continuous with soft light coming through a drape covering a window behind me, light that had appeared momentarily to him to be "very bright."[3]

---

3. Studies done since Lewin's seminal work suggest that the dream screen, rather than representing the breast, flattened after nursing, may represent an early perception of the continuity or fusion of the skin surfaces of the mother and infant that has been written about extensively as early object relations have been understood better (Anzieu 1970, 1985, Bick 1968, 1986, Biven 1982, Cachard 1981, Lacombe 1959, McDougall 1989, Ogden 1986, 1989).

Rosenfeld (1984, 1990, Rosenfeld and Pistol 1986) detected what he termed a psychotic body image among patients who had regressed under special circumstances. That image is the notion that the body contains only liquids or blood, coated by arterial or venous walls that take over the psychological function of the skin, muscles, and skeleton. During psychotic regressions, the notion of the wall disappears and the patient perceives himself to disappear in a boundaryless mass. My patient, at times when our ties to one another were threatened by her intense fear of her aggression, pictured us as bleeding into pools of liquid, which might or might not mingle. She consciously symbolized sanity by being within one's skin.

SUMMARY

Thinking of the interview as if it were a dream facilitates analytic work with regressed patients. Seeing the day residue of the imaginary dream, the interview, as the principal unresolved transference issue of the preceding session or sessions enhances the therapist's understanding of the content presented initially and the cathected conflict to which it refers. Keeping in mind the evacuative function of the "dream" at times alerts the therapist to the possibility that the patient seeks at least predominantly to empty himself or herself of tension and mental contents that have been stripped defensively of symbolic meanings rather than to seek improvement through understanding.

References

Anzieu, D. (1970). Skin ego. In *Psychoanalysis in France*, ed. S. Lebovici and D. Widlocher, pp. 17–32. New York: International Universities Press.
——— (1985). *The Skin Ego. A Psychoanalytic Approach to the Self.* New Haven, CT: Yale University Press, 1989.
Bick, E. (1968). The experience of the skin in early object relations. *International Journal of Psycho-Analysis* 49:484–486.
——— (1986). Further considerations on the function of the skin in early object relations. *British Journal of Psychotherapy* 2:292–299.
Bion, W. R. (1956). Development of schizophrenic thought. In *Second Thoughts. Selected Papers on Psycho-Analysis*, pp. 36–42. New York: Jason Aronson.
——— (1962a). *Learning from Experience.* New York: Basic Books.
——— (1962b). A theory of thinking. In *Second Thoughts. Selected Papers on Psycho-Analysis*, pp. 110–119. New York: Jason Aronson.
Biven, B. M. (1982). The role of the skin in normal and abnormal development, with a note on the poet Sylvia Plath. *International Review of Psycho-Analysis* 9:205–228.
Boyer, L. B. (1983). *The Regressed Patient.* New York: Jason Aronson.
——— (1986). Technical aspects of treating the regressed patient. *Contemporary Psychoanalysis* 22:25–44.
——— (1989). Countertransference and technique in working with the regressed patient: further remarks. *International Journal of Psycho-Analysis* 70:701–704. Also in *Master Clinicians on Treating the Regressed Patient*, ed. L. B. Boyer and P. L. Giovacchini, pp. 303–324. Northvale, NJ: Jason Aronson, 1990.
Cachard, C. (1981). Enveloppes de corps, membranes de rêve. *L'Evolution Psychiatrique* 46:847–856.
Ellenberger, H. (1954). The life and work of Hermann Rorschach. *Bulletin of the Menninger Clinic* 18:173–219.

Fenichel, O. (1929). The dread of being eaten. *International Journal of Psycho-Analysis* 10:448–450.

Freud, S. (1886). Hypnotism and suggestion. *Collected Papers* 5:11–24. London: Hogarth.

——— (1900). The interpretation of dreams. *Standard Edition* 4/5.

——— (1907). Delusions and dreams in Jensen's *Gradiva. Standard Edition* 9:3–144.

Frosch, J. (1976). Psychoanalytic contributions to the relationship between dreams and psychosis—a critical survey. *International Journal of Psychoanalytic Psychotherapy* 5:39–63.

Garma, A. (1969). Present thoughts on Freud's theory of dream hallucination. *International Journal of Psycho-Analysis* 50:486–494.

Grinberg, L., Apter, A., Bellagamba, H. F., et al. (1967). Función del sonar y clasificación clínica de los sueños en el proceso psicoanalítico. *Revista de Psicoanálisis* 24:749–789.

Grotstein, J. S. (1987). Making the best of a bad deal: on Harold Boris's "Bion Revisited." *Contemporary Psychoanalysis* 23:60–76.

Isakower, I. (1938). A contribution to the patho-psychology of phenomena associated with falling asleep. *International Journal of Psycho-Analysis* 19:331–345.

Jones, E. (1953). *The Life and Work of Sigmund Freud.* Vol. 1. New York: Basic Books.

Kern, J. W. (1987). Transference neurosis as a waking dream: notes on a clinical enigma. *Journal of the American Psychoanalytic Association* 35:337–366.

Klein, M. (1928). Early stages of the oedipus conflict. *International Journal of Psycho-Analysis* 9:167–180.

——— (1932). *The Psycho-Analysis of Children,* 4th ed. London: Hogarth.

——— (1946). Notes on some schizoid mechanisms. *International Journal of Psycho-Analysis* 27:99–110.

——— (1955). On identification. In *New Directions in Psychoanalysis,* ed. M. Klein, P. Heimann, and R. E. Money-Kyrle, pp. 309–345. New York: Basic Books.

Lacombe, P. (1959). Du role de la peau dans l'attachement mère–enfant. *Revue Française de Psychanalyse* 23:83–102.

Lewin, B. D. (1932). Analysis and structure of a transient hypomania. *Psychoanalytic Quarterly* 1:43–49.

——— (1935). Claustrophobia. *Psychoanalytic Quarterly* 4:227–233.

——— (1946). Sleep, the mouth and the dream screen. *Psychoanalytic Quarterly* 15:419–434.

——— (1950). *The Psychoanalysis of Elation.* New York: W. W. Norton.

——— (1953a). Reconstruction of the dream screen. *Psychoanalytic Quarterly* 22:174–199.

——— (1953b). The forgetting of dreams. In *Drives, Affects, Behavior,* ed. R. M. Loewenstein, pp. 191–202. New York: International Universities Press.

——— (1954). Sleep, narcissistic neurosis and the analytic situation. *Psychoanalytic Quarterly* 23:487–510.

——— (1955a). Clinical hints from dream studies. *Bulletin of the Menninger Clinic* 19:73–85.

——— (1955b). Dream psychology and the analytic situation. *Psychoanalytic Quarterly* 24:169–199.

McDougall, J. (1989). *Theaters of the Body. A Psychoanalytic Approach to Psychosomatic Illness.* New York: W. W. Norton.

Meltzer, D. (1983). *Dream Life.* London: Clunie Press, for the Roland Harris Trust Library.

M'Uzan, M. de (1976). Countertransference and the paradoxical system. In *Psychoanalysis in France*, ed. S. Lebovici and D. Widlocher, pp. 437–451. New York: International Universities Press.

Ogden, T. H. (1986). *The Matrix of the Mind.* Northvale, NJ: Jason Aronson.

——— (1989). *The Primitive Edge of Experience.* Northvale, NJ: Jason Aronson.

Rosenfeld, D. (1984). Hypochondriasis, somatic delusion and body schema in psychoanalytic practice. *International Journal of Psycho-Analysis* 65:377–388.

——— (1990). Psychotic body image. In *Master Clinicians on Treating the Regressed Patients*, ed. L. B. Boyer and P. L. Giovacchini, pp. 165–188. Northvale, NJ: Jason Aronson.

Rosenfeld, D., and Pistol, D. (1986). *Episodio psicótico y su detección precoz en la transferencia.* Paper presented at the 16th Latin American Psychoanalytic Congress, Mexico City, July.

Segal, H. (1981). The function of dreams. In *The Work of Hanna Segal*, pp. 89–97. New York: Jason Aronson.

Vold, J. M. (1910–1912). *Über den Traum. Experimental Psychologische Untersuchungen.* 2 vol. Leipzig: Barth.

Winnicott, D. W. (1965). *The Maturational Process and the Facilitating Environment.* New York: International Universities Press.

Zusman, W. (1974). A transferencia como mecanismo de defesa. *Revista Brasileira de Psicanálisis* 8:545–570.

Regression in Treatment:
On Early Object Relations

In this chapter a fragment of the case history of a patient with an unusual psychosomatic syndrome is used to discuss the psychic evolution of the infant prior to the development of the transitional object relationship and the role of regression in treatment.

During the past forty years or so, many clinicians have come to treat patients who suffer from the narcissistic neuroses by dynamic psychotherapy; an ever-increasing number use psychoanalysis with few parameters (Eissler 1953). The broadening scope of therapeutic psychoanalysis has been accompanied by an immense burgeoning of the literature pertaining to the so-called borderline patient[1] and a vastly heightened recognition of the roles of countertransference in treatment.[2] To include such patients in analytic practice requires permitting them to regress to early preoedipal

---

1. Abend and colleagues 1983, Bion 1962, Bollas 1987, Boyer 1983, Boyer and Giovacchini 1980, 1990, Frosch 1988, Giovacchini 1972, 1975, 1979, 1986, Giovacchini and Boyer 1982, Green 1986, Grinberg 1977, Grotstein and colleagues 1987, Kernberg 1975, 1986, McDougall 1985, 1989, Meissner 1984, Modell 1984, H. A. Rosenfeld 1965, 1987, Searles 1986, Volkan 1976, 1981, 1987, Wilson and Mintz 1989.

2. Epstein and Feiner 1979, Giovacchini and colleagues 1975, Little 1957, Meyer 1986, Racker 1968, Searles 1979, Slakter 1987.

states; the study of the effects of that regression on transference–countertransference interactions has provided new data that have permitted a more detailed study of early internalized object relations. There is general agreement that such controlled regression cannot occur if the holding environment provided by the analyst and the therapeutic milieu is inadequate.

As Anna Freud (1969) noted, one reason Freud recommended that psychoanalysis be used solely for the treatment of the transference neuroses was that he believed that displacements to the therapist from the early pregenital years were too unstable to be amenable to interpretations. However, it has been demonstrated repeatedly that interpretations dealing with dyadic relationship displacements can be mutative in a conducive milieu. A significant element of such a milieu is the analyst's tolerance of the patient's regressions. Many therapists who treat regressed patients using psychoanalytic principles hold as a highly important aspect of therapy that the interpretation of all regressive phenomena, including psychotic symptoms, as defensive at least in part, and in the service of resistance (Arieti 1959, 1961). Bion (1977), with his concept of not fostering memory, sought to start from the origins in each session. Origins for him, as well as for others who have studied defensive fantasies as mental processes (E. Gaddini 1982), meant early sense data as relived in the analytic situation, a position consistent with Freud's idea that the ego is ultimately derived from bodily sensations, chiefly those arising from the surface of the body.

Let us briefly review some current thoughts about the process of internalization of object relationships. These notions are the product of studies that have added to and refined the ideas of structuralization developed by Freud, who conceptualized the ego to develop from the id and later wrote: "The ego (the I) is first and foremost a bodily ego [and] is ultimately derived from bodily sensations, chiefly from those springing from the surface of the body" (1923, p. 26 fn. added in 1927).

Those current thoughts stem primarily from inferences drawn from ongoing caregiver–infant and –child observations, the psychoanalyses of children, and the psychoanalytic therapy of regressed adults. Such studies stress ultimately the building up of dyadic intrapsychic representations, self and object images that reflect the original infant–mother relationship, and their subsequent development into triadic and multiple internal and external interpersonal relationships. In this chapter discussion will be limited to the effects of very early caregiver–infant relations preceding the development of the transitional object and phenomena (Winnicott 1953) and potential space (Ogden 1986).

Studies of the development of internalized object relations continue to attempt to account for the influences of constitution and heredity as well as the effects of caregiver–child interactions. Bowlby (1988) and Emde (1988a,b) have reviewed comprehensively the research knowledge about innate and motivational factors from infancy gained in disciplines other than psychoanalysis as well as our own discipline in order to advance our own theory. Emde has focused on studies of innate and motivational factors from infancy. He wrote: "Research points to the centrality of the infant–caregiver experience and of emotional availability for establishing both continuity and the potential for later adaptive change. Basic infant motivations are proposed that consist of activity self-regulation, social fittedness and affective monitoring. These influences are biologically inherent and are necessary for development and persist throughout life" (Emde 1988a, p. 38). He found the psychoanalytic relationship to the extent that it recapitulates positive aspects of the normative processes involved in the infant–caregiver relationship to offer a special opportunity for developmental thrust, to offer a new beginning (Balint 1948, Fraiberg 1980), depending on the emotional sensitivity of the analyst, his or her responsiveness to a range of emotions, and the development and analysis of the transference–countertransference relations. The importance of the nature of the psychoanalytic setting and of the development of actual object relations in achieving the new beginning have received and continue to receive attention (Bleger 1967, Greenson and Wexler 1969, Loewald 1960, Modell 1984, 1988, Spruiell 1983). Clinical data too extensive to warrant citation have illustrated that not all primitive patients are amenable to psychological, or, for that matter, any known means of treatment. Most observers assume organic causes for such refractoriness to therapy; no doubt inherited modes of organizing experience are relevant (Lorenz 1937, Ogden 1986, Tinbergen 1957).

Researchers who have conducted infant observations in hopes of ascertaining the beginnings of internalized object relations have found that these object relations have their beginnings in the infant's bodily sensations and that bodily sensations at the skin surface and in the mucosal membranes of the mouth are particularly important (see also Hoffer 1949). These sensations are the basis for the very earliest fantasies that constitute the initial sense of self and experience of going-on-being.

As Freud (1914) and Spitz (1965) note, the beginning of human life is probably characterized by a purely physiological existence and sensory impressions have as yet no psychological meaning. Meaningful sensations depending on the accumulation and reduction of tension constitute the first primitive engrams. The first mnemic registrations take place in an entirely undifferentiated sphere and it is usually not until the second half of the first year that there will be evidence of the infant's mental representations having become grouped into the first crude images of self and an object (Tähkä 1988; see also Jacobson 1974). Of importance in clarifying this area are the clinical and observational work of Meltzer (1967, 1975, Meltzer et al. 1975) and Tustin (1972, 1981, 1986) developed in the context of their work with autistic children and the clinical work of Bick (1968, 1986) and D. Rosenfeld (1982, 1984, 1990, Rosenfeld and Pistol 1986). Ogden (1986, 1989) too writes of the precursors of mother–infant interactions. He considers the development of British object relations theory over the past twenty years to contain the beginnings of an exploration of a realm of experience that precedes the states addressed by Klein, Winnicott, Fair-bairn, and Bion. Ogden (1989) has coined the term *autistic-contiguous position* as a way of conceptualizing a psychological organization more primitive than either the paranoid-schizoid or the depressive position, a mode of organizing experience that stands in a dialectical relationship to the paranoid-schizoid and depressive modes, holding that each creates, preserves, and negates the others. The autistic-contiguous mode is highly germane to an exposition of the development of internalized object relations. It is a sensory-dominated presymbolic mode of generating experience that provides a good measure of the boundedness of human experience and the beginnings of a sense of the place where one's experience occurs. It is beyond the purview of this chapter to discuss further the autistic-contiguous position beyond noting some of its properties. "Anxiety in this mode consists of an unspeakable terror of the dissolution of bounded-ness resulting in feelings of leaking, falling or dissolving into endless shapeless space" (Ogden 1989, p. 68). Such fears have been described similarly by Anzieu (1980), Bick (1968, 1986), and D.Rosenfeld (1984). It will be seen below that Ogden's views are consonant with the presumed presymbolic mentation ascribed by the Gaddinis (R. Gaddini 1970, 1974, 1976, 1985) to infants before they have reached the transitional phase, a position with which Giovacchini (1980) agrees.

At this point let us regard the notion of caregiver–infant relationships and internalization, starting with fantasy, for thought begins with fantasy. Freud (1923) told us that what becomes conscious is the concrete subject matter of the thought, and that thinking in pictures is but a very incomplete form of becoming conscious; that it stands nearer to unconscious processes than does thinking in words. McDougall (1989) writes: "Since babies cannot yet use words with which to think, they respond to pain only psychosomatically. The concept of fantasy, when it begins and its vicissitudes, remain unsettled" (p. 9). E. Gaddini (1982) postulated that before fantasy can become visual there is an experience of it *in* the body. It might be more accurate to designate such experiences as proto-thoughts.[3, 4] Anzieu (1989) has stressed the importance of skin sensations and their effects on the early development of thought and has held that an early fantasy is that of a skin shared by mother and child. He refers to the surface of the body as an inner envelope and the maternal environment as an outer envelope. On this basis a physical function can be altered according to its mental significance, and meaning can be given to its somatic expression. Such fantasies in the body are not available to elaboration as are visual fantasies, and account for early somatic pathology and psychophysical syndromes that begin in infancy and continue into adulthood as well as cases of alexithymia (Demers-Desrosiers 1981, Marty et al. 1963, Taylor 1984).[5, 6] Such crude unvisualized fantasies in the body occur during the

---

3. Wilson and Mintz (1989) hold that deep defensive regression renders a renewed merger of psyche and soma in which whatever capacity to symbolize remains is expressed predominantly through somatic avenues.

4. Such "fantasies in the body" had been inferred previously by Isakower (1938, 1954), Lewin (1946, 1950, 1953), and Spitz (1955). Here I cite Wangh's (Boyer 1956) paraphrasing of Spitz.

> Lewin deduces logically that if a regression occurs from the visual imagery level at which the dream functions, then there should be memory traces older than these pictures. Thus, as I do, he sees these memory traces "more like pure emotion," made up of deeper tactile, thermal and dimly protopathic qualities which are in their way "memory traces" of early dim consciousness of the breast or of the half-sleep state. And, if I read him correctly, he believes it to be at this level of integration that the subject regresses in the so-called blank dream. It follows that the level of regression involved in the Isakower phenomenon harks back to an earlier period, that which precedes the reliable laying down of visual mnemic traces or at least to a period at which a significant number of visual mnemic traces has not yet been accumulated. I would be inclined to say that while the regression of the dream screen goes to the level of the mnemic traces laid down somewhere between the ages toward the end of the first half year and reaching to the end of the first year, in the Isakower phenomenon the regression reaches to the traces of experiences preceding this period. Obviously, these ages represent extremely wide approximations. [pp. 19–20]

5. Lipowski (1988) reminds us that Stekel (1911) introduced the term *somatization* to refer to a hypothetical process whereby a "deep-seated" neurosis could cause a bodily disorder, and Menninger (1947) defined "somatization reactions" as the "visceral expression of the anxiety which is thereby prevented from being conscious."

None of the contributors to the book *Psychosomatic Symptoms*, edited by Wilson and

period of *personalisation*, one of Winnicott's (1971) terms for infant being at one with mother a time for which he used also the term *subjective-object* (Winnicott 1969). They are followed by fantasies *on* the body that represent the first mental image of the separate self. Mahler's (1968, Mahler et al. 1975) studies have established, as have so many others, that continuity of consistent care that is sensitive to the needs of the infant makes it possible for him to move away from his earlier, essential concern with needs and sensations toward a capacity of desiring where the time factor is involved, toward individuation. The work of Mahler and the many other observational students, such as Roiphe and Galenson (1981), of caregiver–child interactions concern themselves primarily with later periods of development than those being considered here. Renata Gaddini (1987) describes the precursor objects as functioning to support the baby's illusion that she or he *is* the mother and the mother *is* the baby. These precursor objects are the sole content of primitive internal phantasies that will develop eventually into transitional objects and self and other internalized object relationships. The precursor objects belong to a period of development where there is no differentiation as they reinforce the baby's sensation of being at-one with the mother.

Sucking and skin contact are for the neonate and the young infant the main consolers and the main physical precursors. The nipple (or its substitute) and the mouth together reestablish the baby's sense of continuity and cohesion. R. Gaddini (1987) thinks of the existence of the intraoral precursors (nipple and substitutes) as a step toward relating to the transitional object. While orality has traditionally been thought of in terms of eroticism and sexuality, sucking, even on a nonnutritive object, more importantly reestablishes ideas of continuity with the mother not only in

Mintz (1989), agrees with Nemiah and his collaborators (Nemiah et al. 1976), nor does McDougall (1989), that a hereditary constitutional defect in psychosomatic patients results in a failure of the ego's capacity to fantasize and dream. Wilson and Mintz hold such failure to report to constitute an analyzable resistance and McDougall adds that some patients can develop the capacity to verbalize fantasies theretofore unexpressed in words during the analysis of regressed states. The data of the current contribution would seem to affirm that position.

6. The relevant work of Viktor von Weizsacker (1946, 1954, 1962) is rarely mentioned in the literature written in English, but has stimulated a school of psychoanalysts in Argentina (Centro de Consulta Médica Weizsacker) whose work is devoted primarily to studying the psychosomatic border and its affects in early object relations development and the treatment of patients with psychosomatic disorders (Chiozza 1976, 1980, Chiozza et al. 1979).

infants but, regressively, in adults as well (Gaddini and Gaddini 1959). The mouth's original function is sensory and only later (when separation has begun) does it become a potentially incorporating organ. It is then that instinctual orality can be mentioned (E. Gaddini 1981). Of greatest importance: the mouth is essentially the place where physical and mental models convene.

To repeat, these precursors (of transitional objects) are based on tactile sensations of continuity, be they intraoral or clearly based on skin sensations such as mother's nipple or its substitute, whether nutritive or otherwise; mother's hair or other parts of her body; or also the infant's body, which is the same at this early stage of development (R. Gaddini 1987).

In our investigation of earliest development, the value of precursors is paramount because, being so primary, their study allows us to understand significant vicissitudes of the initial sense of being. Because of the equation early = severe in psychopathology, we find that the pathology that is based on the failure of their development or on their premature loss is particularly severe: perversions (especially fetishism), fixed ideas, compulsions, adulthood conviction of the reality of the imaginary companion, and so on. In these cases the precursor has not led to the bridge between me and not-me—the transitional object. When the precursor object is prematurely lost, the early self is lost, and the accompanying sensation is presumed to belong to the "primary agonies" or catastrophe, which is at best organized in the mind in a very elementary way. This can be contrasted with the sense of loss experienced by the child who has been deprived of his transitional object, which is closer to mourning.

A mother's pathological symbiotic ties to her infant may interfere with symbolization of reunion with her after loss. Children do not create a transitional object if the mother remains available physically, as sometimes occurs if the mother's symbiosis with her baby is excessive. The protracted use of precursor substitutes for the breast and tactile contact interferes with the development of symbolization. Psychosomatic patients rarely create a transitional object because of their impaired capacity for symbolization. Psychosomatic symptoms appear when the child's use of the object has been adversely affected and in later development language and symbolization prove to be impaired by this early interference with prestages of object relationship, mind–body differentiation and interaction, symbolization, and communication with the object (R. Gaddini 1987). Precursors thus can be viewed also as defenses against differentiation, against the development of the transitional-phase phenomena and an early sense of self. Such objects and phenomena during the subphase of differentiation, when mind and mental operations are developing, are described by Mahler and colleagues (1975) as typical of hatching.

Pathology based on the deficiency or loss of these precursors-not-yet-symbols (see also Segal 1957) consistent with the equation early = severe includes, as mentioned formerly, some cases of psychosomatic syndromes that persist from infancy into adulthood and at least some cases of autism, perversions (especially fetishism), compulsions persistence into adulthood of a belief in the imaginary companion, and fixed thinking.

At the same time, researchers have found little predictability in behavior from infancy to later ages and Emde (1988a) wrote of a "central developmental paradox" (p. 24). Pointing to the degree of flexibility and plasticity that has been found in infants, he stressed the influence of the environment and the "matching" of the growing infant and his caregiver. The developmental orientation in fact indicates a particular view about adaptation and pathology. What is not adaptive is a lack or variability in an individual who is faced with environmental demands necessitating alternative choices and strategies for change (Emde 1988a). Freud (1937) felt that one of the reasons for poor results of psychoanalysis was the rigidity of some analytic practitioners and poor matching between patient and therapist.

IMPLICATIONS FOR TREATMENT
OF REGRESSED PATIENTS

To the extent that it recapitulates or offers positive aspects of normative processes involved in the infant–caregiver relationship, the psychoanalytic relationship occurring later in life offers a special opportunity for a new beginning. A corrective emotional experience takes place that is based on the emotional availability of the analyst and the constancy of the therapeutic environment rather than the therapist's manipulation. To a degree that has been underrecognized in our literature, the optimal availability of the analyst is based on his emotional sensitivity and his security and responsiveness to a wide range of emotions. Stated otherwise the analyst must be able to tolerate emotionally the patient's need to regress to very primitive psychological, even psychosomatic, states, including in some cases those in which the proto-thoughts or fantasies are *in* the soma. It is in this type of atmosphere that a therapeutic alliance can develop within which appropriate interpretations will be effective. In Emde's (1989) words: "If the process goes well the analytic relationship becomes fortified by a new executive sense of we and an analytic we-ego" (p. 291).

Freud's (1910) "countertransference" came to be considered as the repetition of the analyst's irrational unconscious previously acquired attitudes now directed toward the patient. Today most analysts would consider this view to be Racker's (1953) countertransference neurosis. Hann-Kende (1933) may have been the first to have suggested that the countertransference could be turned to purposes beneficial to therapy. Today countertransference is viewed generally as the analyst's total emotional response to his patient's needs (Little 1957).

Analysts have sought long to understand what constitutes Reik's (1948) listening with the third ear or Isakower's analyzing instrument. Spiegel (1975) noted that both analyst and analysand operate in similar states of mind (free-floating attention and free association, respectively), and that this results in a type of conversation that is unique to psychoanalysis. Balter and colleagues (1980) speak of the analyzing instrument as operating within a subsystem of the ego of the analyst, who is more likely to perceive connections between words, ideas, and images that are products of the patient's primary process because his subsystem is itself in part freed from the constraints of secondary process thinking, reality testing, and so on.

I have noted (Boyer 1986) that the analyst's being aware of his fantasies, emotional states, and physical sensations that occur during his free-floating attention (and at times his subsequent dreams) enables him to be more in tune with his patient's communications and that such awareness is especially useful in working with the regressed patient. His tolerance of the patient's primitive regressions (those that might lead to or involve the fantasies *in* the body), transitional relatedness, and subsequent developmental phases as they are relived in the analytic situation entails his capacity to regress concomitantly with his patient while simultaneously retaining the observing function of his ego (Searles 1979).

CLINICAL MATERIAL

A 54-year-old immigrant Levantine, still physically beautiful, had been periodically hospitalized as "schizophrenic" in her native country from the age of 16 to 20, under the care of a renowned psychoanalyst. She had perceived herself to have no will of her own, but rather to be her mother's "organic extension" and "Barbie-doll puppet." During one interview she said, consecutively, "Until I was 4, I was an autonomous body protecting itself against becoming a dead puppet"; "At 13 I turned into non-animate

matter, dead bits of a popped balloon, that is, broken bits of body boundaries swaying helplessly in the waves of an ocean, my mother, without
autonomous movement"; "At 33 I turned into a rotting piece of flesh,
organic matter, devoured by nuggets, fragments of my mother"; and "A few
years later I was a dead puppet whose mother was pulling the strings which
made it look alive, but there were some signs of hidden life at the core, a
secret woven with guilt."

At 21 she decided to live with a rich and influential foreigner old
enough to be her father, "as *his* puppet." She called him "Daddy" and he
called her "Baby." He made no demands on her beyond the satisfaction of
his lust and that she dress magnificently and behave appropriately at
embassy functions, while serving as his highly efficient secretary.

For her, as had been true for her mother, others' external reality was
but a dream and her reality consisted of an inner dream life that continued
during the day. While she had intense orgasms and her physical activities
were graceful and appropriate, her conscious mental life was unassociated
with such outer events. Her privately experienced alienation from the world
and others' experience was recognized but vaguely by them. During this
period of her life, she lived in the same country as did her extended family
and visited with them frequently. No one appears to have recognized her as
being odd.

When the consul returned to his homeland, she became inexplicably
terrified that she would be mysteriously annihilated. At the same time, she
was terrified that were her family to know of her fear, her mother would
"seduce" her to return home where she believed she would become a
"zombie," living her mother's life as fantasied "martyr–world saver." Thus
she lived alone, supporting herself as a secretary, "seeking emotional
sustenance" from the sperm of countless men she "charmed and discarded."
"They had no emotional significance for me whatever as people; they were
but physical objects on whom to nurse." She secretly sought orthodox
psychoanalysis from her former therapist but was seen instead vis-à-vis
once weekly, receiving advice and support that accompanied interpretations that seemed to her to "belong to the private mythology" of her
therapist, since they presumed that the patient's view of reality coincided
with hers and that when the patient talked about lust and sexual activities
"she thought I was confusing the men with my father while I was trying to
fuse with my mother again, after I had become afraid our protective
membrane had ruptured."

In desperation she left treatment and soon found and immediately
married another man old enough to be her father, a renowned scientific

investigator whose expectations of her were similar to those of the consul, and who took her abroad as his assistant.

It was a very strange marriage, again involving the names "Daddy" and "Baby." She served brilliantly as his "puppet," as she had done previously for her other male protector and, while overtly psychotic, her mother. She discovered important data that furthered her husband's career but she claimed no credit for them since she believed they belonged to an irrelevant reality. So far as she was concerned, she was content in her life of puppetry while her inner mental reality consisted of her being the world's heroine savior, an idolized martyr or literally a sun or other planet. Periodically she was quite aware that the "world" symbolized her mother, but that knowledge was of no use to her. At the same time, her husband spent months on end with his "mummy" in another country, apparently living some sort of symbiotic or psychologically fused relationship with her.

Following her psychotic break when she was 12 or 13, she was convinced that she was a literal, physical, and mental extension of her mother, whose existence depended on[7] the patient's thoughts and actions, as, reciprocally, hers did on her mother's. She was consciously aware of believing that she and her mother inhabited the same skin and that any injury, physical or psychical, to either of them, during brief periods when she simultaneously transiently perceived them to be separate, would result in their bleeding out their bodily contents and ceasing to exist. This emphasis on the skin and its implications of continuity with the mother is reminiscent of the Gaddinis' position that the intrapsychic preservation of such continuity is a precursor that precedes and defends against the development of the transitional object, which for her would have constituted premature separation, and of D. Rosenfeld's psychotic body image (1982, 1989). This patient never had a transitional object.

At 35 she had the first of two daughters, born three years apart, both of whom she perceived to be literal extensions of herself. She believed their every anxiety to be the product of uncontrollable and insatiable physical needs. As was true of herself, they were capable solely of "animal and not human communication" and were continuous with her as she was with her mother, inside a membrane that changed character from time to time but clearly symbolized fragile skin. "Animal communication," as I learned after many months, meant unwitting, reflexive response to internal, solely physi-

---

7. The specific stimulus for her regression into a psychotic state appears to have been her mother's accusing her of wanting to seduce her father, that is, a sharp revivification of her unresolved oedipal conflict.

cal needs, particularly alimentary and tactile needs. Now she was terrified that her daughters would eat her up from inside and became aware that she had feared earlier that her mother and she would empty one another by devouring each other from the inside.

She interpreted her husband's fear of impregnating her to mean that he was terrified that orgasm would destroy him through turning him literally into an animal whose flinty eyes were those of a prehistoric reptile, as she saw her mother's eyes at times, and that were he to become sexually excited he would become unable to revert to human rather than animal communication; her sympathetic response would result in their fusion into a fragile membrane, the contents of which would consist of unbridled instinctual urges, largely cannibalistic. Thus she refused sexual relations following the birth of their second daughter, apparently to her husband's relief, and had no further intercourse although she masturbated endlessly with sadomasochistic fantasies in which she was raped serially while tied to a post as an "unpaid victim, a white slave."

Her husband's work took them to various European countries in which she received transient reduction of anxiety from psychotherapists so long as she could hope that they could communicate with her on a "human" rather than an "animal" level, where the "intelligence of the organism" prevailed. Then her husband left her for two years for reasons pertaining apparently solely to his work. She returned to her home with her parents and seemingly became fused anew with her mother, now being incapable of any activities beyond looking after the welfare of her daughters. Otherwise she vegetated in a darkened room where her mental life consisted of fantasies she believed herself to be sharing with her mother.

When her husband rejoined her, they and their daughters moved to the United States where she was hospitalized and medicated as psychotic, with no apparent amelioration. During that period, her parents died and she responded to their deaths by using the negation defense. After a year, her husband's work took them to California, where she continued to live in isolation, bestirring herself solely to cook for and otherwise look after her husband's and daughters' physical needs, or to attend and hostess social activities necessary to her husband's work. At such times she functioned in totally appropriate ways, secretly smiling to herself because all about her, as it seemed to her, lived in an unreal reality. At the same time she held her activities to be automatic or "robotic." She was quite consciously aware of both realities at times and was mildly curious about her need to keep them separate. Her family seemingly were unaware that she was seriously disturbed. When alone, she spent much time writing stream-of-consciousness ideation in a secret code, a shorthand of an actual language unknown to her husband and children. Once her ideas were recorded, their content was repressed but she saved the many written volumes in hopes that at some future time she would be able to face her fantasies and memories, were she to be able to comprehend the reality of others around her. Her family believed she was writing a novel for publication and respected her privacy.

Although she hid her fears of reciprocal cannibalism from her family members, and her husband did not perceive her anxiety, he "babied" her "whim" to seek treatment once again. She was seen by a psychoanalyst, one to three times weekly, for some seven years. Treatment consisted of her bringing her secret writings to her analyst's office and trying to learn the meanings of what she discovered herself to have written. Apparently, her therapist became discouraged and eventually sought to deal with her by arguing about what constituted reality. After the fourth year she interpreted his behavior to mean he was anxious and wanted her to leave his care, but by then she believed that they had fused and that were she to leave him, their enclosing membrane would rupture and their beings would leak out. Nevertheless, after seven years, she had come to the conclusion that taking care of her family had more priority than taking care of her psychoanalyst and she asked to be transferred to my care, having heard I "treated patients everyone else had given up on," and was "tough."

The highly abbreviated material that follows deals with data pertaining to her psychological precursors.

I offered to see her in orthodox psychoanalysis on an experimental basis. She agreed, although she was terrified that the deprivation of eye contact would make all "human communication" impossible and that "the intelligence of the organism" would prevail. Her insatiable "animal needs" would make her burrow into my body like a baby rodent and my eyes would become her mother's eyes, those of a prehistoric, cold-blooded reptilian, totally impersonal and inhuman, watching for any evidence of her stirring that would give me–mother an opportunity to devour her. She likewise feared that were she not to be allowed to translate her writings to me, she would have nothing to say, since without them to come between us and protect us, the "bridging function of words" would lead to our fusion. Our words carried different realities and their fusion would cause our physical fusion.

Although much of what she said made very little sense to me, at no time did I feel uncomfortable with her and my principal initial activity consisted of asking her to restate what she meant for me to understand in different words; I frequently iterated to her what I believed I had understood her to have sought to communicate and asked for further clarification.

Despite her terror, she was intrigued that I encouraged rather than impeded her efforts to verbalize aloud her contorted thinking and images—"The remaining cerebration that has persisted inside me since my mental breakdown when I was 13. I've kept it secret from everyone but my psychoanalysts and they've all discouraged me from trying to tell them about it and to learn about myself from it." She sensed that for the first time she had met someone who was not afraid that her "looniness" was contagious and therefore did not believe she would harm him with her experiences, thoughts, dreams, or hallucinations. She said, "No one has ever encouraged me to look further inside of me. I've never known before that I could say things I've thought aloud and not have the verbalizing make our reality change, that is, turn you or me literally into what I had only become aware I thought after hearing my words." She said that she had always known that her only hope for salvation was to learn to understand her unconscious motivations and conflicts, and consequently each of her previous seventeen therapists had been a certified psychoanalyst.[8] None, however, was willing to give her the experience of seeking a psychoanalytic experience that could have entailed, potentially, psychotic regression. She had believed that she had to take care of them as well as herself.

After some weeks she revealed a secret she had previously imparted to no one, namely, that she lived in constant pain "due to the stirring of animal life" in her lower brain and spinal cord, sometimes extending to her "tail." Her higher, "human" brain was nonfunctional. Her nervous system was the repository of her previous mental life, which had become fused with it "as it was in the beginning before I learned human rather than animal communication."

She quite literally believed that she was motivated solely by neurophysiological manifestations of primitive animal urges, primarily insatiable hunger, which could be gratified solely through physical fusion and devouring a mother surrogate from the inside.

Soon after she reported the pain in her "lower brain and spinal cord," it became apparent to me that anxiety resultant from any conflict whatever

---

8. I have written previously of the successful psychoanalysis of a "schizophrenic" patient who repeatedly had requested and been refused orthodox analysis (Boyer 1977).

was quickly dissipated and replaced by the physical symptoms. Thus my interpretive efforts were directed toward helping her understand this somatization as a defense. As an example, I would recall for her that she had been speaking of uneasiness, fear, or anxiety; then the emotional discomfort had disappeared and been replaced by the pain in her lower brain and spinal cord. I said that her body was colluding with her mind in seeking to protect her from feeling discomfort and learning what internal conflicts had caused the emotional discomfort. Intrigued, she was nevertheless frightened and incredulous, but gradually came to seem to understand the defensive maneuver.

Sometimes screaming and writhing, she described endless permutations of pain radiation and used material taken from her extensive reading of neurophysiological literature to support her position that her symptoms were solely of organic origin whenever I sought to trace her systems of logic and to learn against what such regressive episodes during her interviews served to defend her. As would be expected, the majority of her reported pain radiations followed hysterical paths, and her associations to the pains and the syndromes they reportedly caused revealed fused orality and genitality (Marmor 1953), but she was then impervious to useful knowledge of symbolism. Later, of course, we would learn that "tail" gained symbolic meanings having to do with sexual and perineal activities and desires. Sometimes such knowledge would emerge when she hallucinated my taking an actual active role in her relivings in the consultation room of her sadomasochistic fantasies or dreams of being raped serially. At the same time as she screamed with pain as I raped her vaginally and anally, she retained a grasp on reality and laughed aloud as she told me she had to regress to relive her childhood properly "this time" and I should know that to gratify her sexually at this period of her development would be indulging in "child molestation."

Her life outside the consultation room held no interest for her during her interviews and I had but the vaguest of ideas what she did. From time to time she briefly commented that her husband and daughters had said that she was more energetic and communicative than previously.

It was over a year after she entered treatment with me before she remembered that her pains had begun when she moved with her husband and children to the United States, a move she feared would rupture the membrane surrounding her mother and her and result in their bleeding into nothingness. She reasoned that, so long as she spent much of her time isolated and in a dream state, she was effectively dead and that her being "asleep dead" in fact would prevent her mother's death.

She had interpreted her previous analyst's willingness to let her use her writings as a protective screen between them to mean that he feared that spontaneous recital of her thoughts would damage him. My position that she was to speak rather than read she took as evidence that she did not have to take care of both of us and that she had a better chance to regain the capacity for "human communication" in her work with me.

A change in her symptomatology that occurred six months into her treatment frightened and encouraged her: she began to have "spasms" and "contractions" in her "lower brain and spinal cord" and interpreted them to mean that "humanity" was stirring concurrently with her animality, "the intelligence of the organism." She reported a dream: "A baby's hand came out through my navel inside the membrane-skin from the womb. I was awed and amazed. I showed it to my husband, my beginning to emerge as a human." She then talked of mother animals' kicking hungry babies away and became afraid. My interpretation that she had become fearful that her growing human wishes pertaining to me as a representative of her mother would lead to my rejection of her alleviated her anxiety.

During the next few months, continuing spasms frightened and encouraged her; at the same time her periods of self-isolation became briefer and she undertook many activities, now being able consistently to experience both realities concurrently. She was greatly encouraged. Subsequently, intermittent periods occurred when there were no pains ascribed to her lower brain and spine, and when the symptoms recurred, interpretations of their serving defensive purposes were effective. Then came some sessions in which her dreams and fantasies involved her being an infant or a small child who had a security blanket. She said: "It's hard to believe that my reliving of my past even includes being happy the same way my daughters were." Subsequently, she secretly bought and privately treasured a teddy bear.

About a year into her analysis, following a period of several weeks during which she had experienced no pains or spasms from her "lower brain or spine," she delightedly told me one day that she had reacted to an insensitive act of her husband's by experiencing "spasms" and finally knew that what she had called "the intelligence of the organism" had a psychological meaning and served psychological purposes; that it was not solely a reflex, organic symptom related only to "neurophysiological metabolism." The following session she presented data that support Gaddini's notion of fantasies in the soma as follows. She said, "I woke up with 'sick' pain in my shoulders, arms, neck, and tail. It has a life of its own. It's coming out. It used to be stronger than I was. Then I saw a latent, blurred image which meant I was closer to being able to talk about it." Suddenly she cried, as the blurred image became a clear picture that she later identified as an actual memory of herself sewing and unable to remember what she was doing because she was fearful of her mother's vitriolic ridicule. After talking about having read that men are sexually excited by cripples and thus Chinese men bind women's feet so that they'll be crippled and helpless, she sobbed loudly, saying, "She *smelt* cripples, any psychological weakness in people, and her power gave her immense sexual excitement. I can see her. She made everyone and everything dependent on her and then got so excited when she tortured the helpless ones. She had cats and kept them caged and wouldn't let anyone else feed them. Then she'd take them food and just before they'd get to the food, she'd kick them with her sharp, high-heeled shoes that look like those deformed Chinese women's feet and she'd flush and quiver with what must have been an orgasm." Startled, she became aware that her physical pains had left. She said, "They became a blurred image, then a clear image, and finally words."

At another time, following her telling me with delight and awe that she could now risk loving and trusting me as someone separate from her and not use me solely as a "container for the parts of me that are my mother and torture me," and repeating that she knew for her to get over her "looni-ness" she had to relive her past "from its beginning" in her experiences with me, she described in another way how she perceived her sensations to become words that made "human communication" become possible. "I wake up (from dreams that are only feelings) thinking in images. This morning I saw myself sitting beside a pile of my inner content, content made up only of sensations and emotions; it is quite a big pile. I am taking small pinches of stuff from the pile and hammering it into small containers, rather than bringing it here and believing it is inside you; the containers look like dental crowns. They are strung to each other to form a visible pattern but there are no actual teeth any more. I know what I am doing, I am putting my inner content into containers of words. I am separating and diffusing the content of the heap. I wonder why do I have to hammer the stuff so forcefully into inflexible containers, why it takes so much effort to force my inner content into ready-made shapes. My inner content becomes visible when it is put into the small, hard containers that are how I see words. Nothing in this world can be visible and used for human commu-nication unless it is put into matter and thus given the form of words. As long as energy loaded with emotions and the meaning that is my inner content is not related to matter, it remains invisible, that is, unconscious to me, refuse in a pile, unusable and shapeless. Nothing can be distinguished and identified. As long as patterns of emotions and thoughts are fused together into small knots in a pile made of sensations, nothing can become visible; human communication through words does not really exist."

COMMENT

This chapter has consisted of a brief literature review followed by the presentation of a fragment of the case history of a patient who presented, so far as is known to the author, a unique psychosomatic syndrome. The data suggest that the earliest internalized object relations are to be found in a fusion of psychological and somatic phenomena. The data suggest also that psychoanalytic treatment that encourages controlled regression can enable the patient who has been partially fixated at such an early level of psychic organization to develop to higher levels of organization.

References

Abend, S., Porder, M., and Willick, M. S. (1983). *Borderline Patients; Psycho-analytic Perspectives*. New York: International Universities Press.

Anzieu, D. (1980). Skin ego. In *Psychoanalysis in France*, ed. S. Lebovici and D. Widlocher, pp. 17–32. New York: International Universities Press.

——— (1989). *The Skin Ego. A Psychoanalytic Approach to the Self*. New Haven, CT: Yale University Press.

Arieti, S. (1959). Schizophrenic thought. *American Journal of Psychotherapy* 13:537–552.

——— (1961). Introductory notes on the psychoanalytic therapy of schizophrenics. In *Psychotherapy of the Psychoses*, ed. A. Burton, pp. 69–89. New York: Basic Books.

Balint, M. (1948). Individual differences of behavior in early infancy and an objective way of recording them. *Journal of Genetic Psychology* 73:57–117.

Balter, L., Lothane, Z., and Spencer, J. R., Jr. (1980). On the analyzing instrument. *Psychoanalytic Quarterly* 49:474–504.

Bick, E. (1968). The experience of the skin in early object relations. *International Journal of Psycho-Analysis* 49:484–486.

——— (1986). Further considerations on the function of the skin in early object relations. *British Journal of Psychotherapy* 2:292–299.

Bion, W. R. (1962). *Learning from Experience*. New York: Basic Books.

——— (1977). Attention and interpretation. In *Seven Servants. Four Works by Wilfred R. Bion*. New York: Jason Aronson.

Bleger, J. (1967). Psycho-analysis of the psycho-analytic frame. *International Journal of Psycho-Analysis* 48:511–519.

Bollas, C. (1987). *The Shadow of the Object. Psychoanalysis of the Unknown Thought.* New York: Columbia Universities Press.

Bowlby, J. (1988). Developmental psychiatry comes of age. *American Journal of Psychiatry* 145:1–10.

Boyer, L. B. (1956). Maternal overstimulation and ego defects. In *The Regressed Patient.* New York and London: Jason Aronson, 1983.

——— (1977). Working with a borderline patient. In *The Regressed Patient*, pp. 137–166. New York: Jason Aronson, 1983. Abstracted in *Therapies for Adults*, ed. H. L. Millman, J. T. Huber, and D. R. Diggins. San Francisco: Jossey-Bass, 1982.

——— (1983). *The Regressed Patient.* New York and London: Jason Aronson.

——— (1986). Technical aspects of treating the regressed patient. *Contemporary Psychoanalysis* 22:25–44.

Boyer, L. B., and Giovacchini, P. L. (1980). *Psychoanalytic Treatment of Schizophrenic, Borderline, and Characterological Disorders*, 2nd ed., rev. New York: Jason Aronson.

——— (1990). *Master Clinicians on Treating the Regressed Patient.* Northvale, NJ: Jason Aronson.

Chiozza, L. A. (1976). *Cuerpo, Afecto y Lenguaje. Psicoanálisis y Enfermedad Somática.* Buenos Aires: Paidos.

——— (1980). *Trama y Figura del Enfermar y del Psicoanalizar.* Buenos Aires: Paidos.

Chiozza, L. A., Aizenberg, S., Bahamonde, C., et al. (1979). *La Interpretación Psicoanalítica de la Enfermedad Somática en la Teoría y en la Práctica Clínica.* Buenos Aires: Ediciones Universidad del Salvador.

Demers-Desrosiers, L. (1981). Influence of alexithymia on symbolic formation. *Psychotherapy and Psychosomatics* 38:103–120.

Eissler, K. R. (1953). The effect of the structure of the ego on psychoanalytic technique. *Journal of the American Psychoanalytic Association* 1:104–143.

Emde, R. N. (1988a). Development terminable and interminable. I. Innate and motivational factors from infancy. *International Journal of Psycho-Analysis* 69:23–42.

——— (1988b). Development terminable and interminable. II. Recent psychoanalytic theory and therapeutic considerations. *International Journal of Psycho-Analysis* 69:283–296.

Epstein, L., and Feiner, A. H. (1979). *Countertransference. The Therapist's Contribution to the Therapeutic Situation.* New York: Jason Aronson.

Fraiberg, S. (1980). *Clinical Studies in Infant Mental Health; The First Year of Life.* New York: Basic Books.

Freud, A. (1969). *Difficulties in the Path of Psychoanalysis.* New York: International Universities Press.

Freud, S. (1910). The future prospects for psycho-analytic therapy. *Standard Edition* 11:141–151.

——— (1914). On narcissism: an introduction. *Standard Edition* 14:67–102.

——— (1923). The ego and the id. *Standard Edition* 19:12–68.

——— (1937). Analysis terminable and interminable. *Standard Edition* 23:211–253.

Frosch, J. (1988). *Psychodynamic Psychiatry.* 2 vols. New York: International Universities Press.

Gaddini, E. (1981). Il problema mente-corpo in psicoanalisis. *Rivista di Psicoanalisi* 27:3–29.

——— (1982). Early defensive fantasies and the psychoanalytic process. *International Journal of Psycho-Analysis* 63:369–388.

——— (1986). La maschera e il cerchio. *Rivista di Psicoanalisi* 32:175–186.

Gaddini, R. (1970). Transitional objects and the process of individuation. *Journal of the American Academy of Child Psychiatry* 9:347–365.

——— (1974). Early psychosomatic symptoms and the tendency toward integration. *Psychotherapy and Psychosomatics* 23:26–34.

——— (1976). Formazione del se e prima realta interna. *Rivista di Psicoanalisi* 2:206–225.

——— (1985). The precursors of transitional objects and phenomena. *Journal of the Squiggle Foundation* 1:49–56.

——— (1987). Early care and the roots of internalization. *International Review of Psycho-Analysis* 14:321–333.

Gaddini, R., and Gaddini, E. (1959). Rumination in infancy. In *Dynamic Psychopathology in Childhood*, ed. E. Pavenstedt and J. L. Lesser, pp. 166–185. New York: Grune & Stratton.

Giovacchini, P. L., ed. (1972). *Tactics and Techniques in Psychoanalytic Therapy.* New York: Science House.

——— (1975). *Psychoanalysis and Character Disorders.* New York: Jason Aronson.

——— (1979). *Treatment of Primitive Mental States.* New York: Jason Aronson.

——— (1980). Primitive agitation and primal confusion. In *Psychoanalytic Treatment of Schizophrenic, Borderline, and Characterological Disorders*, 2nd ed., eds. L. B. Boyer and P. L. Giovacchini, Chapter 9. New York: Jason Aronson.

——— (1986). *Developmental Disorders: The Transitional Space in Mental Breakdown and Creative Integration.* Northvale, NJ: Jason Aronson.

Giovacchini, P. L., and Boyer, L. B., eds. (1982). *Technical Factors in the Treatment of the Severely Disturbed Patient.* New York: Jason Aronson.

Giovacchini, P. L., Flarsheim, A., and Boyer, L. B. (1975). *Tactics and Techniques in Psychoanalytic Therapy. Vol 2: Countertransference.* New York: Jason Aronson.

Green, A. (1986). *On Private Madness.* Madison, CT: International Universities Press.

Greenson, R. R., and Wexler, M. (1969). The non-transference relationship in the psychoanalytic situation. *International Journal of Psycho-Analysis* 50:27–39.

Grinberg, L., ed. (1977). *Prácticas Psicoanalíticas en las Psicosis.* Buenos Aires: Paidos.

Grotstein, J. S., Solomon, M. F., and Lang, J. A. (1987). *The Borderline Patient.* 2 vols. Hillsdale, NJ: Analytic Press.

Hann-Kende, F. (1933). On the role of transference and countertransference in psychoanalysis. In *Psychoanalysis and the Occult,* ed. G. Devereux, pp. 158–167. New York: International Universities Press.

Hoffer, W. (1949). Mouth, hand and ego integration. *Psychoanalytic Study of the Child* 3–4:49–56.

Isakower, O. (1938). A contribution to the pathopsychology of phenomena associated with falling asleep. *International Journal of Psycho-Analysis* 19:331–345.

——— (1954). Spoken words in dreams. *Psychoanalytic Quarterly* 23:1–6.

Jacobson, E. (1974). *The Self and the Object World.* New York: International Universities Press.

Kernberg, O. F. (1975). *Borderline Conditions and Pathological Narcissism.* New York: Jason Aronson.

——— (1986). *Severe Personality Disorders. Psychotherapeutic Strategies.* New Haven, CT: Yale University Press.

Lewin, B. D. (1946). Sleep, the mouth and the dream screen. *Psychoanalytic Quarterly* 15:419–434.

——— (1950). *The Psychoanalysis of Elation.* New York: W. W. Norton.

——— (1953). The forgetting of dreams. In *Drives, Affects, Behavior,* ed. R. M. Loewenstein, pp. 191–202. New York: International Universities Press.

Lipowski, Z. J. (1988). Somatization: the concept and its clinical application. *American Journal of Psychiatry* 145:1358–1368.

Little, M. (1957). "R"—The analyst's total response to his patient's needs. In *Transference Neurosis and Transference Psychosis.* New York: Jason Aronson, 1981.

Loewald, H. (1960). The therapeutic action of psychoanalysis. In *Papers on Psychoanalysis,* pp. 221–256. New Haven, CT: Yale University Press, 1980.

Lorenz, K. (1937). *Studies in Animal and Human Behavior.* London: Methuen.

Mahler, M. S. (1968). *On Human Symbiosis and the Vicissitudes of Individuation.* New York: International Universities Press.

Mahler, M. S., Pine, F., and Bergman, A. (1975). *The Psychological Birth of the Human Infant.* New York: Basic Books.

Marmor, J. (1953). Orality in the hysterical personality. *Journal of the American Psychoanalytic Association* 1:656–671.

Marty, P., M'Uzan, M. de, and David, C. (1963). *L'Investigation Psychosomatique. Sept Observations Cliniques.* Paris: Universitaires de France.

McDougall, J. (1985). *Theaters of the Mind. Illusion and Truth on the Psychoanalytic Stage.* New York: Basic Books.

———— (1989). *Theaters of the Body. A Psychoanalytic Approach to Psychosomatic Illness.* New York: W. W. Norton.

Meissner, W. W. (1984). *The Borderline Spectrum. Differential Diagnosis and Developmental Issues.* New York: Jason Aronson.

Meltzer, D. (1975). Adhesive identification. *Contemporary Psychoanalysis* 11:289–310.

Meltzer, D., Bremner, J., Hoxter, S., et al. (1975). *Explorations in Autism.* Perthshire, Scotland: Clunie.

Menninger, W. C. (1947). Psychosomatic medicine: somatization reactions. *Psychosomatic Medicine* 9:92–97.

Meyer, H. C., ed. (1986). *Between Analyst and Patient. New Dimensions in Countertransference and Transference.* Hillsdale, NJ: Analytic Press.

Modell, A. H. (1984). *Psychoanalysis in a New Context.* New York: International Universities Press.

———— (1988). The centrality of the psychoanalytic setting and the changing aims of treatment: a perspective from theory of object relations. *Psychoanalytic Quarterly* 57:577–596.

Nemiah, J. C., Freyburger, H., and Sifneos, P. E. (1976). Alexithymia: a view of the psychosomatic process. In *Modern Trends in Psychosomatic Medicine*, vol. 3, ed. O. W. Hill, pp. 403–409. New York: Appleton-Century Crofts.

Ogden, T. H. (1986). *The Matrix of the Mind. Object Relations and the Psychoanalytic Dialogue.* Northvale, NJ: Jason Aronson.

———— (1989). *The Primitive Edge of Experience.* Northvale, NJ: Jason Aronson.

Racker, E. (1953). A contribution to the problem of counter-transference. *International Journal of Psycho-Analysis* 34:313–324.

———— (1968). *Transference and Countertransference.* New York: International Universities Press.

Reik, T. (1948). *Listening with the Third Ear. The Inner Experience of a Psychoanalyst.* New York: Farrar, Straus.

Roiphe, H., and Galenson, E. (1981). *Infantile Origins of Sexual Identity.* New York: International Universities Press.

Rosenfeld, D. (1982). *The notion of a psychotic body image in neurotic and psychotic patients.* Paper presented before the Norwegian Psychoanalytic Society, Oslo.

———— (1984). Hypochondriasis, somatic delusion and body schema in psychoanalytic practice. *International Journal of Psychoanalysis* 65:377–388.

———— (1989). Psychotic body image. In *Master Clinicians on Treating the Regressed Patient*, ed. L. B. Boyer and P. L. Giovacchini, pp. 165–188. Northvale, NJ: Jason Aronson.

Rosenfeld, D., and Pistol, D. (1986). *Episodio psicótico y su detección precoz en la transferencia.* Paper presented at the XVIth Latin American Psychoanalytic Congress, Mexico City, July.

Rosenfeld, H. A. (1965). *Psychotic States; A Psychoanalytical Approach*. London: Hogarth.

——— (1987). *Impasse and Interpretation. Therapeutic and Anti-Therapeutic Factors in the Psychoanalytic Treatment of Psychotic, Borderline, and Neurotic Patients*. London: Tavistock.

Searles, H. F. (1979). *Countertransference and Related Subjects. Selected Papers*. New York: International Universities Press.

——— (1986). *My Work with Borderline Patients*. Northvale, NJ: Jason Aronson.

Segal, H. (1957). Notes on symbol formation. In *The Work of Hanna Segal*, pp. 49–68. New York: Jason Aronson, 1981.

Slakter, F., ed. (1987). *Countertransference*. Northvale, NJ: Jason Aronson.

Spiegel, L. A. (1975). The functions of free association in psychoanalysis: their relation to technique and therapy. *International Review of Psycho-Analysis* 2:379–388.

Spitz, R. A. (1955). The primal cavity: a contribution to the genesis of perception and its role for psychoanalytic theory. *Psychoanalytic Study of the Child* 10:215–240. New York: International Universities Press.

——— (1965). *The First Year of Life*. New York: International Universities Press.

Spruiell, V. (1983). The rules and frame of the analytic situation. *Psychoanalytic Quarterly* 52:1–33.

Stekel, W. (1911). Zur Differential diagnose organischer und psychogeniseber Erkrankungen. *Zentralblatt für Psychoanalyse und Psychotherapie* 1:45–47.

Tähkä, V. (1988). On the early formation of the mind. I: Differentiation. *International Journal of Psycho-Analysis* 68:229–250.

Taylor, G. T. (1984). Alexithymia: concept, measurement, and implications for treatment. *American Journal of Psychiatry* 141:725–732.

Tinbergen, N. (1957). On anti-predator response in certain birds: a reply. *Journal of Comparative Physiologic Psychology* 50:412–414.

Tustin, F. (1972). *Autism and Childhood Psychosis*. London: Hogarth.

——— (1981). *Autistic States in Children*. Boston: Routledge and Kegan Paul.

——— (1986). *Autistic Barriers in Neurotic Patients*. New Haven, CT: Yale University Press, 1987.

Volkan, V. D. (1976). *Primitive Internalized Object Relations*. New York: International Universities Press.

——— (1981). *Linking Objects and Linking Phenomena*. New York: International Universities Press.

——— (1987). *Six Steps in the Treatment of Borderline Personality Organization*. Northvale, NJ: Jason Aronson.

Weizsacker, V. von (1946). *Casos y Problemas Clínicas*. Barcelona: Editorial Pubul.

——— (1954). *Natur und Geist*. Gottingen: Vandenhoeck & Ruprecht.

——— (1962). *El Círculo de la Forma*. Madrid: Editorial Morate.

Wilson, C. P., and Mintz, I. L., eds. (1989). *Psychosomatic Symptoms; Psycho-*

dynamic Treatment of the Underlying Personality Disorder. Northvale, NJ: Jason Aronson.

Winnicott, D. W. (1953). Transitional objects and transitional phenomena. In *Collected Papers. Through Paediatrics to Psychoanalysis*, pp. 229–242. New York: Basic Books, 1958.

———— (1969). The use of an object. *International Journal of Psycho-Analysis* 50:711–716.

———— (1971). *Playing and Reality*. New York: Basic Books.

Countertransference, Regression, and an Analysand's Uses of Music[1]

WITH THE ASSISTANCE OF
LAURA L. DOTY

INTRODUCTION

Clinical and experimental investigations have demonstrated that music may serve subtle and complex psychological functions, the sounds per se serving more primitive roles than the themes and lyrics. The present study offers data obtained during the psychoanalysis of a musically talented man who had suffered life-threatening croup and asthma to the age of 6. Regression that was achieved as the result of interpretations based on the analyst's countertransferential responses revealed that the analysand was unable to achieve psychological separation from his mother and that music served the function of retaining a life-supporting connection with her. (For

1. The author is heavily indebted to the members of the Center for the Advanced Study of the Psychoses, San Francisco, which he co-directs with Dr. Thomas H. Ogden, for their immense help in the preparation of this chapter, especially to Drs. Charles Dithrich, Rose-Anne Donner, Laura Doty, Sara Hartley, Thomas H. Ogden, Doreen Rothman, and Andrea Walt. He is grateful also for remarks made by members of the audience at the presentation of this paper at the meeting of the Friends of the San Francisco Psychoanalytic Institute and the Candidates' Colloquium of the Institute, notably Drs. Peter Goldberg, Hillie Harned, Jane Hewitt, and Joseph E. Lifschutz.

alternate views concerning the usefulness and applicability of the term *countertransference*, see McLaughlin [1981, 1988], Moore and Fine [1967], and Poland [1988].) Presumably as the result of a complex elaboration of respiratory and auditory introjection, music came to symbolize the noise of air flowing through tubes into the steam tents and blood coursing through the umbilical cord, conceptualized as connecting the patient with his mother and making them permanently interdependent. Diagnostically, this patient might be characterized by Giovacchini (1986) as suffering from a severe characterological disorder or by Abend and colleagues (1983) or Meissner (1984) as belonging to a low-level borderline category.

The patient's early ego defect was overcome through a transference–countertransference interaction that is elaborated in detail. Then, the less primitive meanings and psychological uses of musical themes and lyrics were elucidated, again in response to interpretations based on countertransference reactions.

BACKGROUND DATA PERTAINING TO THE PSYCHOLOGICAL FUNCTIONS SERVED BY MUSIC

Experimental and observational studies have demonstrated that infants of 2 to 5 months can group tones on the basis of proximity and that pitch contours play a critical role in the infant's response to, and identification of, his mother's voice (Cheng and Trehub 1977, Fernald 1985, Mehler et al. 1978, Papousek and Papousek 1977, Trehub et al. 1985, 1987).

Many observers have noted that music as a phenomenon serves more primitive psychological functions "by virtue of its relationship to an archaic emotional form of communication" (Kohut 1957, p. 407) than do its themes and lyrics, which symbolize, express, and defend against more specific and less primitive unconscious conflicts (Aizenberg et al. 1986, Friedman 1960, Juni 1987, Langer 1953, Rechardt 1987).

Niederland (1958) found in the young child and the psychotic the functions of hearing to be extended to concrete thinking, and closely related to physical contact. The subjection of a schizophrenic patient of mine to her mother's shrill, hostile voice had contributed to her development of early ego defects. She ascribed her improvement to the introjection of my "sweet, purring voice" that "babied" her in her mind and said, "I don't care what you say, I just listen to the music" (Boyer 1956). Another psychotic patient said, "I always recover from being crazy in here because I hear your voice as music that permeates my skin and becomes your healthy blood, mixing with mine and purifying it, as must happen in dialysis." Later, "My father cut out the cannibalism of my mother's voice by always listening to music" (Boyer 1990a,b).

Racker (1952) found music per se to serve against anxiety related to untamed aggression, and to maintain a reactive defense against persecutory and paranoid fears. He stressed the magic, omnipotent, and animistic qualities of human breath and singing and inferred that ideas of fusion with the mother sustained the magical and omnipotent beliefs.

Jaffe (1983), no doubt referring to a variety of what Grinberg (1979, 1990) has called *counteridentification*, wrote of his resolution of a "counter-identificatory block" to result from his associations to a tune he heard when awakening from a dream. A similar event was significant in the treatment of the present patient. Reik (1953) found that the empathy of the analyst may involve the sounding of a theme that carries the tone of the affect appropriate to the situation.

What has been said about music in psychoanalytic writing deals predominantly with pathography or psychobiography and the development of musical ability (Bychowski 1951, Esman 1951, Feder 1978, 1990). However, Spitz (1987) delineated how a contemporary musical work evoked in a patient the separation–individuation interaction with all its nuances as an aesthetic experience. Bornstein (1977) analyzed a musically talented blind patient who suffered from life-threatening respiratory infections from age 2 to 5. His analytic regression demonstrated clearly the more primitive functions played by music per se in contrast to its themes and lyrics. He relived in the transference regression early relations with his musically gifted mother.

All psychoanalysts who have studied or treated patients suffering from childhood psychosomatic illnesses have stressed that the handling of pre-genital aggression constitutes a major problem of psychological maturation.

As do blind children, those with early severe respiratory ailments have a marked tendency to regress, remaining fixated to prephallic phases of drive development, and have particularly serious problems in dealing with their aggression, as do the vast majority of other psychosomatically or organically handicapped children (Carta et al. 1986, Deutsch 1987, Fraiberg 1980, Marty et al. 1963, McDougall 1989, Monday et al. 1987, Sperling 1978, Tustin 1972, Wilson and Mintz 1989).

COURSE OF ANALYSIS

Like Greenacre (1975) and others, I keep detailed process notes during interviews, data that often include my emotional reactions, fantasies, and physical sensations to the patient's verbal and nonverbal productions (Boyer 1986, 1989), and, as does McDougall (1989), sometimes those of my dreams, which I believe deal with unresolved transference–countertransference questions. It is my assumption that many of my emotional and physical reactions result from introjection of the patient's projective identifications (Money-Kyrle 1956). The material presented here results from painstaking review of more than some 3,000 pages of process notes. Historical data appeared in such a bewildering, piecemeal fashion that I have presented them in conjunction with the emergence of the transference–countertransference interrelationship.

Patient M was a 30-year-old married medical doctor who had worked as a research biologist for five years. He had become a physician in an effort to gain his father's approval. He could not prescribe medications because he had not taken requisite examinations, and he remained a Ph.D. candidate because he had failed to write his dissertation. He suffered from writer's block for which he came to blame his father, whom he had always felt himself unable to please, and who took hereditary or financial credit for any of M's accomplishments.

Two major problems were obvious from the outset: M's lifelong dependency on predominantly masochistic relationships that he sought to make irrevocable and his need to protect others from his repressed rage. He did his elective medical school work with patients who suffered from terminal cancer and for whom, as we learned later in his treatment, he aspired to achieve "miraculous, religious cures." He interned as a pathologist "to study the murderous mistakes of other doctors and to learn to avoid killing people." He made a special study of all aspects of the respiratory and sexual systems, becoming fascinated with the possibilities both of artificially controlling future generations genetically and of making them capable of bisexual functioning, including childbearing.

M was the third of four boys. His multimillionaire father, the son of destitute immigrant parents, taught foreign languages in a private school and then, following marriage, earned advanced degrees pertaining to business and law in night school. Later he worked on weekends at his office, which was located an hour's distance from his home. Although he laid tfillin, wore a tallis, chanted every morning, and was generous with his financial contributions to Jewish welfare, he was an unscrupulous businessman and an overt philanderer who humiliated his family by shouting lewd remarks to women on the street while driving the family, even to synagogue.

M's mother was the daughter of immigrants who retained a heavy accent from their central European country. As a boy, he did not believe her to be Jewish, despite her numerous Hadassah activities, since the parents spoke her native language in private. Some years into his analysis, he remembered that they also spoke Yiddish. M's mother did all of the managing of the family real estate, as well as all of the manual repairs, including carpentry, plumbing, and electrical work. She owned duplicate complete sets of appropriate tools, which the four sons were forbidden to use. M's father was rarely at home and bitterly resented his wife's insisting that the family eat dinner together.

Max, his father's obvious favorite and eight years M's senior, became a physician and later also a certified public accountant and real estate dealer. Robbie, two years M's senior, made M the butt of his frustrations and "tried to drown" him on many occasions. A girl was stillborn six years after M's birth, and thereafter the mother was bitterly disappointed that M had not been a daughter. Sam, born eight years after M, was his mother's obvious favorite and became unmistakably effeminate. For reasons we never discovered, throughout his childhood, when M was angry with his mother, he called her a witch.

During M's postmedical school research, he became emotionally involved with Alvin, a sadistic genius mentor, a noted cellular biologist, a plagiarist who used all of M's ingenious research solely to his own ends. M literally believed that he and Alvin were mysteriously inextricably connected and that neither could exist without the other. During a session when he was undergoing transferential regression, he said, "I don't know why my coming into this room changes me instantly into a frightened child. Today I believed immediately that you were Alvin and I saw a tube leading from your navel to my mouth or navel, through which we were sharing our blood and oxygen and thus keeping each other alive."

Alvin's psychological resemblances to M's father were striking but unrecognized by M. Alvin's gross exploitations satisfied M's need to be misused, as he had perceived his mother to have been misused by his father, but, using the primitive denial that we often observe in autistic patients (Tustin 1972), Alvin was perceived by M solely as his benefactor and protector. Alvin decided to enter a commercial laboratory in a city far from M's family and M eagerly accompanied him, although his position in the new venture depended totally on Alvin's whim. M had been similarly involved for some years with an exceedingly self-centered and childish girl, Rebbie. Marriage was her price for accompanying him. As his mother had been content to be exploited grossly by M's father, Rebbie was similarly involved with her mother.

After three years, during which the nature of their relationships was unchanged and M willingly acceded to Alvin's getting credit and even promoted for M's brilliant scientific contributions, Alvin announced that he had decided to move soon to a remote area where there was no room for M. M suffered what Bion (1967) called "nameless dread"; Mahler (1968), "organismic distress"; Pao (1977), "experimental core disturbance"; and Glass (1989), "private terror," in which there appears to be a paralysis of ego functions. Volkan (1990) has suggested that at such times the patient holds onto his psychotic self stubbornly, in order to protect himself from experiencing another organismic panic.

M's mentally contentless panic at being left resulted in an incapacity to work and reversion to childhood nightmares of attacks by bisexual monsters who would "possess" him, that is, whose sadistic, cannibalistic natures would govern him from within. Having renounced relations with his family and being unable to obtain emotional support from his equally frightened wife, he sought psychoanalysis. He simultaneously established a relationship with one of his technicians that strikingly resembled the relationship with Alvin, one in which M sought and received blatant exploitation.

As he had done earlier with both Alvin and Rebbie, he required nocturnal verbal reassurance of continuous connection by direct or telephonic contact before he dared to sleep and risk separation from fantasies of being united with them. Later he volunteered the thought that the telephone line had substituted for the oxygen-carrying umbilical cord.

In contrast with Greenson (1969), who believed analysis begins only after the establishment of the "working alliance," and that interpretations are to be made when the oedipal transference was established, but in agreement with Giovacchini (1969), Ogden (1989), and Volkan (Volkan and Ast 1992), I believe the patient to be in analysis from the moment he enters the consultation room door—sometimes before—and that even an initial negative transference can be utilized and interpreted usefully.

Particularly in the treatment of regressed patients, the analysis of material stemming from transference phenomena reflecting preoedipal dyadic relationships is initially more meaningful than that stemming from oedipal triadic relationships. In the experience of many, the presentation of triadic relationship transferences early in working with the primitive patient usually serves defensive purposes and its early analysis is fruitless (Boyer 1966, Ornstein and Ornstein 1975, H. A. Rosenfeld 1966, Volkan 1976).

From the beginning of my psychoanalytic treatment of regressed patients, I have found it advantageous to deal with the vicissitudes of their defenses against the magical fears of their untamed aggressive urges (Boyer

1961). Obviously, such interpretations are more indirect when dealing with schizoid patients (Fairbairn 1952).

From early childhood M had uncontrollably "twitched" his shoulders. He was quite conscious that he "shrugged like my mother's forebears" "to show indifference" and to "dodge expected blows." He blinked his eyes frequently "to shut out seeing things I don't want to observe" and "to show I am afraid I'll be slapped," although he did not remember having been struck. In the initial session, after relating these data, he expressed disappointment that I had granted him fewer hours than he wished. Then he talked without apparent affect of his feeling unimportant to his father. My interpretation that his shrugging and blinking substituted for annoyance at me delighted him, making him feel important and heard. To be sure, the intervention affected his actions but briefly.

For the first four years M's verbal content pertained almost solely to his unhappy relationships with Alvin, and substitutes for him, and with his wife. My attempts to link what he said to the transference–countertransference relationship appeared to be ignored. Similarly, he paid scant attention to my interpretations pertaining to his periodic brief references to relationships with family members and history, which seemed to be affectless asides.

Nevertheless, during those years his fear of the magical effects of his hostility were greatly modified, and he had begun to allow himself to claim credit for his scientific work and accept invitations to give lectures abroad. Presumably his progress can be ascribed primarily to the consistent holding and facilitating environment afforded by the analytic situation, which is largely dominated by the analyst's behavior, and to introjection of some of his perceived qualities (Boyer 1983, Fromm-Reichmann 1950, Gabbard 1991, Giovacchini 1979, Lindon 1991a,b, Nacht 1962, H. A. Rosenfeld 1965, 1987, Searles 1965, Winnicott 1956, 1960, 1965, 1986). M also bought copies of books I had authored to keep me with him during our separations, although he could not as yet read their contents.

Some months later, when a technician, a psychological replacement for Alvin, was threatening to diminish the intensity of their close relationship, M reexperienced panics similar to those that caused him to enter analysis and became overtly fearful that I would "kick him out." For the first time, he was breathless and wheezed, although he was unaware of either phenomenon. With Arlow (1969), Arlow and Brenner (1964), Schwaber (1983, 1990), Smith (1990), and countless others, I have found that calling the analysand's attention to his unnoticed experiences and activities while on the couch often opens new avenues for analysis. Accordingly, I spoke of his respiratory symptoms.

Then, for the first time, he said he had been told in adulthood that he had suffered from unrecalled life-threatening croup and asthma until he was 5 or 6 years old and that he had spent much time in steam and oxygen tents. He then mentioned in an affectless aside that he had been a musician but had renounced playing his instrument ten years earlier when he moved in with a "girlfriend" who then supported him. He had not mentioned music previously in any context. During the next few years, he gradually revealed with increasing emotionality that he had been intensely involved in competitive violin playing throughout his grammar and high school years and that his mother and brothers all had played musical instruments seriously. Following his bar mitzvah, he had served as a cantor for several years, renouncing his pursuit only when he left home and rebelliously ceased any formalized Jewish activities.

Five years later I learned that when he moved in with his girlfriend, he had left the violin at home to retain an unconscious link with his mother, when he relived early relations with her in the transference regression. He never subsequently played the violin. Only then did the nature of his unconscious uses of music emerge.

During the first four to five years of M's analysis, his attention was limited largely to his interactions with Alvin and replacements for him. In his relationships with the substitutes, he came to assume the role—previously assigned to Alvin—of protector and benefactor. His role as sadistic exploiter was much more subtle, but in his interactions with his wife he became progressively more obvious, his treatment of her resembling in many ways his father's treatment of his mother.

As is customary, my activities dealt principally with the vicissitudes of M's aggression. Unlike the modern work of Gill (1983) and his followers, my interventions generally included not only obvious transference interpretations but, wherever possible, historical antecedents. In my experience such a practice contributes to the patient's capacity to confine episodes of psychotic transference to the consultation room and to enhance their lasting effectiveness.

By the time the degree of intimacy M had sought with successive protégés had made them feel "smothered" and driven them away, his transference involvement had become focused in his relationship with me, where it periodically assumed psychotic proportions (Little 1958, H. A. Rosenfeld 1952, Searles 1963). At times he pictured first my holding him as a small boy, then his clinging to my back "like a limpet or barnacle with long claws" and penetrating my body. The sequence would terminate with my becoming pregnant with him; we shared our blood through an umbilical cord through which blood "swooshed." Rarely did M's belief in the reality of those hallucinatory experiences persist for more than a few hours after he left the office.

The primitive natures of M's experiences depicted variously the operations that were described by Bick (1968, 1986) and Anzieu (1970, 1989) as representing the earliest functions served by skin, and D. Rosenfeld's (1975, 1984, 1990, 1991) psychotic body image. His perceptions at such times had more the concreteness of the symbolic equations that Segal (1957) linked with the schizoid-paranoid position than the true symbols linked with the depressive position.

M's defenses against his aggression were manifold, some obvious and some highly subtle. Many dealt with his behavior in the consultation room. Attempts to reduce their effectiveness were often disappointing and boring, and involved my dealing privately with disagreeable countertransference issues involving discouragement, guilt, and quiet rage (Boyer 1989, Gabbard 1990, Grolnick 1990, Poggi and Ganzarain 1983, Winnicott 1949).

For years M entered the consultation room and lay on the couch quickly, always rigidly on his back, with his motionless limbs parallel to his body. He remained unaware of his surroundings, although I redecorate my office every few months, characteristically with varying archeological or anthropological artifacts. His unelaborated wondering about the meanings of my physical actions was a dominant theme.

Accompanying the implied paranoia was ongoing evidence of his belief that I could read his mind. Years into his treatment he revealed that a major reason he had chosen me as his analyst was that he had read that I had been designated a shaman by a Native American group (Boyer 1979), which meant to him that I could combat supernatural evil with my disembodied soul, to which I retained attachment by an invisible tube. In his picture of that encounter my soul devoured the evil monster, pictured concretely either as an eternally pregnant maternal surrogate or as a bisexual. M disclaimed factual knowledge about shamanism, but his notions closely resemble those described by anthropological and psychological scholars (Boyer et al. 1985, Ducey 1979, Eliade 1951, Lommel 1967, Merkur 1985).

M had always avoided eye contact, fearing that his hostile sentiments could be detected. Much later I learned that a more terrifying conviction was that the line of vision "would become an invisible tube through which souls and body contents could be transported and commingle."

For years, until his aggression had become relatively tamed, M defended himself against transference rage, not only by his refusing to observe the contents of the room, but by using two speech patterns, the meanings of which were long obscure to me.

In the first, his talk might appear to be relatively lively, but consisted primarily of intellectual ramblings. In the other, which might be heavily laden with depressive ideation ("There is no point in my working or even living, no one appreciates my efforts and no one ever wants to be with me") or paranoid declarations ("You and my so-called colleagues and technicians plan to steal my ideas and use them to get rich"), his delivery was so flat and monotonous that my process notes often included the words "He droned on again." Both speech patterns left me feeling disgruntled, drowsy, empty, and guilty, wishing I had not accepted him as an analysand. At times when I was sleepy, M said I had left him, so I assume my breathing pattern had altered, although he denied perceiving such a change.

One of the steps I employ while seeking to avert or overcome an analytic stasis or impasse is to remember relevant psychoanalytic literature (Boyer 1983). Eventually recalling Racker's (1968) and Zelig's (1960) thesis that the analyst of the silent patient responds with hunger and wants revenge enabled me to regain objectivity. I then found myself fantasizing that I saw a blank dream screen (Lewin 1948) and turned our attention to M's behavior, saying I wondered whether he was voluntarily withholding thoughts, sensations, and visual perceptions. M then revealed awareness that he was experiencing being inside a plastic sheath, a balloon or transparent skin that kept us separated and made each of us safe from the other's anger. He had had the experience for weeks without mentioning it. I discovered later that the sheath served other purposes as well. It protected us against mutually self-destructive fusion, was a screen onto which he "projected horror movies," as though it were a dream screen, and, in his words, was "an umbilical cord, through which our common blood coursed," but at the same time was shared skin (Anzieu 1989, Bick 1968, 1986, D. Rosenfeld 1975, 1976, 1990, 1991). Later he equated the effectively contentless speech with humming and placental blood and said that "the sheath is filled with music without lyrics."

Following his having finally established me as an early preoedipal maternal figure, probably representing the mother before the development of the transitional object phase (Boyer 1990b, Gaddini 1985, 1987, Winnicott 1953), and frequently experienced transitory psychotic transference regressions, other countertransference experiences led to further progress. I offer an example.

One time following my noting that he was droning again, I became aware of a humming noise in my head and eventually a tune I did not recognize. I assumed I was experiencing the product of a projective iden-tification (Boyer 1986, 1989). I inquired whether he might be listening to a tune rather than the content of his spoken words. He became aware that he heard a lullaby. This experience proved to be a major turning point that enabled M to disclose much more of his involvement with music. This was when he first remembered that his father had sung Hebrew lullabies to him when he was 4 or 5 years old, while holding him and enabling him to fall asleep, an event to which he then ascribed the cure of his childhood asthma. Then he could reveal that he had listened to music almost constantly from early grammar school days, even to the degree that he had worn earphones during sleep. Subsequently we learned that no matter what activity involved him, whether at work or play, or even while talking with others, he was, with varying degrees of awareness, listening to music in his mind, fre-quently tuneless, and thereby retaining a primitive, unconscious connection with his mother.

Concurrently with his making of me a stable early mother surrogate, his relations with his wife became more considerate and he began to contemplate his marriage to be potentially permanent. Soon he acceded to her wish to buy a house, and they began to seek to have children.

In my experience the analyst should insist on discussing contacts that occur between analysand and analyst outside the consultation room. Only because M did not recognize me on the street before an interview did I learn that he had a lifelong inability to retain mental images of his parents when separated from them. It took many months to elicit this information. In his teens, when at a summer camp, his (now remembered) breathless and wheezing anxiety necessitated his calling them every night to be sure they existed. He could visualize them only after hearing their voices, when the respiratory symptoms would disappear. I then learned that an important element behind his confusing speech when with me was that his attention was directed frequently toward determining whether any noise emanated from me. Until he could hear me move, write, or breathe, he was afraid that I had died or left. Sometimes he hallucinated my floating through the ceiling in a clear plastic balloon or sheath; the ceiling itself had changed into a translucent material resembling the steam tents in which he was treated for croup and the shower curtains which surrounded the tub in which he and his mother had bathed together. He revealed also that he continued to bathe in steaming hot water.

One further example of M's concretizing music per se will be followed by an exposition of how a countertransference experience led to our beginning to become aware of less primitive meanings of music to him.

It is to be remembered that when he first moved in with Rebbie, he had renounced playing the violin, leaving it in his parents' home. M rationalized that there was no place to play with adequate acoustics for his perfect pitch perception. During his adolescence, aside from performing for teachers and, on command, for his father, and in class competitions, he had played voluntarily only for himself, accompanying virtuosi while listening to records in a draped bathroom where acoustics were "perfect." The drapery consisted of bedsheets, as did the majority of the tents in which he isolated himself in childhood games and retreats from others. Later, at a time when he believed I had understood an obscure message "perfectly," he became aware that when he played in the bathroom, he believed that his mother was listening and secretly joined to him through aural introjection, the music having become concretized as a fluid that went from his "caressed instrument" into them to become part of their flowing blood. My "understanding perfectly" his message was visualized similarly. Additionally, he became aware that he had believed that the existence of the unplayed violin in his parents' house constituted an unseen umbilical cord that connected him with each of them.

My becoming aware of a memory of my own during the sixth year of our work provided the stimulus to M's revealing what he had thus far concerning meanings to him of themes and lyrics in contrast to primal qualities of the music itself, such as rhythm, instrumentation, chords, and interplay of counterpoint. For some time he had reverted to talking semi-incoherently and did not appear to pay attention to what he said, although the emotional tone was sad and lonely. I understood his behavior to be an imitation of the use of language by the child who still understands both primary and secondary process language, but who has not yet learned to suppress or repress idiosyncratic symbols and who did not appear to heed his own words (Spiro 1992). I found myself responding emotionally but without conscious fantasies to the sad and lonely emotional tone, listening, as it were, to the melody but not the content.

That night I had a dream to which I associated. I recalled that when I had been in military service in a culturally deprived area and was lonely, I had hallucinated symphonic and operatic scores and lyrics while listening to my patients' often saddening accounts. I recalled Gustav Mahler's *Das Lied von der Erde*, specifically the words "Dunkel ist das Leben, ist der Tod," which I translate as "Life and death are equally depressing." Then I was able to inquire whether M heard music as he was talking. He responded that my question made him aware that he had done so throughout his analysis and just then had been hearing music by Mahler. As mentioned previously, he had listened to the radio, records, tapes, or compact discs continuously at home, in the car, or while studying or working, and until recently had even worn earphones during his sleep.

Then he revealed that for perhaps ten years he had listened to *The Ring*, always sung in German. In adolescence he had learned that Wagner had some Jewish forebears, and that, at his wife's insistence, had composed "Christian music" in order that it would possess him and transform him into an Aryan. M had hoped aural introjection of *The Ring* would similarly "cleanse him of Jewish blood," although he claimed he never listened to the lyrics. He recalled with great affect a repeated preschool childhood experience he had related previously without apparent emotion: an aggressive and exhibitionistic neighbor girl had convinced him that if he did not convert to Catholicism and thus rid himself of his Jewish blood, he would be castrated and sent to Hell.

M still maintains that he does not know, and is uninterested in, the mythology depicted in *The Ring*, having been content to be transported by the tonal themes alone. However, he knows that the Valkyries were equated with witches in England. He even knew the correct Old English word *waelcyrgean* for witches. There is no evidence that he heard Wagnerian music or knew any Scandinavian mythology during the period when he called his mother a witch. However, there have been hints that he identifies himself with Siegfried. He believes that although of noble birth, Siegfried grew up bereft of parental care, conquered a dragon to rescue a maiden who may have been a witch, and was eventually killed by Brunhild to whom he had lied concerning his love for her. During the period when he ruminated about the themes of *The Ring*, M recalled having believed himself to have been adopted by a witch and wondered whether he had been orphaned by Aryan nobility. During this period he recalled "Hansel and Gretel" and was surprised to discover that he had believed the children eventually ate the witch who had sought to cannibalize them. He had never had knowledge of the original version of the Grimm brothers' unexpurgated "Hansel and Gretel," which, by implication, included the children's cannibalism of the witch after Hansel pushed her into the oven (Grimm and Grimm 1819).

Finally, he told me that he had begun listening constantly to requiems and Bach cantatas since seeing the movie *Amadeus* some months previously. He had not mentioned the film before. M owned complete sets of most composers' operas; now he had collected all of the recorded requiems and cantatas, hoping that listening to them would infuse him aurally with "Christian music," and thus transform him into an Aryan.

Amadeus opened for us less primitive meanings that he ascribed to the lyrics as contrasted with the music itself. One theme of the movie was of particular importance. This was the unsuccessful sibling rivalry that, in M's view, motivated Salieri to murder Mozart by poisoning him or causing him to starve to death. M was struck by Mozart's having provoked Salieri to attack him, as he himself had provoked earlier Rebbie, Alvin, and his father. Even more important was what M saw as Mozart's ambivalent relationship with his father and his attempt to atone for his guilty hostility by composing the requiem, beyond the point of exhaustion. M ascribed to Mozart a fear of forgiveness by his father lest the resultant intimacy would lead to a homosexual relationship, a negative oedipal resolution. Through listening to the requiems, M appeared to retain a safe, nonsexual connection with his father.

CURRENT STATUS

Having related these data, M obtained his violin from his parents and began to play for his own enjoyment, without magical ideas of umbilical cord connectedness. Simultaneously, he began to listen to spoken as well as musical radio programs, and subscribed to a newspaper for the first time.

Shrugging, twitching, and blinking have been almost absent for years, recurring only at times of intense emotional stress. M has resolved satisfactorily his sibling rivalries.

While he has just begun to work through his oedipal conflicts, his current overt relationships with his parents and wife are largely comfortable. He can confront them directly and realistically and insist on receiving logical responses to previously evaded queries.

Despite his great clinical improvement, to date we have dealt primarily with his fixation on early preoedipal relationships. During the periodic episodes of transference psychosis, we observed and worked through the results of his having regressed to the level of primitive internalized object relations characteristic of those prior to the development of transitional objects and phenomena.

He continues to avoid talking about his actual sexual behavior and toilet activities and about primal scene memories, although he spent his first seven years next to his mother in the parental bed, on the floor of that bedroom, or in an adjoining room that was connected by open French doors. In view of his unconscious fantasy that he retained connection with his mother through an umbilical cord, it is particularly interesting that he did not speak of an awareness of his mother's pregnancy with the stillborn girl until two years after the foregoing material had been written. That material is presented in the discussion below.

M's work relationships have improved greatly, as he has overcome his fear that direct confrontation would lead to someone's death or his abandonment and he has become aware of his use of vagueness and ambiguity to provoke intimate attack by me and others as parental transference figures, attacks that might lead to his being used as and turning into a girl and thereby become mother's purported favorite.

His writer's block has disappeared since he learned that it resulted from his wish to frustrate his father's desire for his professional productivity and his mother's wish to possess his feces. He has become a prolific scientific writer, whose articles and reviews are sought internationally. At the same time, he has not begun to compose music or lyrics, nor has he any interest in doing so. Although he has begun to consider preparing for and taking examinations that would qualify him to practice medicine and write prescriptions, he has not done so, nor has he considered seriously writing his doctoral dissertation, although his data are all in order. Oedipal elements of his success neurosis have just begun to emerge.

Between the sixth and eighth years of his analysis, music was scarcely mentioned. Then came a period in which his work relationships improved dramatically and were rewarded by his being promoted to an important administrative position that included his being a principal designer for his company's research programs. No longer did he invite exploitation; he was at ease with important scientists, debating esoteric subjects unemotionally and insisting on objective evaluation of his program suggestions through sophisticated experimentation. At the same time, he served as a model, encouraging, nonexploitative teacher for junior scientists. It was then that he became aware that he had been able to renounce his imaginary fusion with me.

Piecemeal through the analysis, M revealed that various individuals in both his mother's and father's families, over a period of several generations, had been reported to have suffered from undiagnosed psychotic and severe psychosomatic disorders, some of which had necessitated brief hospitalizations in various central European countries (see Tienari 1991).

Following a series of interviews in which he spoke of new relations with his parents, whose continuing manifestations of psychopathology did not disturb him but instead prompted him to help them through direct, kind, verbal confrontation, advice, and interpretation, he surprised me by opening an interview dealing overtly with material to which he had alluded tangentially earlier. After looking about the room for the first time overtly and interestedly as though it had been his habit to do so, he said, "It feels so odd to experience the change in me of becoming separate from you and to identify the objects in the room that to me before today seemed to be direct extensions of your body, and to feel that they, too, were parts of me. Before I came in I became aware that I wanted to crawl into the belly of the woman who was leaving here. Then I knew I'd wanted to crawl into any patient leaving here, especially the women, to continue to be with you while they were with you and to buffer myself against my parents' hostility."

I reminded him that he had never talked of his mother's pregnancies, although he slept with or near her during both of them. He replied, "I have no memory, but it must be clear that I am guilty because of the wish the little girl would die and then she did. Now my brain is drowning in amniotic fluid, suffocating. I keep erasing the pregnancies because they meant that three children were not enough. I keep forgetting that my youngest brother was an accident. I'd thought I was mother's favorite because of all the time that she gave me with my croup and asthma. My father held me and sang to me when mother was pregnant with her. When my sister was born dead, and my father no longer sang to me, my asthma disappeared, as though I had no further use for it to try to distract my mother from my sister. . . . Being inside you or another patient is not protection . . . being inside mother didn't protect my little sister from my wish she'd die." Further on he said, "My parents always put their anger through prisms, never went to the source, and nurtured their anger. . . . I've had secret coexistences, secret from myself. I didn't know about peaceful coexistence. My separate existences and co-parts are in harmony . . . these parts of you scattered about the room. I don't think I learned that from you. I think I introjected it."

At the next interview, after talking of no longer feeling as though he were split into two people, his father and mother, M returned to talking about music. He said that after he left the previous session, he thought the woman who preceded him was my pupil and also the pupil of my eye, in the sense that he might be able to get information about me from looking into her eyes. Recalling his thinking when playing the violin in the bathroom that he could transmit his mental and emotional contents into his mother through an invisible tube, as though they were looking into each others' eyes, he said he had awakened from a dream, hearing Siegfried's funeral theme from *Götterdämmerung*, but that now he could see the dawn. "It's the same, here, death and rebirth," he mused. "Many places are no longer dangerous; the only danger remaining is of my own splitting into representatives of my mother and father, and that's almost gone. Now my hearing and sight and physical feelings are all interwoven and intact." He went on, speaking of music as having been the most important rescuing and integrating part of his life.

DISCUSSION

As was noted in the earlier section on background data, previous observers have found that music serves more primitive functions than do its themes and lyrics. M is still in therapy. To date, he has dealt much less with the meanings to him of lyrics and themes. Although he knows by heart the music of numerous operas, he has never read their lyrics. He understands no German or Italian and, on the rare occasions when he has heard an opera in a language he knows, has avoided understanding the words, just as he avoided understanding the secret language of his parents. Essentially, this chapter applies psychoanalytic object relations theory to the treatment of a severely regressed patient whose unconscious early preoedipal ties to his mother were expressed through the concretization of music in a fantasized umbilical cord.

The clinical data clearly support the findings of previous observers that music serves more primitive psychological functions than do its themes and lyrics, which symbolize, express, and defend against more specific unconscious conflicts. Briefly, the case material validates the conclusion of Niederland (1958) and many others that the functions of hearing may be extended in the regressed patient to concrete thinking and are closely related to physical contact. It also affirms Racker's (1952) and others' view that music itself, simultaneously using primary and secondary process modes of dealing with mental activities, serves to ease anxiety related to untamed aggression and to maintain a reactive defense against persecutory and paranoid fears; further, that ideas of fusion with the mother sustain the magical and omnipotent beliefs associated with the breath, of which Róheim (1921) wrote so long ago, based on anthropological work with so-called primitives.

Clearly, M could not tolerate the reality of separation. His masochistic relationships, as exemplified most clearly in his interactions with Alvin, helped him sustain a fantasy of merger, and being exploited enabled him to use his great intellectual capacities, working without suffering the devastating sense of differentiation he would have had to experience were he to receive and accept credit for his achievements. Maintaining such a relationship with his father had enabled him to get through university and medical school, receiving the highest honorary degrees. Far more primitively, through his use of music, he sustained a fantasy of fusion with and containment within the maternal object, which probably prevented total mental collapse.

For M, music may have served as a concrete representation of what Grotstein (1985) has called the background object of primary identification.[2] This self-object, which forms the basis for a sense of individual identity and self-integration, begins to emerge with the infant's earliest experiences of separation and individuation and aids in the formation of boundaries. Grotstein, Anzieu (1989), Bick (1968, 1986), and D. Rosenfeld (1975, 1990, 1991) assert that the development of the body boundary located at the skin surface serves as the first boundary this object facilitates. It later functions by helping to establish other boundary formations that allow for differentiation. It is an early internalization of the figure of self-care, one that mediates and gives meaning to experience and provides room for the development of thoughts and feelings. In cases with a defective background object, individuals have a poorly developed sense of identity and persistently fear fragmentation. Like the dream screen (Lewin 1946), to which Grotstein compares it, the ordinary "good-enough" background object is rarely in evidence, providing as it does the backdrop for ordinary functioning. Again, like the dream screen, it mediates affect and thought and is linked to early experiences of separation from the maternal object.

During the early years of his analysis, being unable to let the background fall back, M required that it be constantly present to reassure him that he too had continued existence. It can surely be no coincidence that his hallucination of gaining access to the interior of the analyst's body began with being a limpet on and then clawing his way through the analyst's back. At various periods during his analysis, he used the ceiling and a hallucination of the analyst's back as if they were a dream screen. His incessant playing or recalling of music afforded him a precarious sense of continuity of being. Such a use of music, to sustain a sense of existence, can be seen as characteristic of what Ogden (1989) has called the autistic-contiguous position, thus extending the paranoid-schizoid and depressive positions of which Melanie Klein (1946) wrote.

In the autistic-contiguous position, psychological experience is developed and processed by the dialectical interplay among these positions, all of

2. The remainder of this discussion was written collaboratively with Laura Doty.

which function and interact throughout one's lifetime. In the autistic-contiguous position, psychological meaning is derived from early sensory experiences that provide a sense of cohesion and boundedness, particularly those occurring at the surface of the skin. These form the structure for the rudimentary experiences of subjectivity and incipient experiences of an integrated self. This position delimits less a realm of experience than a plane in which little or no separation exists between self and object, a presymbolic area where potential space has yet to be generated. Ogden (1989) suggests that the anxiety characteristic of this position involves the experience of the dissolution of self, and that certain rhythmic activities—such as exercise, bingeing, purging, and head banging—and autostimulations—such as face stroking, humming, and foot tapping—and mental preoccupations—such as working on computer programs, thinking about numbers or geometric shapes, or recalling music—are ways that people restore or support a sense of self, experienced as disintegrating. The singsong speech of certain patients may also be a manifestation of an effort at warding off this kind of anxiety, by stripping words of their meanings and diminishing the experience of language to one of shapes on the tongue and palate (Tustin 1972, 1981, 1986), vibrations or other sensations in the throat (Isakower 1938), and tones in the ear. All of the aforementioned phenomena characterized M's behavior with the exception of bingeing, purging, and head banging; his droning speech may itself have had such a meaning. The Gaddinis (R. Gaddini 1985, 1987, 1990; see Boyer 1990a,b) have been similarly impressed by the early affinity and meanings of somatic and psychical processes.

Continuing this line of thinking, it may be that M not only defended himself against transference rage by refusing to look at the contents of the office, but may have fought desperately an entire order of being that he experienced as being too threatening to him. It may have been that he dared not risk introjecting the analyst's background, lest doing so obliterate his own.[3]

Facilitated by the analyst's countertransference fantasy of a dream screen, M could describe a screen that provided both differentiation and fusion between himself and the analyst, whose tolerance of paradox created a safer environment for continued regression that could then lead to the patient's revealing more clearly the importance music held in structuring

---

3. Dr. Jane Hewitt has suggested that the author's repetitive changes of office decor may assist patients, by introjection, to begin to view fragmentations of their own selves as tolerable.

and containing the experience. The use of the countertransference experience allowed the patient the opportunity first to disclose and then to transfer over to the analyst the functions of the containing environment he had created in infancy. That made it possible for a potential space to exist between the two and thence to explore M's various uses of music.

Let us shift now more specifically to the concept of transference–countertransference relationship as it is used here; namely, that there is a constant interplay between the analyst and the analysand that consists of their mutual introjection of the other's projective identifications (H. A. Rosenfeld 1987). I will limit my remarks to the countertransference. It is held here that whatever the analyst experiences during the analytic session constitutes his idiosyncratic introjection of the patient's projections and his predominantly unconscious reactions to that introjection. We should not be misled into thinking our stray, apparently unrelated thoughts and physical or emotional reactions can be dismissed as idle preoccupations taking us away from the business at hand, interfering with our free-floating or evenly hovering attention. In the present case, the analyst's unconscious realization that an unrecognizable tune was the product of a projection specifically provided the information that led to the understanding of the role of music in the patient's psychological life.

In point of fact, the analyst resisted strongly the recognition of his reaction to the projective identification because of his own painful memories. Subsequent to his having ultimately become aware of the tune in his head, he recalled that for months he had heard a humming noise during many of M's sessions. Review of his careful and extensive process notes shows no entry recording this information.

Evenly hovering attention and countertransference are closely associated links in the chain of relationships between analyst and analysand. As early as 1912, Freud equated the analyst's evenly suspended attention with the analysand's task of free association and recommended that the doctor turn his unconscious like a receptive organ toward the transmitting unconscious of the patient. Freud suggested that the analyst would be incapable of such activity without his having undergone previous psychoanalysis and recommended self-analysis of the professional's own dreams as a starting point.

We see here an ambivalent position that continues to underscore the disagreement between the classical and totalistic approaches to countertransference. While Freud insisted that the analyst be purified so that he has no blind spots, at the same time he said that the analyst's unconscious should be in contact with that of the analysand. How can this be understood other than implying that the analyst have available for use not only his thoughts, but emotions, sensations, and fantasies—in short, all channels through which the unconscious communicates? Ferenczi (1919) pointed to this problem when he suggested that attempts at "mastering" the countertransference would inhibit the analyst's free-floating attention to his own unconscious processes, from which empathic understanding of the patient arises.

When we continue to think of this paradox, we return to Freud's original term for evenly hovering attention, *gleichschwebende Aufmerksamkeit*, the literal translation of which is accurate. But how did Freud come upon this term? What sorts of things hover evenly? The term implies a comparison between two or more things, as though one's attention should operate like the pans of a scale in a state of equilibrium. And consultation of an etymological dictionary begun by the brothers Grimm (1984) reveals that *gleichschwebende* equates it with equilibrium and that all of the examples of its use, beginning in 1661, involve the comparisons of two concepts of equal importance or weight.

At its simplest level, this can be seen as meaning that there is a way of considering equally both the content and the process presented by the analysand, an equal way of considering one's own internal process as well as what the patient presents. Again, we must question, how? How do we apply the concept of equilibrium to the use of our attention? It cannot be a matter of simply measuring amounts of process, of content, of one's own and the other's experience, and the like. It may be here that the method of interpreting dreams comes into play, as Freud mentioned each time he discussed evenly hovering attention.

As with dreams, we give equal weight to all of the elements that are presented, associating not only to large, attention-grabbing details, but also to the seemingly insignificant ones, so in the use of our attention we must give equal weight to all of the details, regardless of the degree to which they may appear to be extraneous. It is common in the perusal of the literature to find that experiences designated as belonging to countertransference are unpleasant, ego-dystonic, or even bizarre. The awareness of phenomena that appear to be unremarkable, trivial, or familiar is ignored, while the analyst seeks to record the anticipated alien experience. In doing so, we lose the opportunity to see ways in which our identifications with our patients are sometimes to aspects that are very similar to ourselves, or to aspects of the patients' experiences that are unthreatening and easy to manage, but that, like M's use of music, are vital, albeit pathological, adaptations that enable the patient's to cohere.

Let us return to other meanings that have been ascribed by readers and listeners to aspects of this patient's personality and uses of music.

It has been suggested that in this case music in its various forms served many purposes, including that of being both an autistic barrier, perhaps against mother's witchery, and, later, as a transitional object, and that the hearing of music served as an anxiety-reducing container.

We must assume that among M's significant psychological injuries was his mother's pregnancy with and the death of the stillborn girl, as he himself affirmed in interview material cited above. Although we do not have clear supporting evidence to offer, it may be that his notion of being possessed by bisexual monsters may represent his wish to keep alive the sister who was born dead, and that the constant hearing of music may have served the purpose of screening out and keeping repressed primal scene and prechildbirth sounds. Many anthropologists have noted that on an experiential basis, possession trances reflect aspects of sex and power. This applies to males in many of the cults studied, who are often referred to as effeminate and/or homosexual (cf. Spiro 1967 for Burma, Leacock and Leacock 1972 for Brazil, and Onwuejeogwu 1971 for the Hausa). Bourgignon (1992) writes,

> These, however, are only two of the aspects of the symbolism of the possession trance, those dealing with power relations and sexuality. Underlying all of this is the basic aspect of belief that makes the conceptualization of possession possible: the image of a separation between body and indwelling spirit. What is the source of such an image? Where, in human experience, is the body double, inhabited by another? Phrased in this manner, the answer is clear: the model is pregnancy. [p. 164]

See also Bourgignon (1965, 1973) and, discussing the psychology of Henry Moore, Neumann (1959).

The case fragment affirms anew that the permission, indeed the invitation, granted to the patient to regress in psychoanalysis to levels of early internalized object relationships can be salutary. Further, it demonstrates once again that judicious use of the emotionally available analyst's empathic or intuitive responses can facilitate the growth of higher levels of internalized object relations (Boyer 1986, 1989, Costa and Kataz 1989, Giovacchini 1989, Green 1975, Grinberg 1979, Grotstein 1985, Hann-Kende 1933, Heimann 1950, Khan 1964, Ogden 1986, 1989, Reich 1951, Reik 1948, 1953, H. A. Rosenfeld 1965, 1987, Searles 1979, Segal 1977;

see also Balter et al. 1980 and Fleming and Benedek 1966, who discuss Isakower's "analyzing instrument"). Without this patient's having been allowed to regress deeply in the transference–countertransference relationship, we could not have learned that he had reached the psychological level in which he could develop a transitional object but that he reacted to a combination of traumata by regressing to more primitive internalized object relationships (Boyer 1990b, Meltzer 1975, Meltzer et al. 1975, Tustin 1981, 1986, Winnicott 1953, 1958, 1965, 1971, 1986).

SUMMARY

Clinical and experimental investigations have demonstrated that music may serve subtle and complex psychological functions, the sounds per se serving more primitive roles than the themes and lyrics. The present study offers data obtained during the psychoanalysis of a musically talented man who had suffered life-threatening croup and asthma until the age of 6. Regression that was achieved as the result of interpretations based on the analyst's countertransferential responses revealed that the analysand was unable to achieve psychological separation from his mother and that music served predominantly the function of retaining a life-supporting connection with her. Presumably as the result of a complex elaboration of respiratory and auditory introjection, music came to symbolize the noise of air flowing through tubes into the steam tents and blood coursing through the umbilical cord, conceptualized as connecting him with his mother and making them permanently interdependent.

The early ego defect was overcome through a transference–countertransference interaction that is delineated in detail. Then, the less primitive meanings and psychological uses of musical themes and lyrics were elucidated, again in response to interpretations based on countertransference reactions.

References

Abend, S. M., Porter, M., and Willick, M. S. (1983). *Borderline Patients: Psychoanalytic Perspectives*. New York: International Universities Press.

Aizenberg, D., Schwartz, B., and Modal, I. (1986). Musical hallucinations, acquired deafness, and depression. *Journal of Nervous and Mental Disease* 174:309–311.

Anzieu, D. (1970). Skin ego. In *Psychoanalysis in France*, ed. S. Lebovici and D. Widlöcher, pp. 17–32. New York: International Universities Press, 1980.
——— (1989). *The Skin Ego*. New Haven, CT: Yale University Press.
Arlow, J. A. (1969). Unconscious fantasy and disturbances of conscious experience. *Psychoanalytic Quarterly* 38:1–27.
Arlow, J. A., and Brenner, C. (1964). *Psychoanalytic Concepts and the Structural Theory*. New York: International Universities Press.
Balter, L., Lothane, Z., and Spencer, J. H., Jr. (1980). On the analyzing instrument. *Psychoanalytic Quarterly* 49:474–504.
Bick, E. (1968). The experience of the skin in early object relations. *International Journal of Psycho-Analysis* 49:484–486.
——— (1986). Further considerations of the function of the skin in early object relations. *British Journal of Psychotherapy* 2:292–299.
Bion, W. R. (1967). *Second Thoughts. Selected Papers on Psycho-Analysis*. New York: Science House.
Bornstein, M. (1977). Analysis of a congenitally blind musician. *Psychoanalytic Quarterly* 46:23–37.
Bourgignon, E. (1965). The self, the behavioral environment and the theory of spirit possession. In *Context and Meaning in Cultural Anthropology*, ed. M. E. Spiro, pp. 39–60. New York: Free Press.
——— (1973). *Religion, Altered States of Consciousness, and Social Change*. Columbus, OH: Ohio State University Press.
——— (1992). Women's experience: fantasy and cultural change. *Psychoanalytic Study of Society* 17:143–170.
Boyer, L. B. (1956). On maternal overstimulation and ego defects. In *The Regressed Patient*, pp. 3–22. New York: Jason Aronson, 1983.
——— (1961). Provisional evaluation of psycho-analysis with few parameters employed in the treatment of schizophrenia. In *The Regressed Patient*, pp. 63–88. New York: Jason Aronson, 1983.
——— (1966). Office treatment of schizophrenic patients by psychoanalysis. *Psychoanalytic Forum* 1:337–356.
——— (1979). *Childhood and Folklore. A Psychoanalytic Study of Apache Personality*. New York: The Library of Psychoanalytic Anthropology.
——— (1983). *The Regressed Patient*. New York: Jason Aronson.
——— (1986). Technical aspects of treating the regressed patient. *Contemporary Psychoanalysis* 22:25–44.
——— (1989). Countertransference and technique in working with the regressed patient: further remarks. *International Journal of Psycho-Analysis* 70:701–714.
——— (1990a). Introduction: psychoanalytic intervention in treating the regressed patient. In *Master Clinicians on Treating the Regressed Patient*, ed. L. B. Boyer and P. L. Giovacchini, pp. 1–32. Northvale, NJ: Jason Aronson.
——— (1990b). Regression in treatment. On early object relations. In *Tactics and Techniques in Psychoanalytic Therapy. Vol. 3: The Implications of Winnicott's*

Contribution, ed. P. L. Giovacchini, pp. 200–225. Northvale, NJ: Jason Aronson.

Boyer, L. B., De Vos, G. A., and Boyer, R. M. (1985). Crisis and continuity in the personality of an Apache shaman. *Psychoanalytic Study of Society* 11:63–113.

Bychowski, G. (1951). Metapsychology of artistic creation. *Psychoanalytic Quarterly* 20:592–602.

Carta, I., Clerici, M., Pantò, C., et al. (1986). Representation of psychosomatic disturbances: metaphor and metonymy. *Psychotherapy and Psychosomatics* 46:177–183.

Cheng, H. W., and Trehub, S. E. (1977). Infants' perception of temporal grouping in auditory patterns. *Child Development* 48:1666–1670.

Costa, G. P., and Kataz, G. (1989). A importancia da identificação proyectiva no evolução do concepto e na elaboração da contratransferencia. *Revista Brasiliera de Psicanálise* 23:95–117.

Deutsch, L. (1987). Reflections on the psychoanalytic treatment of patients with bronchial asthma. *Psychoanalytic Study of the Child* 42:239–261. New Haven, CT: Yale University Press.

Ducey, C. (1979). The shaman's dream journey. Psychoanalytic and structural complementarity in myth interpretation. *Psychoanalytic Study of Society* 8:71–118.

Eliade, M. (1951). *Shamanism: Archaic Techniques of Ecstasy*. New York: Bollingen Foundation, 1964.

Esman, A. H. (1951). Mozart: a study in genius. *Psychoanalytic Quarterly* 20:603–612.

Fairbairn, W. R. D. (1952). *An Object Relations Theory of Personality*. New York: Basic Books.

Feder, S. (1978). Gustav Mahler, dying. *International Review of Psycho-Analysis* 5:125–148.

——— (1990). Music in mind. *American Psychoanalyst* 24:18–20.

Ferenczi, S. (1919). On the technique of psycho-analysis. *The Theory and Technique of Psychoanalysis*, 2nd ed., pp. 177–188. London: Hogarth, 1950.

Fernald, A. (1985). Four-month-old infants prefer to listen to motherese. *Infant Behavior Development* 8:181–195.

Fleming, J., and Benedek, T. F. (1966). *Psychoanalytic Supervision. A Method of Clinical Teaching*. New York: Grune & Stratton.

Fraiberg, S. (1980). *Clinical Studies in Infant Mental Health: The First Year of Life*. New York: Basic Books.

Freud, S. (1912). Recommendations to physicians practicing psycho-analysis. *Standard Edition* 14:109–120.

Friedman, S. M. (1960). One aspect of the structure of music. A study of regressive transformations of musical themes. *Journal of the American Psychoanalytic Association* 8:427–449.

Fromm-Reichmann, F. (1950). *Principles of Intensive Psychotherapy.* Chicago: University of Chicago Press.

―――― (1991). Do we need theory? *Bulletin of the Menninger Clinic* 55:22–29.

Gaddini, R. (1985). The precursors of transitional objects and phenomena. *Journal of the Squiggle Foundation* 1:49–56.

―――― (1987). Early care and the roots of internalization. *International Review of Psycho-Analysis* 14:321–333.

―――― (1990). Regression and its use in treatment. In *Master Clinicians on Treating the Regressed Patient,* ed. L. B. Boyer and P. L. Giovacchini, pp. 227–244. Northvale, NJ: Jason Aronson.

Gill, M. (1983). *Analysis of Transference.* Vol. 1. New York: International Universities Press.

Giovacchini, P. L. (1969). Modern psychoanalysis and modern psychoanalysts: a review. In *Psychoanalysis of Character Disorders,* pp. 292–315. New York: Jason Aronson, 1975.

―――― (1979). *Treatment of Primitive Mental Disorders.* New York: Jason Aronson.

―――― (1986). *Developmental Disorders: The Transitional Space in Mental Breakdown and Creative Integration.* Northvale, NJ: Jason Aronson.

―――― (1989). *Countertransference Triumphs and Catastrophes.* Northvale, NJ: Jason Aronson.

Glass, J. M. (1989). *Private Terror/Public Life: Psychosis and the Politics of Community.* Ithaca, NY: Cornell University Press.

Green, A. (1975). The analyst, symbolization and absence in the analytic setting. In *On Private Madness,* pp. 30–59. Madison, CT: International Universities Press, 1986.

Greenacre, P. (1975). On reconstruction. *Journal of the American Psychoanalytic Association* 23:693–712.

Greenson, R. R. (1969). *The Technique and Practice of Psychoanalysis.* New York: International Universities Press.

Grimm, J. L. K., and Grimm, W. K. (1819). *Grimm's Tales for Young and Old. The Complete Stories.* Newly translated by Ralph Mannheim. Garden City, NY: Doubleday, 1977.

―――― (1984). *Deutsches Wörterbuch, Band 7.* Munich: Deutscher Taschenbuch Verlag.

Grinberg, L. (1979). Countertransference and counteridentification. *Contemporary Psychoanalysis* 15:226–247.

―――― (1990). *The Goals of Psychoanalysis.* London: Karnak.

Grolnick, S. A. (1990). *The Work and Play of Winnicott.* Northvale, NJ: Jason Aronson.

Grotstein, J. S. (1985). The Schreber case revisited: schizophrenia as a disorder of self-regulation and interactional regulation. *Yale Journal of Biological Medicine* 58:29–314.

Hann-Kende, F. (1933). On the role of transference and countertransference in psychoanalysis. In *Psychoanalysis and the Occult*, ed. G. Devereux, pp. 158–167. New York: International Universities Press, 1953.

Heimann, P. (1950). On counter-transference. *International Journal of Psycho-Analysis* 31:60–76.

Isakower, O. (1938). A contribution to the pathopsychology of phenomena associated with falling asleep. *International Journal of Psycho-Analysis* 19:331–345.

Jaffe, D. S. (1983). On words and music: a personal commentary. *Psychoanalytic Quarterly* 52:590–593.

Juni, S. (1987). From the analysis of an obsessive hummer. Theoretical and clinical implications. *Psychoanalytic Review* 74:63–81.

Khan, M. M. R. (1964). Ego-distortion, cumulative trauma and the role of reconstruction in the analytic situation. In *The Privacy of the Self*, pp. 9–68. New York: International Universities Press, 1974.

Klein, M. (1946). Notes on some schizoid mechanisms. In *Developments in Psycho-Analysis*. London: Hogarth, 1952.

Kohut, H. (1957). Observations on the psychological functions of music. *Journal of the American Psychoanalytic Association* 5:389–407.

Langer, S. (1953). *Feeling and Form*. New York: Scribner's.

Leacock, S., and Leacock, R. (1972). *Spirits of the Deep*. New York: Doubleday, Anchor.

Lewin, B. D. (1946). Sleep, the mouth and the dream screen. *Psychoanalytic Quarterly* 15:419–434.

——— (1948). Inferences from the dream screen. *International Journal of Psycho-Analysis* 29:224–231.

Lindon, J. A. (1991a). Does technique require theory? *Bulletin of the Menninger Clinic* 55:1–21.

——— (1991b). Treatment techniques in evolution. *Bulletin of the Menninger Clinic* 55:30–37.

Little, M. I. (1958). On delusional transference (transference psychosis). In *Transference Neurosis and Transference Psychosis*, pp. 81–92. New York: Jason Aronson.

Lommel, A. (1967). *Shamanism: The Beginnings of Art*. New York: McGraw-Hill.

Mahler, M. S. (1968). *On Human Symbiosis and the Vicissitudes of Individuation*. Vol. 1: *Infantile Psychosis*. New York: International Universities Press.

Marty, P., M'Uzan, M., and David, C. (1963). *L'Investigation Psychosomatique. Sept Observations Cliniques*. Paris: Presses Universitaires de France.

McDougall, J. (1989). *Theaters of the Body. A Psychoanalytic Approach to Psychosomatic Illness*. New York: W. W. Norton.

McLaughlin, J. T. (1981). Transference, psychic reality and countertransference. *Psychoanalytic Quarterly* 50:639–664.

——— (1988). The analyst's insights. *Psychoanalytic Quarterly* 57:370–389.

Mehler, J., Bertoncini, J., Barriere, M., and Jassik-Gerschenfeld, D. (1978). Infant recognition of mother's voice. *Perception* 7:491–497.

Meissner, W. W. (1984). *The Borderline Spectrum. Differential Diagnosis and Developmental Issues.* New York: Jason Aronson.

Meltzer, D. (1975). Adhesive identification. *Contemporary Psychoanalysis* 11:289–310.

Meltzer, D., Bremner, J., Hoxter, S., et al. (1975). *Explorations in Autism.* Perthshire, Scotland: Clunie.

Merkur, D. (1985). *Becoming Half Hidden. Shamanism and Initiation among the Inuit.* Stockholm: Almqvist & Wiksell International.

Monday, J., Montplaisir, J., and Malo, J.-L. (1987). Dream process in asthmatic subjects with nocturnal attacks. *American Journal of Psychiatry* 144:638–640.

Money-Kyrle, R. E. (1956). Normal counter-transference and some of its deviations. *International Journal of Psycho-Analysis* 37:360–366.

Moore, B. E., and Fine, B. D. (1967). *A Glossary of Psychoanalytic Terms and Concepts.* 2nd Edition. New York: American Psychoanalytic Association.

Nacht, S. (1962). Curative factors in psychoanalysis. *International Journal of Psycho-Analysis* 43:206–211.

Neumann, E. (1959). *The Archetypal World of Henry Moore.* Bollingen Series, LXVIII. New York: Pantheon.

Niederland, W. (1958). Early auditory experiences, beating fantasies, and primal scene. *Psychoanalytic Study of the Child* 13:471–504. New York: International Universities Press.

Ogden, T. H. (1986). *The Matrix of the Mind. Object Relations and the Psychoanalytic Dialogue.* Northvale, NJ: Jason Aronson.

——— (1989). *The Primitive Edge of Experience.* Northvale, NJ: Jason Aronson.

Onwuejeogwu, M. (1971). The cult of the Bori spirits among the Hausa. In *Man in Africa*, ed. M. Douglas and P. M. Kaberry. Garden City, NY: Anchor Books/Doubleday.

Ornstein, A., and Ornstein, C. H. (1975). On the interpretive process in schizophrenia. *International Journal of Psychoanalytic Psychotherapy* 4:219–271.

Pao, P-N. (1977). *Schizophrenia Disorders: Theory and Treatment from a Psychoanalytic Point of View.* New York: International Universities Press.

Papousek, M., and Papousek, H. (1977). Musical elements in the infant's vocalization: their significance for communication, cognition and creativity. In *Advances in Infant Research*, vol. 1, ed. P. Lipsitt, pp. 163–224. Norwood, NJ: Ablex.

Poggi, R., and Ganzarain, R. (1983). Countertransference hate. *Bulletin of the Menninger Clinic* 47:15–37.

Poland, W. S. (1988). Insight and the analytic dyad. *Psychoanalytic Quarterly* 57:341–369.

Racker, E. (1952). Aportación al psicoanálisis de la música. *Revista de Psicoanálisis* 3–29.

——— (1968). *Transference and Countertransference.* New York: International Universities Press.

Rechardt, E. (1987). Experiencing music. *Psychoanalytic Study of the Child* 42:511–530. New Haven, CT: International Universities Press.

Reich, A. (1951). On countertransference. *International Journal of Psycho-Analysis* 32:25–31.

Reik, T. (1948). *Listening with the Third Ear.* New York: Farrar, Straus.

——— (1953). *The Haunting Melody. Psychoanalytic Experiences in Life and Music.* New York: Farrar, Straus & Young.

Róheim, G. (1921). Das Selbst. *Imago* 7:1–39.

Rosenfeld, D. (1975). Trastornos en la piel y el esquema corporal. Identificación proyectiva y el cuento infantil *Piel de Asno. Revista de Psicoanálisis* 2:309–330.

——— (1976). *Clínica Psicoanalítica. Estudios sobre Drogadicción, Psicosis y Narcissismo.* Buenos Aires: Galerna.

——— (1984). Hypochondriasis, somatic delusion and body schema in psychoanalytic practice. *International Journal of Psycho-Analysis* 65:377–388.

——— (1990). Psychotic body image. In *Master Clinicians on Treating the Regressed Patient*, ed. L. B. Boyer and P. L. Giovacchini, pp. 165–188. Northvale, NJ: Jason Aronson.

——— (1991). *Psychosis and Body Parts.* London: Karnak.

Rosenfeld, H. A. (1952). Transference-phenomena and transference analysis in an acute catatonic schizophrenic patient. In *Psychotic States: A Psychoanalytic Approach*, pp. 63–103. New York: International Universities Press, 1965.

——— (1965). *Psychotic States: A Psychoanalytic Approach.* New York: International Universities Press.

——— (1966). Discussion of "Office Treatment of Schizophrenia" by L. B. Boyer. *Psychoanalytic Forum* 1:351–353.

——— (1987). *Impasse and Interpretation. Therapeutic and Antitherapeutic Factors in the Psychoanalytic Treatment of Psychotic, Borderline and Neurotic Patients.* London: Tavistock.

Schwaber, E. A. (1983). A particular perspective on analytic listening. *Psychoanalytic Study of the Child* 38:519–546. New Haven, CT: International Universities Press.

——— (1990). Interpretation and the therapeutic action of psychoanalysis. *International Journal of Psycho-Analysis* 71:229–240.

Searles, H. F. (1963). Transference psychosis in the treatment of schizophrenia. *Selected Papers on Schizophrenia and Related Subjects*, pp. 654–716. New York: International Universities Press, 1965.

——— (1965). *Collected Papers on Schizophrenia and Related Subjects.* New York: International Universities Press.

——— (1979). *Countertransference and Related Subjects.* New York: International Universities Press.

Segal, H. (1957). Notes on symbol formation. In *The Work of Hanna Segal*, pp. 9–68. New York: Jason Aronson, 1981.

——— (1977). Countertransference. In *The Work of Hanna Segal*, pp. 81–88. New York: Jason Aronson.

Smith, H. F. (1990). Cues: the perceptual edge of the transference. *International Journal of Psycho-Analysis* 71:219–228.

Sperling, M. (1978). *Psychosomatic Disorders in Children*. New York: Jason Aronson.

Spiro, M. E. (1967). *Burmese Supernaturalism*. Englewood Cliffs, NJ: Prentice Hall.

——— (1992). The "primary process" revisited. *Psychoanalytic Study of Society* 17:171–180.

Spitz, E. H. (1987). Separation-individuation in a cycle of songs. George Crumb's *Ancient Voices of Children*. *Psychoanalytic Study of the Child* 42:531–543. New Haven, CT: Yale University Press.

Tienari, P. (1991). Finland: interaction between genetic vulnerability and rearing environment. Address presented at the 10th International Symposium for the Psychotherapy of Schizophrenia, Stockholm, August 13.

Trehub, S. E., Thorpe, L. A., and Morrongiello, B. (1985). Infant's perception of melodies. Changes in a single tone. *Infant Behavior and Development* 8:213–223.

——— (1987). Organizational processes in infants' perception of auditory patterns. *Child Development* 58:741–749.

Tustin, F. (1972). *Autism and Childhood Psychosis*. London: Hogarth.

——— (1981). *Autistic States in Children*. Boston: Routledge and Kegan Paul.

——— (1986). *Autistic Barriers in Neurotic Patients*. New Haven, CT: Yale University Press, 1987.

Volkan, V. D. (1976). *Primitive Internalized Object Relationships*. New York: International Universities Press.

——— (1990). The psychoanalytic therapy of schizophrenia. In *Master Clinicians on Treating the Regressed Patient*, ed. L. B. Boyer and P. L. Giovacchini, pp. 245–270. Northvale, NJ: Jason Aronson.

Volkan, V. D., and Ast, G. (1992). *Eine Borderline Therapie*. Göttingen: Vandenhoeck and Ruprecht.

Wilson, C. P., and Mintz, I. L., eds. (1989). *Psychosomatic Symptoms. Psychodynamic Treatment of the Underlying Personality Disorder*. Northvale, NJ: Jason Aronson.

Winnicott, D. W. (1949). Hate in the countertransference. In *Collected Papers: Through Paediatrics to Psycho-Analysis*, pp. 194–203. New York: Basic Books, 1958.

——— (1953). Transitional objects and transitional phenomena. In *Collected Papers: Through Paediatrics to Psycho-Analysis*, pp. 229–242. New York: Basic Books, 1958.

———— (1956). Primal maternal preoccupation. In *Collected Papers: Through Paediatrics to Psycho-Analysis*, pp. 300–305. New York: Basic Books.

———— (1958). *Collected Papers: Through Paediatrics to Psycho-Analysis*. New York: Basic Books.

———— (1960). The theory of the parent–infant relationship. *International Journal of Psycho-Analysis* 41:585–595.

———— (1965). *The Maturational Process and the Facilitating Environment*. New York: International Universities Press.

———— (1971). *Playing and Reality*. New York: Basic Books.

———— (1986). *Home Is Where We Start From*. New York: W. W. Norton.

Zelig, M. A. (1960). The role of silence in transference, countertransference and the psychoanalytic process. *International Journal of Psycho-Analysis* 41:407–412.

Countertransference and Technique in Working with the Regressed Patient: Further Remarks

Thirty-seven years ago I introduced into the North American literature a concept that to my knowledge was new, the idea that unresolved countertransference constitutes a major impediment to the successful psychoanalytic treatment of regressed patients (Boyer 1961).[1] I became aware later that such an idea had been implied earlier or contemporaneously in the writings of Searles (1953) and certain British and French authors and their followers in Latin America (Balint 1968, Garma 1962, Grunberger 1971, Heimann 1950, Khan 1964, Nacht 1963, Racker 1968, Winnicott 1947). Subsequently, that position has found much support, although it is not universally accepted.[2]

Following my initial communications, I have written of the roles of other factors in the treatment of the regressed patient that are aimed at the resumption of ego development (Loewald 1979) and his becoming more

---

1. I even erroneously believed that I had introduced the term *countertransference neurosis*, a phrase used by Racker in 1953. So far as I am aware, my use of the term *countertransference psychosis* was original.

2. Thus Waldinger and Gunderson (1987), in their recent *Effective Psychotherapy with Borderline Patients*, scarcely mention countertransference.

alive as a subjective, historical being (Ogden 1986) who emerges from analysis as an empathic, effective, and creative person (Giovacchini 1986): (1) the establishment of the working or therapeutic alliance; (2) the holding or facilitating environment; (3) timely empathic interpretations; and (4) the analyst's internal security and optimism in the face of inevitable transference regressions.

In the introduction to the book from which this chapter is taken (Boyer and Giovacchini 1990), I discussed the advantages of the therapist's being selectively aggressive in his search for usable data in analysis and how interpretations based on his awareness of his own physical, emotional, and ideational responses to the patient's veiled messages can be effective in treatment. Analysts have become progressively aware of the potentially beneficial therapeutic uses of countertransference phenomena (Boyer 1983, Giovacchini 1989, Hann-Kende 1933, Little 1981, Racker 1968, Searles 1979). Yet Waldinger's (1987) overview of the work of North American psychoanalysts who treat borderline patients considers the role of countertransference but in passing.

In this chapter I hope to demonstrate that interpretation facilitated by countertransference experiences constitutes an important agent of psychic structuring in the treatment of at least some regressed patients.

As illustrative material, I discuss the treatment of a group of patients whose use of projective identification appears to be excessive; it very heavily influences their relationships with others as well as their psychic equilibrium. Their principle conscious goal in therapy is to relieve themselves immediately of tension. Often they greatly fear that the experience of discomfort is intolerable and believe that failure to rid themselves of it will lead to physical or mental fragmentation or dissolution. Bion (1962) holds that "excessive projective identification should be understood to apply not to the frequency only with which projective identification is employed but to excess of belief in omnipotence" (p. 114).

The principal data of this chapter consist of a precis of the psychoanalysis of a woman who, during a period of regression that was limited almost entirely to the consultation room, attempted to empty herself totally of mental contents and deposit them into me or into space. I believe that the data demonstrate that interpretation facilitated by countertransference experiences constituted in this case an important agent of psychic restructuring. I have treated three other similar patients who confirm to my satisfaction that interpretation thus facilitated proved to be equally beneficial.

COUNTERTRANSFERENCE

In my experience, both the most effective interpretations and the recovery of the most relevant repressed memories are based frequently on information gathered through transference–countertransference interactions. In working with regressed patients, many of those interactions depend on the patient's projective, and the analyst's introjective, identification. Searles (1976) found that effective interpretations also can be based on the analyst's projective and the patient's introjective identifications.[3]

Psychoanalytic impasses can be traced to the analyst's faulty use of his introjections, based on his idiosyncratic psychology (Grinberg 1979, Racker 1968). Especially during the patient's inevitable regressions, the analyst at times undergoes experiences that enable him to reach previously hidden material (Green 1975, Searles 1976). Freud (1912) recommended that the therapist "turn to his own unconscious like a receptive organ towards the transmitting unconscious of the patient . . . so that the doctor's unconscious is able to reconstruct the patient's unconscious" (pp. 115–116).

Khan (1964) conceives of countertransference as an instrument of perception, and McDougall (1985) holds that she articulates her introjections of the patient's preverbal and presymbolic experiences. At times she becomes aware of the meanings of countertransference disturbances through analysis of her own dreams (McDougall 1978). Winnicott (1971) and Ogden (1985, 1986) have stressed the need of the analyst to be able to allow the existence of potential space in which creativity can occur, and Bion (1967), the need for the analyst to enter a "reverie" allowing a similar development.

Apparently it has become usual for some analysts to include quite consciously their countertransference reactions in their interpretations, particularly with regressed patients. (See also Loewald 1986.)

When working with neurotics, the analyst is frequently able to make significant interpretations from a position of technical neutrality, although Jacobs (1986) reminds us that "neutrality, too, may become involved with countertransference reactions" (p. 197). To judge from the literature and my own experience, mutative interpretations made to regressed patients often are made from a position tinged with the analyst's emotions. Searles

---

3. It has been assumed for many years that countertransferences are determined largely by the analyst's introjections of qualities of the patient that come into contact with the therapist's unresolved infantile conflicts (Federn 1952, Fenichel 1945, Fliess 1953).

(personal communication) reminds us that the "neutral" psychoanalyst "is all too likely to project into the patient all sorts of far-from-neutral emotions."

The range of experiences the analyst must be able to tolerate, understand, and interpret meaningfully extends from his feeling like an excluded object (Giovacchini 1967, McDougall 1972) whose interventions, if acknowledged, are treated by the patient as evidence of the analyst's madness, to reacting to the patient's fusional regression and dependence as though the analyst is an extension of his mind and/or body, and to his sometimes startling somatic displays when on the couch.

Many regressed patients present psychosomatic syndromes that have been interpreted as masking symbolic thought or interfering with the patient's capacity to symbolize, through what McDougall (1985, 1989) has called *psychic shortcutting*. In order to reach the level of regression that will enable them to develop a new kind of object relations and experience transference in such a way that it can be interpreted profitably, some patients may require that the process of shortcutting through somatization, which more or less separates psyche and soma, be reduced. Reducing the shortcutting process may result in *symbolic formation* (Chiozza 1976, Demers-Desrosiers 1982, Fain 1966, Marty et al. 1963, Tayler 1984). With others, psychic shortcutting is accomplished through acting out. The analyst's tolerance may be taxed severely as he observes such developments in the course of analysis of patients who seemed relatively psychologically mature when treatment started; we know that many therapists refuse analysis to psychosomatic patients or to those who customarily deal with their problems through action.

CLINICAL DATA

The following information emerged in a highly fragmentary manner during the course of the analysand's treatment, because her conscious goal was to use each interview solely for the purpose of relieving herself of tension or "internal pressure." When she was very tense and felt such internal pressure, she panicked, and for periods of varying length believed quite literally that her mind would explode and her body would fragment. A major therapeutic task was to enable her to see the value of understanding internal conflicts. Doing so involved my being, for me, unusually aggressive in insisting that she listen to, associate to, and think about what she and I had said, and her emotional and physical responses to our interactions.

Prior to our understanding of a rather spectacular regression and my reaction to it, no direct information had emerged pertaining to real events in her early life, information crucial to our comprehension of her intrapsychic problems and her resumption of more accelerated ego development.

Mrs. T was a 39-year-old housewife with four children, all under 7 years of age. She was the baby of her family by five years, an "accident." She and her older siblings, two boys and two girls, were reared by maids and cooks, because her mother was so busy in pursuits pertaining to Zionism and Jewish social welfare. Her husband was physically unlike her father but his psychological twin. Both were physicians, passive, easygoing gastronomic bon vivants who were unperturbed by their domineering and shrewish wives' behavior and saw no necessity to help their children develop a capacity to control themselves and think of the rights of others. Mrs. T established some contact with her mother by joining her from early childhood in her auxiliary religious activities and by serious involvement in Judaism. She studied eagerly for her *bat mitzvah* and became fluent in Hebrew.

Undisciplined as a child, she easily ruled her parents with screaming, kicking, biting, and clawing temper tantrums. She had close relations only with her age-mates. Parents, caregivers, teachers, and siblings found her to be an intolerable brat.

During early childhood she was severely troubled with typical phobias. In her grammar school years, the phobias receded in intensity, being gradually replaced by almost continuous obsessive thinking related to problems of living and dying and forbidden sexuality. Beginning in preadolescence, those symptoms were replaced by discharging tension through immediate action and the development of asthma and a spastic colon. A teenage truant, she ran with a delinquent crowd, smoked marijuana, shoplifted, and was promiscuous. Before and following her period of rampant action, she resentfully followed her mother's dictum that she was to be pretty and popular and "hook a rich doctor."

The high school psychologist had recommended professional help, but upon her graduation she joined a kibbutz in Israel. Uncomfortable there, she soon left. She met and felt needed by a gentile "hippie" and lived happily with him as beggars in a commune in Jerusalem. For her, sex was "like nursing and being nursed." When she faced the obvious, that he was sleeping with several women, she returned home, entered psychotherapy, and attended college.

During the next five years she lived a passive, apparently almost

catatonic-like existence at home. Aside from auxiliary religious activities
and rather casual involvement with mundane craft productions, she masturbated more or less compulsively and daydreamed. The contents of her
renewed phobias and obsessions symbolized simultaneously dyadic and
triadic relationship anxieties.

At 30 she met her husband-to-be at a Jewish social function, immediately idealized and adored him largely as a good combined parental
surrogate, and, after finding him to be the first man who could bring her to
orgasm, married him within a few weeks. From the moment of marriage,
however, she saw him as contemptible and inadequate, was furious that she
was dependent on him for orgasms, and vowed to make his life as miserable
as she had known her father's to have been at the hands of her mother.

She resumed seeking to identify with her mother in some roles, being
more interested in the welfare of Jews as a group than of her nuclear family.
It was easy for her, having felt emotionally starved, to adopt one of her
mother's means of belittling and frustrating her gourmet husband. As
mother had refused to cook except for company, Mrs. T ignored her
husband's requests, got dinner solely after he arrived home at night, and
served only raw vegetables and bland dishes she thought to be healthy for
her children. She tried to establish a kosher home despite her husband's
sharp objections, limited her extra-domestic activities to Jewish issues, and
set out to have five children immediately.

Mrs. T came for treatment reluctantly. She had been in therapy almost
continuously for twenty years for a variety of complaints, for each of which
she received transient mild relief. She chose me as her therapist because she
had heard that I was a harsh disciplinarian and treated patients everyone
else rejected. Her specific reason for seeking assistance was worry about
what she called her "destructive, intrusive, uncontrollable anger." From the
first interview she spoke about the presence from childhood of overt sexual
fantasies involving her father. She said she supposed having them should
have bothered her, but that they were useful to calm herself and enable her
to go to sleep. Apparently unconcernedly, she said her first reaction to me
was to imagine sucking my penis. While the incest fantasies did not bother
her consciously, she had been unable to touch her father or permit his touch
from girlhood and it was over a year before she could allow her hand to
touch mine as she gave me her check.

During the first few vis-à-vis interviews she seemed to enter a mild
fugue state as she talked loudly and continuously. The manifest content
belittled me although she acted also as though I were not in the room. In
response to a question, she said she visualized her anger and words to be

going either into space or into me; they were seen as enclosed in balloons emanating from mouths in cartoons. During the fourth session she announced very angrily that she had decided to go to a "competent" Jewish female psychiatrist. My first interpretation dealt with the interpersonal aspects of projective identification and enabled her to enter psychoanalysis. I told her that she sought to establish safe links with me by believing she had put some of her anger into me and then by seeking to pick fights in which she imagined that I would help her to behave by dominating her and thereby reassure her that she could not hurt me. Vastly relieved, she introduced the subject of night terrors, and said that she often woke in the morning convinced that she had murdered her husband in her sleep.

I believe that if I had not subsequently forgotten my early conviction that her primary need was to empty herself into me, her treatment would have been less confusing and I would have been able to make synthesizing interpretations more often.

Her everyday life was chaotic. She displaced her need to be in control of her internal urges to a need to control her husband's and children's activities absolutely; much of her time was spent in rages because one or another of them had disobeyed some mandate.

She could not establish priorities. The house and her very existence were littered with projects enthusiastically begun and soon interrupted. She did all household repairs and improvements. Although she was terrified by thoughts of voyeurs, attacks, and rape, neither blinds nor curtains had covered the windows of the master bedroom or the bathroom for eight years. She followed her mother's custom of parading naked before husband and children, "to show them that I am not ashamed that I have breasts and no penis."

She took charge of family finances and transacted them solely by check. She did not record deposits or withdrawals and, since her husband used credit cards over her objections, threw his bills away. Each month she was surprised to discover that her finances were a shambles, detecting no contribution on her part. Yet she paid me accurately and on time although my patients are asked to keep track of their obligation to me and to pay me on the last interview of the month.

The same chaos characterized her behavior in treatment. Ordinarily she talked continuously and loudly, attaching equal emotional intensity to every utterance. Subjects shifted rapidly and there was no orderly time sequence. For months the predominant affect expressed was mixed aggrieved anger and suspiciousness. At times her paranoia was temporarily delusional. She perceived herself as being wronged and deprived by almost everyone and in every imaginable way. Nothing outside of her session relieved her tension for more than a few minutes, whether she thoughtlessly ate ravenously, masturbated frantically, engaged in orgies of insulting neighbors and hired help, or physically beat her husband or children. She was surprised to discover that she felt calmed in my presence, even while the suspiciousness and transitory persecutory delusions shifted over a period of months from the actions and motivations of people in her domestic environment to those of people near the consultation room and eventually to my behavior and secret intentions.

My most helpful intervention during the first year was to speak repeatedly of the defensive use of the regressive behavior. I suggested that the disordered presentation and failure to listen to herself or me were in the service of hiding connections from herself and internal conflicts that she sought to externalize. In order for me to get her attention, I sometimes had to command her forcefully to stop talking and listen to me or to try to remember what she had said during the previous few minutes and to seek to link the subjects. Her reactions to such actions on my part were complex. She was surprised to become aware that I did not read her mind and automatically understand what she meant even though she didn't, while she railed at me for hopeless stupidity and incompetency. She was grateful that anyone would discipline her, take the trouble to try to help her present herself in an orderly and understandable way, and assume that she had the capacity to learn.

By the end of the first year, she tolerated better the examining of her internal conflicts and had developed an interest in remembering her past and understanding her life and identity as a continuity. Her interview experiences were so much with her that her everyday life seemed to her to be superposed upon what she called her "continuous dream," and my interpreting the initial interview material as day residue (Boyer 1988) was readily accepted by her. During the first year, as I have found to be beneficial with regressed patients in general, I focused my interpretations almost solely on her fears of, and defensive maneuvers against, aggression. In her case, the dominant defense consisted of projective identification or evacuation.

As her adolescent living-in-action and psychosomatic problems were followed by the reemergence of phobias and obsessions, they were recathected in analysis as she gave up much of her psychic shortcutting through action. Neither asthma nor spastic colitis reappeared, although she did experience frightening episodes of tachycardia, tightening of the throat, and intolerable vulvar itching, which she not infrequently attempted to relieve by scratching her perineum during the interviews.

Part of the subject matter of her initial chaotic verbal productions had to do with fury because her husband both deprived her of sex by his passivity, which forced her to humiliate herself by seducing him, and had the capacity to bring her to orgasm by his special oral-genital techniques. Gradually she began to have anxiety attacks while driving to my office through a tunnel and had to drink water en route to relieve the hyperventilation-induced dryness in her throat. Her anxiety and the fluid intake forced her to begin to use the toilet provided for patients. She developed phobias with delusional intensity that black men lurked there to attack her and that other women would hold her helpless while the huge phallus penetrated her mouth, vagina, or urethra. Later her urinary pressure became vaginal excitement and she believed transiently that I had secret mirrors that enabled me to see her vaginal contractions and thereby gratify my voyeuristic wishes. She was sometimes certain that I was masturbating behind her and was simultaneously afraid that I would choke her with my phallus or that she would bite it off, and was furious because I did not rape her.

Largely as a result of my consistently interpreting her reactions to me as transference displacements from earlier relations with her father and older brothers and suggesting reconstructions, we gradually understood her phobias and their attendant obsessive thinking largely in terms of her reactions to observations of her parents' bedroom activities. As a girl of 3 to 5 years of age, she listened at their door or sneaked into the bedroom, observed their polymorphous activity, and was terrified by fantasies pertaining to combined lust and danger and confusion about who had what sexual organs and how they were used. At the same time, she shared their excitement and found herself able to get relief of tension through urination. As the highly eroticized transference abated, her life became quite calm. Her relationships with her husband, children, and parental nuclear family were unbelievably peaceful, and she stopped provoking her children's teachers and the neighbors. She cooked for and socialized with her husband and began to think of leaving treatment and having her fifth child.

This phase of her analysis occupied the first two years, and her rate of improvement left me uneasy. In my experience and that of some others (Ornstein and Ornstein 1975, Rosenfeld 1966, Volkan 1976), the mutative analysis of triadic relationship, oedipal material prior to the understanding of dyadic relationship material, is at best unusual in the treatment of regressed patients. In a sense, her involvement in the eroticized transference could be viewed as a flight into relative health from the basic problem of her need to empty her contents into others, which I understood to mean that her early relationship with her mother was defective and that her ego structure was grossly deficient. Nevertheless, the regression that followed both surprised and bewildered me because I was unaware of connections to be spelled out now, until I reviewed my extensive process notes.

When patients begin analysis with me, I inform them that I shall be absent perhaps six times during the year and that I shall tell them the dates of my planned absences as soon as I know them. This practice helps people focus on issues pertaining to separation, an issue of consummate importance to regressed patients. Mrs. T initially reacted to this information with ambivalence; she was relieved because she could save money and she was infuriated that I treated her like a "second-class citizen" by establishing rules. She forgot the dates of my first absences, and only dream material hinted that she was aware that they were imminent. Her forgetting and the absences themselves were of no conscious interest to her.

During the period when the eroticized transference was in the forefront, her jealousy was intense, and the manifest material of her dreams and interviews was concerned largely with rage at me and the woman or women I was gratifying while I was away. As her sexual reactions toward me were understood in transferential terms as reenacting triadic childhood relationships, they diminished greatly in intensity and my absences became once again of no apparent interest to her.

Although her life outside the consultation room continued to be peaceful, she began to behave periodically as she had during the first months of treatment. Having more leisure than previously to study the regressions during which she entered an altered ego state and sought to evacuate her mental and affectual components into me or into space, I observed that during those periods she concretized thoughts and feelings through somatization. As an example, her pleasure because of an intellectual achievement would be instantly converted into clitoral excitement. Such excitement was unaccompanied by conscious thought, but was followed by feelings of abandonment and an altered ego state during which she was terrified of bodily and/or mental fragmentation. The somatization, thus, was a shortcutting of ideation. At times, we were able to trace the sensation that she had been abandoned to feelings of guilt or shame. Only subsequently were ideas associated with the awareness of guilt or shame. Chiozza (1976) would designate such a somatization a presymbolic equation, used in the service of discharging tension without ideation, or, in Kleinian, Bionian, or Grinbergian terminology, evacuation. Regaining awareness of me removed the feeling of abandonment. Then she was able once again to generate symbols and use them for purposes of communication, signaling her need to use me as a repository.

Review of my notes indicated that such regressive behavior followed by some days as announcement of a forthcoming absence that she had been reminded of by some life event, a connection of which I had been consciously unaware. I also forgot that during the early periods of regression she had mentioned offhandedly several times that she had dreams of, or read about, insects or larvae, and had fleeting thoughts of watching them or other small objects being torn apart. In my experience, insects and larvae most often symbolize small children and fetuses, often siblings. Thus I missed the intense wrenching trauma to her of my leaving her, and her feeling torn from an imaginary continuum. I had recognized, but been unable to use effectively, that the regressive behavior was accompanied by, or followed, talk of some current event involving hostile relationships with various women. The women were not obvious transference figures, but rather appeared to be vehicles to contain her anger and persecute her with it, but my interpretations scarcely warranted her notice.

The dominant theme of the interviews was the change in her view of me. Previously, and for a long time, I had been her kind, good supporter, an ideal father. Now I became incompetent, physically ugly, truly beneath vilification. My attempts to interrupt her increasingly loud flow of imprecations were treated with contempt. Finally, for a period of a week, she spewed out hatred toward me; essentially nothing else occurred during the interviews. She seemed to enter a light trance state; gradually my efforts to interrupt her flow of words were less and less successful. I noted that while she consistently threatened to murder or castrate me, she dressed more attractively, was eager to come for her interviews, and said nothing about wanting to terminate treatment. Retrospectively, I gradually became more passive and periodically drowsy. Ultimately I dozed. Suddenly she sat up, shouted that she would not tolerate such contempt of her, screamed that she was quitting, and ran to and opened the door. I had no doubt that our work was over if I did not respond appropriately and immediately, since she had quit treatment with other therapists suddenly and stormily four times previously. I commanded her to stop and to return for another interview to discuss what had happened and our future plans.

When she appeared for the next session, she was enraged and could scarcely sit, preferring to pace the room while making faces and threatening gestures. I told her that I recommended further analysis and would place her with another therapist, or, should she choose to continue with me, I would seek to handle privately the internal problem that had led to my falling asleep. She continued to fume. Then, to my total surprise, I heard myself saying that her having left me through her altered ego state and having treated me as though I were a worthless thing had made me feel lonely and that I wondered whether her behavior had been designed to do just that. Then, with remarkable clarity, I silently remembered dreams and fantasies that had involved my having been left in many ways as a young child by a disturbed caregiver and also of having torn the wings off flies soon after the birth of my brother.

Her reaction startled me. For the first time during her treatment, she cried. She curled up in the chair like a little girl. She told me I must have been misunderstanding her although she had thought I knew, as she did, what was going on. She had to act as though she hated me and discharge her rage into me and the consultation room to keep from killing her husband and her older son—her husband because his passivity enraged her so and her son because she was unable to help him stop his temper tantrums. She adored me, I was her saviour, her Abba Eban.

She had thought about why I had fallen asleep and decided that she had had to make me feel the loneliness and sense of being unwanted that she knew she had felt as a young girl and thought that she must have felt as an infant. She supposed the only way she could do that was to empty her feelings into me and she had thought I was "strong enough to contain them without being upset." She had "always known" but had never remembered while she was with me that her mother had been hospitalized for some months for postpartum depression after each of her children was born. Mrs. T had had, during her first year, several different caregivers and probably not seen her own mother during her first four or five months. After she spoke of such issues, she returned to the couch.

Thenceforth her analysis proceeded calmly and dealt primarily with dyadic issues. I came to represent the mother of her early years. Concurrently, her need to provoke her husband and children practically disappeared. He came to "wear the pants" much of the time, the children's temper tantrums disappeared, and she became a gourmet cook. As her sexual relations with her husband improved, she stopped her compulsive masturbation. After a year she decided to stop treatment precipitously "on a trial basis."

I did not then discover why or how she made her decision. In my experience, following the meaningful analysis of dyadic material in the treatment of regressed patients, analysis or reanalysis and working through of oedipal issues occurs. Because this had not happened and I did not understand her motives for her sudden decision, I was uneasy about her termination. I suggested that she allow a few months before a planned ending, but she was adamant.

Four years later she requested further analysis. She revealed that she had been pregnant when she terminated her treatment, wanting to savor her "feeling of oneness" with the baby inside her and the early years with her baby, who was a girl, without "analytic interference." She was still troubled by her inability to control her temper. However, she was much changed both in her life and in the consultation room. The most striking differences were that she was much better organized, no longer used projective identification and evacuation as dominant defensive operations, and had the capacity to experience depression. She cried readily. The principal problems that emerged were her identification with the dependent needs of her daughter and problems that ensued from her incapacity to help the little girl to control her impulses, whether libidinal or aggressive. The analysis of that dyadic relationship has now been satisfactorily completed and she has entered into a satisfactory analysis of her oedipal problems.

By chance, I learned from another source that her mother had in fact suffered the postpartum depressions that Mrs. T remembered following the interpretation I made that was influenced so heavily by countertransference, and that Mrs. T had had little if any contact with her mother during the first half year or so of her life. During the second period of her analysis, it became apparent that she had repressed knowledge of that trauma once again.

DISCUSSION

The most singular events of the analysis were her responses to two of my interventions. The circumstances were very similar. During the initial interviews, Mrs. T entered a mild dissociative state, essentially excluding me from an interpersonal relationship with her, as she vilified me interminably. Finally, apparently afraid that I could not help her handle her unmodulated aggression, she threatened to stop and to go to a "competent" female Jewish psychiatrist for treatment, obviously a fantasied idealized mother surrogate who could tolerate Mrs. T's using her as a container. The second event occurred during a dramatic regression that lasted for over a week following episodes of like nature that had become more intense and frequent and had lasted longer, over a period of a year. Ultimately I responded to her having entered an altered ego state, during which she did almost nothing but scream obloquy, by withdrawing in my own way, eventually falling asleep. Again, she felt compelled to stop treatment, for the same reason, as I believe.

The first time, I made an interpretation I had formulated intellectually, one that I thought would enable her to reestablish relationships with me and use me as a container, rather than to continue to seek to evacuate her terrifying aggression "into space."

I viewed her then rather as an autistic child who sought to have relationships solely with something inhuman; I saw her space as an autistic object and sought to force her to pay attention to me rather than to the hypothesized space-autistic object. Tustin (1980, 1984) has found such separation of autistic child and autistic object to be mandatory before she could be used as a container.

The second time, I commanded her to return the next day, having quickly formulated a maneuver, again, as I believe, via secondary process thinking alone. I thought that what had happened had resulted from an emotional problem of my own, although I had no inkling about what it might have entailed.

That night I was insomniac but could not remember my dreams or hypnogogic or hypnopompic fantasies.

My unplanned interpretation to her was clearly the product of my repressed emotional reaction to her having left me during her altered ego states and spoken of her having felt that she was ripped apart while being considered to be an unwelcome pest. It was an intolerable reminder of my own early life experiences and my responses to them. My defensive withdrawal had culminated in my falling asleep. She had forced me to return to a relationship with her with her furious threat to actually abandon me. Subsequently, I forced her back into a relationship with me by my command, offering her logical alternatives and then my interpretation.

As had been the case throughout the year during which she had undergone the increasingly severe regressions while in the consultation room, she had been able to think logically much of the time when alone at home. She had never thought to tell me that she had come to love me deeply and totally platonically and idealized me as incomparably wise, the savior of all the Jews, as extensions of her nuclear family. She assumed that, in my ascribed omniscience, I knew. She had been sure that I could contain for her the rage that she had sought to empty into me to avoid killing her husband and son, and remained certain that that judgment was correct. When at home, she had known that she expected me to serve the functions she had read in Winnicott's writings that a good mother served for her infant, including making possible the "existence of a potential space within which I can be creative."

During the interview while she sat, my interpretation that she had sought to make me feel lonely had gratified her greatly and set off a new line of thought. The night before, she had become aware that her rage because I had fallen asleep had served to keep several painful phenomena from her awareness. She knew retrospectively of an intense fear that I had abandoned her through death as did in fact a previous therapist, although several years after she had left him and even though she had "forgotten" him. Likewise, she became cognizant that she had felt acutely alone when I drowsed. Earlier periods of having felt abandoned, frightened, and lonely returned from the repressed. When she had curled up in the chair, she had wanted to be held in my arms like a baby, and then remembered for the first time in many years what she had "always known," namely, that her mother had suffered from postpartum depressions requiring hospitalization after each child was born, and that she had been deprived of her actual mother throughout most of her early childhood.

H. A. Rosenfeld (1950) found that only precise interpretations were mutative in the psychoanalytic treatment of a man who suffered from confusional states. It will have been noted that the effective interpretations made to my patient were quite exact. In my experience, the potentially beneficial inexact interpretations of which Glover (1931) wrote are helpful more often in the treatment of neurotic than of regressed patients.

It would seem that the interpretation made on the basis of my having become aware of the countertransferential reasons, both intra- and inter-personal, for my falling asleep was markedly mutative. However, it was the culminative event of an overlapping series of phenomena, and it cannot be separated from them. Following the interpretation, Mrs. T was able to put aside using projective identification as a dominant defensive mechanism and to switch to more mature defensive operations. Bychowsky (1952) and Bion (1957) would say that her nonpsychotic personality now remained in ascendancy. The first memory to emerge following the culminative interpretation was her having been abandoned in infancy as a result of her mother's psychotic regression. We could say that in her renunciation of projective identification, that is, her psychotic personality, she renounced an identification with her mother. It then became possible for her to identify further with some of my traits.

The progress of her treatment was very unusual (in my experience) in that some significant degree of meaningful analysis of oedipal material preceded that of preoedipal material, following consistent interpretation of her use of projective identification as a defensive and communicative mechanism. Perhaps this special transference unfolding resulted from her individual constellation of experience. Her lifelong tendency to go into action, modulated somewhat during the oedipal and latency periods by the development of phobias and obsessive thinking, can be ascribed to her having learned only insecurely to use symbols and language to mediate between her feelings and identity or between herself and others (Deri 1984). She could mediate essentially only through action and projective identification, or, when there was no adequate container for the projections, through evacuation. Her father's personality made it impossible for him to serve as a mediator between her and her mother and him, too, she apparently deemed incapable of serving as a container for her projections. At least, however, he was kind.

We remember that throughout her life she openly fantasied sexual intimacy with him. Her actual observations were that no physical intimacy existed between her parents except for the primal scene activities from which she appears not to have been excluded and which she found to be frightening, stimulating, and confusing. During her childhood she secretly idealized her father and ascribed omniscience to him, while pretending that she agreed with her mother's evaluation of him as contemptible and worthless. She believed that he could tame her mother's alternately overt and covert hostility through the use of his penis.

In the transference, at least after I helped her to develop the capacity to order her thoughts and to prioritize behavior, she consciously ascribed omniscience and omnipotence to me, which I would use in helping her subdue her rage. We cannot forget that I was secretly viewed as Abba Eban.

During the year of the analysis of triadic relationship material, fantasies of my helping her control her rage by subduing her with my phallus were succeeded by deeply felt, loving fantasies of sexual relationships involving mutual giving and caretaking. She was able to have them in actual life with her husband during the last year of analysis. Perhaps, then, the reason for the unusual unfolding of the transference stemmed in part from her past and in part from my demonstrating to her that I could help her to develop the capacity to mediate between impulses and identity.

It would be difficult to overstate the importance of the provision of a facilitating environment in the treatment of regressed patients. Its elements are provided largely by the capacities of the therapist. The patient's personal security must ensure that the therapist retain objectivity and equilibrium during the patient's regressions and tolerate modulated experiences that are similar to those of the patient during some of his or her regressions. My temporary incapacity to do so was the basis for the impasse that went on essentially for a year in the treatment of Mrs. T although I did not recognize its presence. But other qualities of therapists are at least as important. They must be able above all to provide constancy and patience, to be able to abide, without more than transient despair, endlessly repetitive maladaptive behavior on the part of the patient, whose personality is being changed slowly while his actual object relationship development and transference experiences influence each other and are understood, as was discussed so well by Loewald (1960).

The question often arises whether analysts can successfully treat someone they do not like. My work with patients whom I viewed initially as disagreeable, contemptible, or otherwise unsavory has been successful in general. I believe this results in part because I see their personalities as indicative of the best they have been able to do in adjusting to their lifelong stresses, internal and external. Additionally, I am convinced that the analytic experience has a good chance of helping them to become less self-oriented and to develop the capacity to behave automatically in ways that seriously consider the rights of others. At the end of his long analysis that had sometimes tried the patience of both of us, a particularly disagreeable man who had changed remarkably said, "While your interpretations were crucial, they would have been useless but for your constancy, patience, and optimism, which gave me self-worth." Therapeutic optimism, then, based on experience, I deem to be a most important element in working with regressed patients.

In the regressed patient's development of a personality structure that is often very different in certain ways than at the beginning of analysis, he reexperiences early childhood in modified form in a better environment. Identifications with pathological aspects of prior caregivers are rendered unnecessary and replaced by healthier identifications with qualities of the analyst, primarily as mother surrogate. Obviously, I have no intention of underplaying the importance of the analyst as the surrogate of other people who are important in the rearing of children; I speak here only of the needs of patients while they are regressed.

CONCLUSION

Some patients whose sole conscious goal in therapy is to relieve themselves of tension can be viewed as continuing to use projective identification as a dominant defensive and interpersonal communicative mechanism. During the inevitable regressions that occur during psychoanalysis, they lose contact with the therapist as a potential container who might be able to hold and process their frightening aggression and/or libido and seek to discharge their terrifying feelings and the mental representations of their impulses into space. At such times the psychotic part of the patient's personality is in the ascendancy, presumably in identification with aspects of the mothering figure(s) of his infancy.

Ordinarily, the analysis of the psychotic part of his personality must be accomplished before the patient will be able to deal adequately with other psychic defects and conflicts. To be effective, interpretations that will help him to renounce his identification with psychotic aspects of his mother's personality and his achieving perhaps for the first time some elements of psychic structure must be made in a facilitating environment. The dominant element of that environment is the therapist who must have the ability to remain calm, objective, and optimistic and, at times, to undergo experiences that are similar to those of the patient during his inevitable and necessary regressions. The analysand is provided with and identifies with aspects of his analyst's personality as he develops the capacity to use symbols and language to mediate between his chaotic emotions and his personal identity.

Not uncommonly, the most effective interpretations are found to be those that stem from the analyst's use of his countertransferential responses to the patient's productions.

Viewing and interpreting the analytic session as if it were a dream facilitates the analyst's comprehension of the analytic process and gives him or her greater objectivity and security. The usual day residue of the session dream is the dominant unresolved transference issue of the preceding interview or interviews.

In working with regressed patients, the most effective interpretations are based frequently on information gathered through transference–countertransference interactions, interactions that often depend on the patient's projective and the analyst's introjective identification.

A group of regressed analytic patients seek to rid themselves of tension predominantly by evacuating or projecting their unconscious fantasies into the analyst. A fragment of the analysis of such a patient illustrates how her fantasies could not be adequately contained by the analyst because they revived in him inadequately resolved conflicts from early childhood, conflicts that resembled closely those being relived by the patient. His reacting by falling asleep created an emergency that was resolved by his making an unplanned interpretation that proved to be significantly mutative, a "turning point."

References

Balint, M. (1968). *The Basic Fault. Therapeutic Aspects of Regression.* New York: Brunner/Mazel, 1979.

Bion, W. R. (1957). Differentiation of the psychotic and non-psychotic personalities. In *Second Thoughts. Selected Papers on Psycho-Analysis*, pp. 43–64. New York: Jason Aronson, 1967.

——— (1962). A theory of thinking. In *Second Thoughts. Selected Papers on Psycho-Analysis*, pp. 110–119. New York: Jason Aronson, 1967.

——— (1967). *Second Thoughts. Selected Papers on Psycho-Analysis.* New York: Jason Aronson.

Boyer, L. B. (1961). Provisional evaluation of psycho-analysis with few parameters in the treatment of schizophrenia. *International Journal of Psycho-Analysis* 42:389–403.

——— (1983). *The Regressed Patient.* New York: Jason Aronson.

——— (1986). Technical aspects of treating the regressed patient. *Contemporary Psychoanalysis* 22:25–44.

——— (1988). Thinking of the interview as if it were a dream. *Contemporary Psychoanalysis* 24:275–281.

Boyer, L. B., and Giovacchini, P. L., eds. (1990). *Master Clinicians on Treating the Regressed Patient.* Northvale, NJ: Jason Aronson.

Bychowsky, G. (1952). *Psychotherapy of Psychosis.* New York: Grune & Stratton.

Chiozza, L. A. (1976). *Cuerpo, Afecto y Lenguaje. Psicoanálisis y Enfermedad Somática.* Buenos Aires: Paidós.

Demers-Desrosiers, L. (1982). Influence of alexithymia on symbolic function. *Psychotherapy and Psychosomatics* 38:103–120.

Deri, S. K. (1984). *Symbolization and Creativity.* New York: International Universities Press.

Fain, M. (1966). Regression et psychosomatique. *Revue Française de Psychanalyse* 30:451–456.

Federn, P. (1952). *Ego Psychology and the Psychoses.* New York: Basic Books.

Fenichel, O. (1945). *The Psychoanalytic Theory of the Neuroses.* New York: W. W. Norton.

Fliess, R. (1953). Counter-transference and counter-identification. *Journal of the American Psychoanalytic Association* 1:268–284.

Freud, S. (1912). Recommendations to physicians practicing psycho-analysis. *Standard Edition* 112:109–112.

Garma, A. (1962). *El Psicoanálisis. Teoría, Clínica, y Técnica.* Buenos Aires: Paidós.

Giovacchini, P. L. (1967). The frozen introject. In *Psychoanalysis of Character Disorders*, pp. 29–40. New York: Jason Aronson.

――― (1986). *Structural Pathology. Transitional Space in Breakdown and Creative Development.* Northvale, NJ: Jason Aronson.

――― (1989). *Countertransference Triumphs and Catastrophes.* Northvale, NJ: Jason Aronson.

Glover, E. (1931). The therapeutic effect of inexact interpretation: a contribution to the theory of suggestion. *International Journal of Psycho-Analysis* 12:397–411.

Green, A. (1975). The analyst, symbolization and absense in the analytic setting (on changes in analytic practice and analytic experience). *International Journal of Psycho-Analysis* 50:1–22.

Greenacre, P. (1975). On reconstruction. *Journal of American Psychoanalytic Association* 23:693–712.

Grinberg, L. (1979). Countertransference and projective counteridentification. *Contemporary Psychoanalysis* 15:226–247.

Grunberger, B. (1971). *Le Narcissisme. Essais de Psychanalyse.* Paris: Payot.

Hann-Kende, F. (1933). On the role of transference and countertransference in psychoanalysis. In *Psychoanalysis and the Occult*, ed. G. Devereux, pp. 158–167. New York: International Universities Press.

Heimann, P. (1950). On counter-transference. *International Journal of Psycho-Analysis* 31:60–76.

Jacobs, T. J. (1986). On countertransference enactments. *Journal of the American Psychoanalytic Association* 34:289–308.

Khan, M. M. R. (1964). Ego-distortion, cumulative trauma and the role of reconstruction in the analytic situation. In *The Privacy of the Self*, pp. 59–68. New York: International Universities Press, 1974.

――― (1974). *The Privacy of the Self.* New York: International Universities Press.

Little, M. (1981). *Transference and Countertransference.* New York: Jason Aronson.

Loewald, H. (1960). The therapeutic action of psychoanalysis. In *Papers on Psychoanalysis*, pp. 221–256. New Haven, CT: Yale University Press, 1980.

――― (1979). Reflections on the psychoanalytic process and its therapeutic potential. In *Papers on Psychoanalysis*, pp. 372–383. New Haven: Yale University Press, 1980.

――― (1980). Transference–countertransference. In *Papers on Psychoanalysis*, pp. 372–383. New Haven: Yale University Press.

Marty, P., M'Uzan, M. de, and David, C. (1963). *L'Investigation Psychosomatique. Sept Observations Cliniques.* Paris: Presses Universitaires de France.

McDougall, J. (1972). L'antianalysant en analyse. *Revue Française de France* 36:167–184.

———— (1978). Countertransference and primitive communication. In *Plea for a Measure of Abnormality*, pp. 247–298. New York: International Universities Press.

———— (1985). *Theaters of the Mind. Illusion and Truth on the Psychoanalytic Stage.* New York: Basic Books.

———— (1989). *Theaters of the Body. A Psychoanalytic Approach to Psychosomatic Illness.* New York: W. W. Norton.

Nacht, S. (1963). *La Presence du Psychanalyse.* Paris: Presses Universitaires de France.

Ogden, T. H. (1985). On potential space. *International Journal of Psycho-Analysis* 66:129–142.

———— (1986). *The Matrix of the Mind. Object Relations and the Psychoanalytic Dialogue.* Northvale, NJ: Jason Aronson.

Ornstein, A., and Ornstein, P. (1975). On the interpretive process in schizophrenia. *International Journal of Psychoanalytic Psychotherapy* 4:219–271.

Racker, H. (1953). The contribution to the problem of countertransference. *International Journal of Psycho-Analysis* 34:313–324.

———— (1968). *Transference and Countertransference.* New York: International Universities Press.

Rosenfeld, H. A. (1950). Note on the psychopathology of confusional states in chronic schizophrenia. *International Journal of Psycho-Analysis* 31:132-137.

———— (1966). Discussion of "Office Treatment of Schizophrenia" by L. Bryce Boyer. *Psychoanalytic Forum* 1:351–353.

Searles, H. F. (1953). Dependency processes in the psychotherapy of schizophrenia. *Journal of the American Psychoanalytic Association* 3:19–66.

———— (1976). Transitional processes and therapeutic symbiosis. In *Countertransference and Related States. Selected Papers*, pp. 503–576. New York: International Universities Press, 1979.

———— (1979). *Countertransference and Related States. Selected Papers.* New York: International Universities Press.

Taylor, G. J. (1984). Alexithymia: concept, measurement, and implications for treatment. *American Journal of Psychiatry* 141:725–732.

Tustin, F. (1980). Autistic objects. *International Review of Psycho-Analysis* 7:27–39.

———— (1984). Autistic shapes. *International Review of Psycho-Analysis* 11:280–288.

Volkan, V. D. (1976). *Primitive Internalized Object Relationships. A Clinical Study of Schizophrenic, Borderline and Narcissistic Patients.* New York: International Universities Press.

Waldinger, R. J. (1987). Intensive psychodynamic therapy with borderline patients: an overview. *American Journal of Psychiatry* 144:267–274.

Waldinger, R. J., and Gunderson, J. G. (1987). *Effective Psychotherapy with Borderline Patients. Case Studies.* New York: Macmillan.

Winnicott, D. W. (1947). Hate in the countertransference. In *Collected Papers*, pp. 194–203. New York: Basic Books, 1958.

——— (1971). *Playing and Reality.* New York: Basic Books.

12

The Verbal Squiggle Game in Treating the Seriously Disturbed Patient

INTRODUCTION

During almost half a century of treating seriously regressed patients psychoanalytically, I have become convinced that working through the countertransference is indispensable for a favorable therapeutic outcome.

My training began in the 1940s in an ultraconservative training institute where the psychoanalytic treatment of Freud's "narcissistic neuroses" was strongly disapproved. Only the patient's intrapsychic dynamics were to determine the nature and timing of interpretations. As was the custom in North America, Freud's oft-reiterated ambivalence and contradictions concerning the nature and utility of countertransference were essentially ignored (Boyer 1994); it was seen solely as the therapist's pathological response. Doubting Freud's bases for eschewing such treatment of regressed patients (Boyer 1967), largely on the basis of lifelong experience with a periodically psychotic mother and lack of success in working in a traditional way with regressed patients, I experimented systematically, despite the heated disapprobation of my mentors (Boyer 1961, 1966).

In my experiment of using psychoanalysis for the treatment of the

226 COUNTERTRANSFERENCE AND REGRESSION

seriously disturbed patient, it soon became apparent that the analysand's fears of his aggression constituted a major obstacle. Setting a framework of conditions of therapy, deviations from which were spoken of overtly and promptly and suitably interpreted, assisted in bringing the patient's and analyst's hostility and/or his or her anxiety about it into focus. This structuring reduced the tendency of both analyst and analysand to express their unconscious thoughts, feelings, impulses, and memories in action (Casement 1982). I am more comfortable when the patient's scrutiny does not hinder my access to my own state of reverie (Bion 1962a); therefore my patients use the couch.

It is now generally agreed that transference–countertransference relations can be studied only in terms of container and contained and that those relations are much more easily understood and interpretable in the presence of a consistent analytic frame, deviations from which are not ignored (Bion 1962a,b, 1963, 1987, Modell 1976). As Ogden (1994) has discussed, the analyst must have the capacity to be aware not only of the patient's transference and simultaneously his own countertransference reactions; in addition he must develop the capacity to allow an analytic (intersubjective) third to be elaborated, understood, and eventually interpreted.[1] I completely agree. Additionally, in my judgment, the maintenance of the analytic frame is *mandatory* for the successful treatment of severely disturbed patients.

It is my view that whatever the analyst experiences during the analytic session is influenced heavily by his idiosyncratic introjection and reformulation of the patient's verbal and nonverbal communications containing his or her projections. We should not be misled into thinking our stray, apparently unrelated thoughts, fantasies, physical or emotional reactions can be dismissed as idle preoccupations, taking us away from the business at hand, interfering with our free-floating or evenly hovering attention (Boyer and Doty 1993).

---

1. Other significant contributors to the development of a theory of countertransference include E. Balint et al. (1993), M. Balint (1968), Blechner (1992), Bleger (1962), Bollas (1987), Etchegoyen (1991), Gabbard (1991), Giovacchini (1989), Green (1975), Grinberg (1957, 1962), Grotstein (1981), Heimann (1950, 1960), Jacobs (1991), Joseph (1975, 1985), Kernberg (1985), Little (1951, 1957), McLaughlin (1991), Meltzer (1975), Milner (1969), Money-Kyrle (1956), Ogden (1982, 1986, 1989), Pallaro (1994), Pick (1985), Racker (1952, 1958), D. Rosenfeld (1992), Sandler (1976), Searles (1979), Steiner (1993), Symington (1983), Tansey and Burke (1989), Volkan (1981, 1995), Winnicott (1947).

However, I do not infer that everything the analyst thinks or feels should be considered countertransference. It is clear that factors other than introjection of the patient's projections are significantly operative in the analyst's perceptions of his patient's communications. The analyst's prevailing emotional state and individual conflicts, repressed or otherwise, will determine his degree of openness to the patient's communications.

THE VERBAL SQUIGGLE GAME

Observing that analysands often continue symbolically the themes of one interview to the next led me to seek to view each analytic session as though it were a dream, in which the major unresolved transference–countertransference issue of the last or last few sessions composes the "day residue" (Boyer 1988). I now assume that *every* communication of the interview very likely may in some way be related to that day residue in the context of the ensuing "dream" and am particularly interested in the symbolic meanings of the opening verbal and/or nonverbal communications. I believe that viewing the interview as if it were a dream serves as a part of, leads to the background for, or constitutes a part of the verbal squiggle game, in which the analyst is prepared to enter a mild reverie. Occasionally, as a session opens, analysands visualize events from the previous meeting as "scenes" on a wall or an imaginary movie screen (Lewin 1948).

My usual technical orientation involves my seeking to be, in the words of E. Balint (1993), "quiet and nonintrusive, but also absolutely *there*," while "the patient is occupied in finding his own words or actions" (p. 4). The length of the period during which I retain this relatively passive role while receiving stimuli actively through all my senses depends on the capacity of the patient to accept and profitably use my tentative interpretations. This state rarely lasts longer than a few months, at the end of which time I usually feel quite relaxed in the presence of my analysand and frequently find myself in a light trance during which fantasies and primary process thinking are often intermixed with my more customary social thinking.

As I find myself progressively both more at ease and able to associate more freely, I usually find myself anxiety-free as I offer trial interpretations to be considered by the analysand. I wait less long for the analysand to recall formerly offered material inconsistent with present data and more actively suggest that the patient's conflictual or genetic explanations of anxiety might be modified by alternate explanations. As we become more accustomed to one another, in my role as analytic third I am aware that my introjections are not infrequently psychosomatic: a tightness in the chest, muscle group tensions, abdominal cramps, or barely perceptible odors or tastes, transient, vague visual phenomena. I assume that they reflect the preverbal or presymbolic nature of the patient's unconscious communication of his anxiety. Further, I become more trusting that my perceptions accurately reflect the patient's unconscious projections and feel freer to interpret on the basis of my countertransference reactions. My notion is that at times when the patient and I are (in varying degrees) simultaneously comfortably regressed, we both enter a sort of recapitulation of the hypothetical symbiotic phase of the mother–infant dual unity (Benedek 1949, Loewald 1980, Mahler and McDevitt 1982). As Poggi (personal communication) observes: Part of the countertransference experience with certain patients is a sharing of body boundary confusion that, for a time, leaves me uncertain of my own sensation and therefore of my own distinct physical response to the presence of the patient. A good deal of what is ultimately imagined in the course of such a countertransference experience is built on these now confused sensations.

Winnicott (1958, 1965) has stressed the need of the analyst to be able to allow the existence of potential space in which creativity can occur, and Bion (1962a) the need for the analyst to enter into a "reverie," allowing a similar development. I find my most exhilarating and productive periods when working with regressed patients to occur during those unusual occasions when, while in the state of reverie to which I believe Bion to refer, I quite comfortably and spontaneously play what I conceive to be a verbal version of Winnicott's (1971) "squiggle game" with the patient. At such times the analysand and I have become subjective objects to one another. We do not use pencils but instead create our "drawings" verbally when the patient's and therapist's associations are obviously contaminated by one another. Then they meet in that potential space in which creativity can occur, enacting an intensification of a verbal squiggle game. (See also Deri 1984 and Grolnick 1990.)

CLINICAL ILLUSTRATION

During the verbal squiggle game the thinking of both analysand and analyst can most flexibly and cogently switch, without conflict, to the uses of autistic-contiguous (Ogden 1989), paranoid-schizoid, and depressive modes of generating experience. It is most doubtful that such an interchange could take place in a therapeutic endeavor in which the analytic frame had not been consistently maintained, or in which the therapist was uncomfortable during the patient's sometimes psychotic regressions (presumably because of anxiety concerning the analyst's own aggressive or libidinal urges, his anxiety concerning his own sanity, his capacity to maintain the analytic frame, and so on).

I record extensive process notes during interviews; in my notes I seek to include my own fantasies, physical sensations, and emotional changes. The clinical example that follows is not literally accurate because it is partially reconstructed.

This reported event is unusual in that it *heralded* a salutary regression during which crucial new information emerged. In the service of time and space, the report, which was quite repetitious, is abbreviated.

Dr. J was a middle-aged psychoanalyst whose three previous analyses had not helped him stop overtly acting out sexually with his clients. During the third year of his treatment with me, he was able to regress sufficiently to be able to recover memories he validated subsequently as portraying actual events in his life. The introductions to the memories were recovered during an interview in which we played for the first time the verbal squiggle game, a spontaneous activity that surprised us only retrospectively, even though his interviews were customarily characterized by emotional flatness and heightened intellectualization. He had never mentioned fairy tales, folklore, or interest in anthropology. He learned consciously of my concern with them when he read many of my writings, beginning some months after our first episode of playing the squiggle game.

He customarily entered the consultation room moving briskly and looking hyperalert. Nevertheless, Dr. J never appeared to be aware of any of the room's contents, noting rarely and only in passing changes in my facial expressions, dress, and/or moods, and never revealing his fantasies concerning them, either spontaneously or when questioned. No stable transference relationship had developed. For brief periods I appeared to be the cold, potentially undependable phallic mother of a preoedipal boy whose rare apparent kindnesses would lead to her suddenly and unexpectedly physically hurting him for vaguely defined pleasures of her own, often associated with bathroom activities. At others I seemed to represent his violent, morally weak, sexually exhibitionistic, paranoid, greedy father who beat his young children during temper tantrums, the causes of which were ascribed by Dr. J to his father's being cheated in business, probably by Nazi agents. Ordinarily, I seemed to be solely an impersonal colleague.

Some months previous to the interview to be reported I had redecorated the consultation room, changing the decor to African, using bright textiles and ebony statuary. At the foot of the couch was the figure of a seated man holding a large musical instrument on his lap, reaching around it to the strings. The top of the instrument consisted of a head facing forward. The head was almost identical to, but just smaller than, that of the man, and barely beneath it. Although Dr. J seemed unaware of the changed appearance of the room, during the interview he remarked, without affect or apparent connection to other thoughts, that he had read that aboriginal women sometimes had retractable dentate penises in their vaginas. Some sessions later he mentioned, apparently totally out of context and without connection to any other verbal material or discernible event or curiosity, that as a young boy he once wondered whether a discoloration on the bathroom wall were blood. During some six subsequent months, there was neither further mention of either of those themes nor reference to the room's decorations.

The day before the session to be described, Dr. J had reported a fragment of a dream in which the vague, immobile figure of a man who reminded him of an infamous and widely known effeminate polo player of whom he had recently read, seated on a horse. The polo player was reputed to be cruel to the mares he rode by choice, sometimes beating or poking them with his mallet. No action occurred in the dream, which was related without emotion or curiosity. I felt certain that the dream depicted symbolically the nature of the dominant transference situation of the previous session, apparently shaped by a fear that as a phallic mother I would use him for my own gratifications. I wondered silently whether the dream was a manifestation of a screen memory of early life events, involving disappointment, sadism, and betrayal in a bedroom setting, because of the inferred horseback riding and the cruelty of the polo player.

The patient's appearance and attitude as he entered the consultation room for his next session were unprecedented. In contrast with his usual brisk motions, hypervigilant, rigid pose on the couch, and matter-of-fact speech, on this day Dr. J came in looking as though he were not yet fully awake, and seemed to float to the couch, where he lay relaxed and silent, and, for the first time, appeared to be in a light trance. I felt myself also entering an altered ego state, and found myself feeling psychologically split, observing him, myself, and our intersubjectivity detachedly, while being simultaneously deeply involved. I revisualized his dream and silently thought he would talk of the statue and turn to passive homosexual fears.

After a time he said he had just noticed the statue for the first time and wondered whether it were of a mother and her son. She seemed to be holding him too intimately and trying to bring his "bottom" closer to her "pelvis."

I heard myself saying, "Perhaps to touch his bottom with the penis that can come out?" Unsurprised and clearly pleased, he immediately responded:

> *Dr. J:* The phallic witch was going to eat Hansel and Gretel but they pushed her into the oven.
> *Analyst:* Then she couldn't eat them or use the dentate phallus.
> *Dr. J:* No.

Dr. J fell silent and dreamily looked about the room, eventually asking whether the previously unmentioned colorful textiles were newly there. After further silence:

> *Dr. J:* There was blood on the wall of the bedroom and I was so terrified I couldn't think or move.
> *Analyst:* Several months ago you mentioned wondering whether a discoloration on the *bathroom* wall were blood.

He became silent, seemed bewildered, lifted his hands in a gesture of self-protection, and spoke what sounded like mumbled Yiddish. I felt distinctly eerie, and wondered silently whether he would imagine that a man were threatening to enter the room through the closed and locked door at his feet. After a few moments of silence, Dr. J said he had thought he had seen a man's shadow on the closed door at his feet.[2]

> *Analyst:* When you were mumbling, I thought I heard you say *golem* and *dybbuk*.
> *Dr. J:* Yes, I thought I did too, although I don't think I know what those words mean, except that I think they pertain to dead people.[3]

---

2. Freud (1899, 1900, 1904, 1922, 1933) and others (Devereux [1953], Major [1983], and Zwiebel [1977, 1984]) have written about the presence of telepathy in psychoanalysis and its part in occasional countertransference reactions.

3. I had an imprecise understanding of the words *golem* and *dybbuk* only because some months previously I had been editing an article on ancient Jewish folklore in conjunction with other work.

I commented that he had never spoken Yiddish previously in my presence. He was unsurprised and said he had thought he had forgotten that childhood language. After a long, contemplative silence, he continued:

> *Dr. J:* It's my uncle. He's coming through the door and I'm glad to see him, especially because my mother is angry with me and hurting me. (*Dr. J did not amplify.*) He was nice to me when he visited, holding me. I think I never saw him after I was about 7.
> *Analyst:* He held you in his lap after mother hurt you?
> *Dr. J (becoming alert):* I didn't know then that he was a *golem* or a *dybbuk.* I only learned that when studying for my bar mitzvah, and reading assigned literature. . . . When I was 4 or 5, he used to lie on the bed with me and hold me. (*Reentering his trance*) I feel warm and comforted and loved. I don't mind when he hurts my little asshole with his big cock, I just want to please him. . . . (*Regaining alertness*) It's only later that I know that he's just using me as a thing and I have to become catatonic.

It is impossible, I think, to judge the degree of transferential compliance with my unconscious wish. Three previous patients had seen the ebony figure as two men in sexual relationships. That I was unaware of a wish that Dr. J would join them in his idiosyncratic use of the statue does not, of course, mean that such a wish was absent. His compliance with his uncle's wish could well have been recapitulated in the transference.

This condensed episode of the squiggle game was the first and most dramatic of several during the three ensuing years of his analysis. It provided the first revelation that Dr. J had suffered a childhood psychosis that he subsequently relived for months in the consultation room. During regressive episodes, Dr. J did indeed relive in the transference–countertransference relationship catatonic-like regressions that recapitulated actual and symbolized psychotic experiences of his boyhood that had occurred between perhaps 3 and 10 years of age. The details recapitulated his being at times convinced that I was one of his parents or a golem or a dybbuk. Such regressed episodes were limited to periods when he was in the consultation room. They closely resembled forgotten episodes during his early grammar school years when he was under psychiatric care and hospitalized briefly.

For some days at a time, while regressed into a mild form of waxy flexibility, he spoke of the man in the transitory hallucination of his uncle coming through the doorway as a previously "unremembered" uncle whom his parents had act as babysitter for Dr. J from age 3 to 7. He never remembered exactly when or how he learned that his uncle, to his parents' knowledge, had been a convicted pederast.

Analysis of aspects of his perceptions and experiences during his "squiggle games" continued until the end of his analysis. The blood that had been visualized initially as on the bedroom wall was eventually identified as being spots on menstrual rags that had been thrown against the bathroom wall, but displaced in the vision to the bedroom, probably because of his earlier conviction that mother bled after being injured by the father's "mallet" and by his own body, during his birth.

Gradually, during various ensuing regressive episodes that included delusions of being possessed by, or himself, an automaton, he reread Jewish folklore and remembered that he had learned about *golems* and *dybbuks* in Hebrew school. He brought examples of the folklore literature to interviews and read aloud that *dybbuk* refers to "an evil spirit possessing man, or the soul of a dead person residing in another's body and acting through it" and that, conversely, *golem* represented both the shapeless stage of Adam or an embryo and an artificial man, an automaton (Neilson et al. 1949). He also brought other references to the consultation room, some written in Hebrew (Dan 1970, Ginsburg 1913, Idel 1989).

Dr. M recalled that in his early childhood he had been singularly frightened after having heard a recitation of Hansel and Gretel (Grimm and Grimm 1819), being concerned with the themes of being deserted by his parents and of cannibalism.

DISCUSSION

In this presentation and elsewhere I have presented examples of ways that analyzing countertransference experience has had salutary effects during the analyses of regressed patients.[4]

Here I further the discussion of work within the countertransference by describing an example of a verbal squiggle game. In such intersubjective play between analyst and analysand, a generative space is available to each through which new understanding and conceptualizations can emerge, the creativity to which Winnicott often refers. I believe this space to be the

---

4. Boyer 1961, 1966, 1972, 1976, 1977, 1978, 1982, 1986, 1989, 1992, 1993, 1994.

space meant by A. Rosenfeld (1952), that is, the most powerful link between the patient's dissociated states.

Such space exists, when it does, through the efforts of the analyst who, within a reverie, adapts himself to the task of attending to both subjective and intersubjective experience. This vital splitting of experience on the part of the analyst is essential to the process of intersubjectivity within the analytic hour, and the sine qua non of the interpretation not only of countertransference material but *through* the countertransference. Accurate interpretation through the countertransference gives lease to a play space through which the analysand, in both his separateness and within the analytic third, newly and creatively expresses his experience.

During such episodes of play, the space's potential for linking dissociated aspects of the analysand's experience is potentiated. I believe that the new connections between previously dissociated states depend on the analyst's ability to tolerate such a type of splitting within himself.

To tolerate such internal flexibility, the analyst himself must have been well analyzed by a therapist who was capable of tolerating deep regressive episodes undergone by his patients during their analyses (Racker 1958). An analyst who does not enable his patient to live through deep regressions during treatment cannot have developed the capacity to experience the inevitable reciprocal countertransference and to learn to use it in the service of treatment, or to teach his analytic trainees. Also, it is possible, although I consider it to be unlikely, that the life experiences of the analyst may have to have been exceptional and his neurophysiological endowments may need to be of a nature that permits special sensitivities. Those sensitivities allow him to experience without great conflict and work through the countertransference he experiences while analyzing such regressions.

It is difficult to tolerate this kind of splitting, particularly to admit the highly personal, private, and embarrassingly mundane aspects of one's subjective experience (Ogden 1994). Beyond this, such experiences can be felt as a threat to one's sense of lucidity. At times one must permit links to fall away in order to perceive the greater trail of the chain: madness may be experienced in fantasy or body.

Equally important as interpretations made through the countertransference are the tolerance and containment of this splitting process. We cannot value too highly the patient's introjection of an analytic object of equanimity, which so clearly rests on the capacity for integration of part-object, whole-object relatedness, the capacity for concern, and a sense of optimism (Doty, personal communication). It must not be forgotten that patients who suffer from Freud's narcissistic neuroses frequently, if not always, have not developed a well-grounded sense of self; this sense of self will arise through the gradual internalization and maturation of the object relationships developed with the analyst during the course of analysis; we can think of Mahler's (1968) "vicissitudes of individuation."

I would like to expand the idea that each interview may be viewed as a dream. As all communications (of both analyst and analysand) are in some way related to the day residue of the enduring "dream," it can be most fruitful for the analyst to apply the tenets of dream analysis to the flow of associations obtained through attention to the subjective/intersubjective process (Doty, personal communication).

SUMMARY

Successful psychotherapeutic work with severely disturbed patients necessitates an intensification of the analyst's attention to his intrapsychic countertransference experiences stemming from his conscious and unconscious interactions with his patient. The countertransference reactions manifest themselves as psychical, emotional, and somatosensory perceptions. The effectiveness of the analyst's work is heightened by his formulating his interpretations on the basis of those intrapsychic experiences. Interpreting *through* the countertransference implies the analyst's ability to tolerate a psychic split, simultaneously thinking for himself while with the analysand. During temporary regressions to presymbolic modes of experience that allow for the retrieval and exchange between analyst and analysand of primary-process-related fantasies in verbal forms of Winnicott's "squiggle game," the analyst must also be capable of concurrently maintaining an observing ego stance that is informed by secondary process thinking.

Case material demonstrates how countertransference-informed interpretations foster the disturbed patient's engagement in the therapeutic process and help him recover repressed memories of early infantile psychic trauma. Through the analyst's complementary regression to and simultaneous interpretation of the analysand's autistic-contiguous and schizoparanoid modes of experience, the patient is enabled to introject the analytic object. This introjection allows for the patient's concurrent experience and integration of part-object and whole-object relatedness, which, in turn, contributes to the development of a stable sense of self.

Interpreting through the countertransference implies not only that the analyst has worked through primitive mental states during his own personal analysis, but that he also works strictly within the analytic frame. Maintaining the frame is essential for the analysis of the patient's hostility, anxiety, and defense mechanisms, and materially reduces the probability of the patient's and the analyst's acting out and acting in.

References

Balint, E., Mitchell, J. L., and Parsons, M., eds. (1993). *Before I Was I. Psychoanalysis and the Imagination.* New York: Guilford.

Balint, M. (1968). *The Basic Fault.* London: Tavistock.

Benedek, T. (1949). The psychosomatic implications of the primary unit: mother–child. *American Journal of Orthopsychiatry* 19:642-654.

Bion, W. R. (1962a). *Second Thoughts.* New York: Jason Aronson, 1967.

——— (1962b). *Learning from Experience.* New York: Basic Books.

——— (1963). *Elements of Psycho-Analysis.* In *Seven Servants.* New York: Jason Aronson, 1977.

——— (1987). *Clinical Seminars. Brasilia and São Paulo,* ed. F. Bion. Abingdon, Scotland: Fleetwood.

Blechner, M. (1992). Working in the countertransference. *Psychoanalytic Dialogues. A Journal of Relational Perspectives* 2:161–179.

Bleger, J. (1962). Modalidades de la relación objectal. *Revista de Psicoanálisis* 19:1–2.

Bollas, C. (1987). *The Shadow of the Object. Psychoanalysis of the Unknown Known.* New York: Columbia University Press.

Boyer, L. B. (1961). Provisional evaluation of psychoanalysis with few parameters employed in the treatment of schizophrenia. *International Journal of Psycho-Analysis* 42:389–403.

——— (1966). Office treatment of schizophrenic patients by psychoanalysis. *Psychoanalytic Forum* 1:337–356.

——— (1967). Historical development of psychoanalytic psychotherapy of the schizophrenias: Freud's contributions. In *Psychoanalytic Treatment of Schizophrenic and Characterological Disorders,* ed. L. B. Boyer and P. L. Giovacchini, pp. 50–75. New York: Science House.

——— (1972). A suicidal attempt by an adolescent twin. *International Journal of Psychoanalytic Psychotherapy* 1:7–30.

——— (1976). Meanings of a bizarre suicide attempt by an adolescent twin. *Adolescent Psychiatry* 4:371–381.

——— (1977). Working with a borderline patient. *Psychoanalytic Quarterly* 46:386–424.

——— (1978). Countertransference experiences in working with severely regressed patients. *Contempory Psychoanalysis* 14:48–72.

——— (1982). Analytic experiences in work with regressed patients. In *Technical*

Factors in the Treatment of the Severely Disturbed Patient, ed. P. L. Giovacchini and L. B. Boyer, pp. 65–106. New York: Jason Aronson.

——— (1986). Technical aspects of treating the regressed patient. *Contemporary Psychoanalysis* 22:25–44.

——— (1988). Thinking of the interview as though it were a dream. *Contemporary Psychoanalysis* 24:275–281.

——— (1989). Countertransference and technique in working with the regressed patient. Further remarks. *International Journal of Psycho-Analysis* 70:701–714.

——— (1992). Roles played by music as revealed through countertransference facilitated regression. *International Journal of Psycho-Analysis* 73:55–70.

——— (1993). Introduction: countertransference–brief history and clinical issues with regressed patients. In *Master Clinicians on Treating the Regressed Patient,* vol. 2, ed. L. B. Boyer and P. L. Giovacchini, pp. 1–22. Northvale, NJ: Jason Aronson.

——— (1994). Countertransference: condensed history and personal view of issues with regressed patients. *Journal of Psychotherapy Practice and Research* 3:122–137.

Boyer, L. B., and Doty, L. (1993). Countertransference, regression and an analysand's uses of music. In *Master Clinicians on Treating the Regressed Patient, Volume II,* ed. L. B. Boyer and P. L. Giovacchini, pp. 173–204. Northvale, NJ: Jason Aronson.

Casement, P. (1982). Some pressures on the analyst for physical contact during the reliving of an early trauma. *International Review of Psychoanalysis* 9:279–286.

Dan, Y. (1970). Maggid (In Hebrew). *Encyclopedia Hebraica* 22:139–140.

Deri, S. (1984). *Symbolization and Creativity.* New York: International Universities Press.

Devereux, G. (1953). *Psychoanalysis and the Occult.* New York: International Universities Press.

Etchegoyen, R. H. (1991). *The Fundamentals of Psychoanalytic Technique.* London: Karnac.

Freud, S. (1899). A premonitory dream fulfilled. *Standard Edition 5.*

——— (1900). The interpretation of dreams. *Standard Edition 4.*

——— (1904). Premonitions and chance: an excerpt. In *Psychoanalysis and the Occult,* ed. G. Devereux, pp. 52–55. New York: International Universities Press, 1953.

——— (1922). Dreams and telepathy. *Standard Edition 18.*

——— (1933). Dreams and the occult. New Introductory Lectures: Lecture XXX. *Standard Edition 22.*

Gabbard, G. (1991). Do we need theory? *Bulletin of the Menninger Clinic* 55:22–29.

Ginsburg, L. (1913). *The Legends of the Jews*. Vol. 4. Philadelphia: The Jewish Publication Society of America.

Giovacchini, P. L. (1989). *Countertransference Triumphs and Catastrophes*. Northvale, NJ: Jason Aronson.

Green, A. (1975). The analyst, symbolization and absence in the analytic setting. (On changes in analytic practice and analytic experience.) *International Journal of Psychoanalysis* 60:347–356.

Grimm, J., and Grimm, W. (1819). *Grimm's Fairy Tales for Young and Old. The Complete Stories*. Newly translated by R. Mannheim. Garden City, NY: Doubleday & Co.

Grinberg, L. (1957). Perturbaciones en la interpretación por la contraidentificación proyectiva. *Revista de Psicoanálisis* 14:23–28.

——— (1962). On a specific aspect of countertransference due to the patient's projective identification. *Contemporary Psychoanalysis* 15:226–245.

Grolnick, S. (1990). *The Work and Play of Winnicott*. Northvale, NJ: Jason Aronson.

Grotstein, J. S. (1981). *Splitting and Projective Identification*. New York: Jason Aronson.

Heimann, P. (1950). Counter-transference. *International Journal of Psycho-Analysis* 31:81–84.

——— (1960). Countertransference. *British Journal of Medical Psychology* 33:9–15.

Idel, M. (1989). Jewish magis from the early renaissance period to early Hasidism. In *Religion, Science and Magic*, ed. J. Neusner et al. New York: Oxford University Press.

Jacobs, T. (1991). *The Use of the Self. Countertransference and Communication in the Analytic Setting*. Madison, CT: International Universities Press.

Joseph, B. (1975). The patient who is difficult to reach. In *Tactics and Techniques in Psychoanalytic Therapy. II. Countertranceference*, ed. P. L. Giovacchini, A. Flarsheim, and L. B. Boyer, pp. 205–216. New York: Jason Aronson.

——— (1985). Transference: the total situation. *International Journal of Psycho-Analysis* 66:447–454.

Kernberg, O. F. (1985). *Internal World and External Fantasy*. Northvale, NJ: Jason Aronson.

Lewin, B. D. (1948). Inferences from the dream screen. *International Journal of Psycho-Analysis* 29:224–231.

Little, M. I. (1951). Counter-transference and the patient's response to it. In *Transference Neurosis and Transference Psychosis*, Chapter 2. New York: Jason Aronson, 1981.

——— (1957). "R"—the analyst's total response to his patient's needs. In *Transference Neurosis and Transference Psychosis*, Chapter 4. New York: Jason Aronson, 1981.

Loewald, H. (1980). *Papers on Psychoanalysis*. New Haven: Yale University Press.

Mahler, M. S. (1968). *On Human Symbiosis and the Vicissitudes of Individuation.* New York: International Universities Press.

Mahler, M. S., and McDevitt, J. B. (1982). Thoughts on emergence of the sense of self, with particular emphasis on the body self. *Journal of the American Psychoanalytic Association* 30:827–848.

Major, R., ed. (1983). *Confrontation: Telepathie.* Vol. 10. Paris: Aubier-Montaigne.

McLaughlin, J. (1991). Clinical and theoretic aspects of enactment. *Journal of the American Psychoanalytic Association* 39:595–614.

Meltzer, D. (1975). Adhesive identification. *Contemporary Psychoanalysis* 11:289–310.

Milner, M. (1969). *The Hands of the Living God.* London: Hogarth.

Modell, A. (1976). "The holding environment" and the therapeutic action of psychoanalysis. *Journal of the American Psychoanalytic Association* 24:285–308.

Money-Kyrle, R. (1956). Normal counter-transference and some of its deviations. *International Journal of Psychoanalysis* 37:360–366.

Neilson, W. A., Knott, T. A., and Carhart, P. W., eds. (1949). *Webster's New International Dictionary of the English Language,* 2nd ed., unabridged. Springfield, MA: G. & C. Merriam.

Ogden, T. H. (1982). *Projective Identification and Psychotherapeutic Technique.* New York: Jason Aronson.

———— (1986). *The Matrix of the Mind. Object Relations and the Psychoanalytic Technique.* Northvale, NJ: Jason Aronson.

———— (1989). *The Primitive Edge of Experience.* Northvale, NJ: Jason Aronson.

———— (1994). Projective identification and the subjugating third. In *Subjects of Analysis,* pp. 97–106. Northvale, NJ: Jason Aronson.

Pallaro, P. (1994). *Somatic countertransference: the therapist in relationship.* Paper presented at the Third European Arts Therapies Conference. Ferrara, Italy, September.

Pick, I. (1985). Working through in the counter–transference. In *Melanie Klein Today. Volume II. Mainly Practice,* ed. E. Spillius, pp. 34–47. London: Routledge, 1988.

Racker, E. (1952). Observaciones sobre la contratransferencia como instrumento técnico; comunicación preliminar. *Revista de Psicoanálisis* 9:342–354.

———— (1958). Classical and present techniques in psycho-analysis. In *Transference and Countertransference.* New York: International Universities Press, 1960, pp. 23–70.

Rosenfeld, D. (1992). Countertransference and the psychotic part of the personality. In *The Psychotic Part of the Personality,* pp. 79–100. London: Karnac.

Rosenfeld, H. A. (1952). Notes on the psychoanalysis of confusional states in chronic schizophrenia. *International Journal of Psycho-Analysis* 31:132–137.

———— (1987). *Impasse and Interpretation.* London: Tavistock.

Sandler, J. (1976). Countertransference and role responsiveness. *International Review of Psychoanalysis* 3:43–47.

Searles, H. (1979). *Countertransference and Related Subjects.* New York: International Universities Press.

Steiner, J. (1993). *Psychic Retreats. Pathological Organizations in Psychotic, Neurotic and Borderline Patients.* London: Routledge.

Symington, N. (1983). The analyst's act of freedom as agent of therapeutic change. *International Review of Psychoanalysis* 10:283–291.

Tansey, M., and Burke, W. (1989). *Understanding Countertransference: From Projective Identification to Empathy.* Hillsdale, NJ: Analytic Press.

Volkan, V. D. (1981). *Linking Objects and Linking Phenomena.* New York: International Universities Press.

——— (1995). *The Infantile Psychotic Self and Its Fates.* Northvale, NJ: Jason Aronson.

Winnicott, D. W. (1947). Hate in the countertransference. In *Collected Papers. Through Paediatrics to Psycho-Analysis*, pp. 194–203. New York: Basic Books, 1958.

——— (1958). *Collected Papers. Through Paediatrics to Psycho-Analysis.* New York: Basic Books.

——— (1965). *The Maturational Processes and the Facilitating Environment.* New York: International Universities Press.

——— (1971). *Playing and Reality.* New York: International Universities Press.

Zwiebel, R. (1977). Der Analytiker Träumt von seinem Patientin. *Psyche* 31:43–59.

——— (1984). Zur Dynamik des Gegenübertragunstraums. *Psyche* 38:193–213.

13

A Conversation with
L. Bryce Boyer

SUE VON BAEYER

A major contributor to psychoanalytic theory and practice for over forty years, Dr. Boyer has influenced generations of psychotherapists through his writing, teaching, and growling. He has been a major influence on my life and work and I eagerly accepted the opportunity to interview him.

I took him a homemade secret-recipe chocolate torte to sooth the annoyance that I expected from him once I began peppering him with my questions. It barely worked. I began by asking him if he could identify a few major ways his thinking had changed over the course of his life work.

LBB: "A few major ways?" You don't want much. What does that mean, "course of my life work"? When does my life work begin? Well, that isn't when my life work began, doing analysis. My life work began on the day I opened my eyes. And I would never think of the course of my life work as beginning when I became a psychoanalyst. Obviously my life work didn't begin with my being a doctor, or being a psychiatrist, or being a medical practitioner, or any such thing. How can one possibly answer a question like this, if one doesn't talk about the life influence of having had parents who hated each other, and a mother who hated her children, and a mother who tried to torture her children? Tortured me, not her second son. A person who in childhood has lived on a farm, lived on the edge of an Indian reservation, has investigated gopher holes and bird nests and pulled turds out of turkeys that were constipated. I early learned that there was no possibility of believing anything I was told. Nothing told to me by my mother at any rate, and she was the only one who was really important to me. No—my father, it turned out, was very important to me, even kept me sane, although I saw him very little. But my mother was a chronic liar and thief, and sadist. At the same time I adored her. I learned from my experience with my mother that there was no possibility of believing anything I was told. This was combined with her having been always grossly hysteric and periodically frankly delusional. So I had to discard what I was told, and I learned never to believe anything I was told, that I had to find out for myself what I should trust and believe. And I was a scientist. I was always a scientist, and I always believed in secondary logic, secondary process logic. At the same time I was highly intuitive. With my mother, for example, I could make a pretty good guess of when she was going to have a temper tantrum, or when she was going to have a paranoid attack, or when she was going to come after me with a knife and try to kill me, or wound me in some way. I usually got some glimpses, so that I was able to divert her attention in some way, sometimes I was able to show her that what she had in mind wasn't so. And I actually only got one knife cut deep enough to leave a scar.

I couldn't even trust what I read, and I read all the books on the second floor of the Salt Lake City Library while I was playing hooky from school. Why they let me stay in school I don't know, except I knew everything that they taught. School was very boring for me and I could give them back the answers that they wanted. I lived in the foothills near Salt Lake City and I learned on my own a good deal about geology and botany, and zoology. Particularly about plants. Life cycles. Collected bird eggs. Postage stamps. And I dreamed every night. My dream was always on the theme of being in some remote country, usually Africa, deep Africa, deep Asia, and learning their customs and learning how to get along with people. Learning that one *could* learn how to get along with people, if one had a steady response to something. I hated, *hated* being at home. But at the same time I thought it was my responsibility to take care of my brother, and I tried to take care of him. By the time I was 8 years old, because of my personal interpretation of a movie—what was the name of the movie? It was a Somerset Maugham movie. And my personal interpretation of that movie was that a young man lost his father, and rescued and saved his father. He met him by chance. His father was a heavy-duty, tuberculosis-ridden porter in a hotel, and the young man became a doctor and saved him. I was 8, I then decided to become a doctor. So I was going to get my father back and save him. Well, I was also going to save my brother from my mother's psychosis. This was the same brother who committed suicide.

Anyway, I couldn't leave my brother to my mother. I simply couldn't. So I didn't go whaling when I had the opportunity at age 16. I looked for work instead for that year. And then I got the scholarship down at Stanford and went down there. And I worked very, very, very hard, because I wanted to get through school as fast as I could. I developed a pattern of sleeping no more than three hours, four hours a night, because I loaded myself up with twenty-six units of science. Sixteen is customary, and what most advisors permit. Most of my classes were science classes. Science and language were all I ever learned, so I never got anything graceful out of college, you know. No art, no literature.

I tried to get into Stanford Medical School after my junior year. That was not permitted, but I got in after my senior year—did okay—I graduated with honors. But I didn't succeed with my brother. And my mother committed suicide when I was an adult. I don't know exactly when she committed suicide. This is a strange story. I had a schizophrenic patient, endlessly screaming and cursing, a schizophrenic patient who started screaming in the hall, and screamed vituperations throughout every interview. Well, anyway, my brother had committed suicide, shot his head off after an argument with his third wife. And she called up and said that he'd killed himself. And I thought that I would be able to see my patients anyway until the plane left later that morning, and I went to work. I'm sitting here, and that guy who screamed, he came to the door and he glanced at me. He said, "I can't do that to you today. I have to take care of you today." Okay. I said not a word during the entire interview. And he knew nothing, literally nothing about my life or family. But on the basis of his fantasies of why I was so depressed—I said nothing—on the basis of his fantasies and my somatic responses to his fantasies, by the end of the interview he told me my brother had committed suicide.

You started to ask a question.

SvB: Maybe you just answered it. I was going to ask what it is that allows your students to understand the way of working that your particular life led you to develop. But it sounds like, given what you've just said about this patient, it's that some people already have the capacity to tune in to you and in so doing, they understand something. You propose that the analyst go into a controlled, complementary regression.

LBB: Those are the right words.

SVB: . . . and your students learn how to do it, or they learn that it's okay to do it, or to not be afraid to do it?

LBB: Yes. I think we have to think of it in terms of Klein's projective identification, introjective identification. When I began training, I was taught ego psychology. And I was taught a very conservative ego psychology. But of course I didn't believe anything I was taught, I found out for myself. One of the things I was taught was that you never try to analyze a patient who suffered from a narcissistic neurosis. Well, I knew that was bullshit, because I could do that with my mother when I was 4. You know, so I went ahead, and worked that way. But I was confused a lot until I had regular, ongoing contact with Tom Ogden, my most recent guru. For me, Bertram Lewin was also a guru. My Christmas "neurosis" paper for example. I wrote that paper in 1953, when I was still a candidate, and it was accepted for presentation at the winter meeting of the American Psychoanalytic Association. Bertram Lewin asked to discuss it, and Sandor Lorand asked to discuss it, and René Spitz asked to discuss it. So I presented the paper, and Bertram Lewin begins to discuss the paper, and his discussion is so interesting, the next scheduled speaker said, "Hey, let's cancel my paper and have this discussion." So that's what happened. And that's the way I started out in national psychoanalytic circles. But among my mentors, Bertram Lewin thought a lot like Melanie Klein except that he was considerably more logical than she was. And I think that he was my main guru, through my correspondence with him. And Sandor Lorand, and others—Kurt Eissler. I couldn't really get along with *him* because he was so imbued with ego psychology, and he was just rigid. There was no talking to him about any of the edges of that. All this by correspondence, you understand. There was nobody in the San Francisco Society who taught me anything, except Siegfried Bernfeld, Erik Erikson, and a little bit Bernhard Berliner and Norman Reider. The person from whom I learned most at the San Francisco was a renegade, Donald Macfarlane, but he was not consistent in the way he taught.

Over the course of my life work I have come to believe, on the basis of my actual learning experiences, that if you can stand for them to, people, no matter how awful they are from the outside, have a wish to do as well as they can do. And this philosophy is in me—and I think that I learned this from these various people I've been talking with while doing field work with my cultural anthropologist wife—American Indians, Eskimos, Quechuas in Peru, and Laplanders in northern Finland, for example. Warlike natives, awfully warlike natives, who assumed I was sweet and wanted to be nice to them, and they didn't want to hurt me, you know?

People do the best they can do. And if the therapist has a notion that regardless of how repulsive or crude or paranoid or whatever a patient apparently is, this is the best he's been able to get to. And psychoanalysis is the method of choice, nothing else works. You must have the personal, emotional interplay of tolerating the introjection of whatever it is that's being projected into you, and must have also the capacity to have the observing analytic third at the side of it so that you don't react crudely to it. And you're also thinking about the meaning of why does the patient have to do this, and why does he have to try to get at me in that way. And the patient is meantime introjecting the kindness and love that you're supplying for him. It's understanding and forgiveness, and evaluating—if you can step aside and look. It's what Tom Ogden described as the essential element, the capacity to have the objective third that watches the way you feel and act, and the way the patient feels and acts, and tries to evaluate what goes on between you and the patient, assessing what your somatic sensations tell you as well as your overt thoughts. The question has to do with the space that in fantasizing is actualizing. It's enough sometimes to open my door and still be in a healthy range of humanness.

SvB: It's that combination, isn't it—the loving, containing, and accepting of the introjection?

LBB: Yes, and psychoanalysis is the method of choice because nothing else works. Secondary process teaching scarcely scratches the surface. And drugs sure as hell don't do anything to affect the psychopathological processes. Why I prefer psychoanalysis is its effectiveness.

SvB: And for some people it may not work?

LBB: For some people, like chronic disorganized schizophrenics, it can't work. And if the therapist doesn't have the capacity to develop this intersubjective third, and feel comfortable with complementary regression.

And also, therapists who do not have the awareness, or are not susceptible to developing the awareness that the person is doing the best he can do.

SvB: I am thinking again of this idea of controlled regression, because it seems like the depth of the understanding of the use of countertransference is the idea that I associate mainly with you. I don't know if you started out with that.

LBB: You can't start with that, you have to learn with it. You have to learn that from working intimately with borderline and psychotic patients. You can't start with it. Having a knowledgeable supervisor, I now know, is an inspiring, invaluable help.

SvB: When you are training people, it seems like what you're training them to do is to use their countertransference, understand it, translate it, so they can understand the deepest levels of the patient. Can you say something about how you teach this?

LBB: I teach by example, by joking, by telling stories. I think I taught more to a group the other day by telling the following story than I had taught them in months.

I was in the Army during World War II. I was in charge of a series of locked wards including one huge one, peopled by soldiers who had to be in straitjackets some of the time, and so forth. And one weekend I had 500 new patients in straitjackets assigned to me. Five hundred new patients, and I'm looking after the whole hospital without backup, for the weekend.

They had come from the South Pacific, and they were all terribly psychotic and had malaria and fungus infection till they looked eaten up. Oh, Jesus, what a sight! And here I am to look after them. And one of them looked so pitiful, and he said, "I really have to talk to you." And I said, "I can't. I can't talk to you now. I want you to write whatever it is that you want to tell me in a couple of notebooks and I'll see you as soon as I can. Okay?" He was well by the time I saw him four or five days later. He was *well*. No trace of psychosis whatsoever. And I asked him, "What the hell goes on here, you know, you were out of your mind?" He said, "I know I was out of my mind." I said, "And you were hallucinating and delusional" and he said, "I know those big words, and I know it's true." And he was smiling at me, and he was touching me. Big, tough, great big tough guy. And he said, "The reason I'm not sick anymore is I gave it to you in the notebooks." Thirty days later he left, well, and ten years later I got a letter from him. The letter said, "I've been watching you very carefully, because I've always been afraid that I had made you crazy by giving you my notebooks, and I am so happy that you're not, that you're famous and you're healthy and you're doing well and your family is doing well." And he knew all about me. He lived in Arkansas or Oklahoma or someplace but he knew all about me from reading I don't know what sources. And that was the story I told the students to make real to them the message of projective identification. And that it can be done by fantasy or words or letter, or it can be done by a dream, any means at all. And this is the way I teach. Some people think I'm joking when I'm telling stories, but most learn quickly that there's much more going on.

I think a very important element of my teaching is my optimism. I am damn sure that if people are able, if they themselves are able, and if they have a good personal analysis and enough life, élan, to be able to allow themselves to experience people's difficulties without being too personally changed themselves, then there's nothing that cannot be accomplished in working with psychological problems.

SvB: And that's where the importance of having had a good analysis comes in?

LBB: I think I'm pretty well analyzed.

SvB: And I've heard you say that it was because you found an analyst who wasn't afraid of you.

LBB: Who would let me regress to a frank psychosis in the office. He was not afraid of it, he wasn't afraid I'd kill him. He was not afraid when I was deluded. My identification with my third analyst is my identification with this capacity to allow a patient's regressions.

SvB: How did you develop your fascination with the Rorschach?

LBB: Fascination with the Rorschach? That's simple. My wife and at times two other anthropologists and I were working together with Apache Indians, living with them for fifteen months continuously. Two anthropologists were working on social structure, religion, economics, kinship, politics, stuff like that. My wife was working on that plus mythology plus child-rearing patterns and the relations between children and their parents and their brothers and sisters, and I was doing psychoanalytic psychotherapy. The Indians were coming to me for help with personal problems. But how could I expect to learn about the personality of the old people? The young and middle-aged people came voluntarily and responded to transference interpretations. So I finally figured the best I could do was to administer the Rorschach test, and see how much of their personalities I could learn from the Rorschach. The way I started out was I did Rorschachs on all of the old people—I have to give you some history, though.

The Chiricahuas were taken as prisoners of war in 1886 and sent to jail in Florida and then Alabama, and eventually relocated in Oklahoma, still as prisoners of war. The Mescaleros who are very closely related to them stayed in their homelands, and they were run by the Bureau of Indian Affairs, and more laxly. The people who were sent to Alabama and Florida and later to Oklahoma gradually identified with the enlisted men of the army, rather than old-time Apache ways. They gradually became more and more like enlisted men in the Army, as did their progeny. The Indians that I dealt with were released from Oklahoma in 1913, that is, after twenty-seven years of being prisoners of war. And I found the Rorschachs of the two groups were very different. The old people of the Mescaleros had very specific kinds of ways of communicating, and the old people of the Chiricahuas had very different ways, which happened to be almost identical to the ways that poor whites respond to Rorschachs. Well, I thought this was fascinating. I didn't know Bruno Klopfer at that time but he was the most famous Rorschachist around. I wrote to him and told him I wanted to experiment with him, and he was delighted. And I sent him some fifty protocols of Rorschachs taken from old Chiricahuas and Mescaleros; I told him I was sending him Rorschachs from two groups of Native Americans and I didn't tell him anything about them. I wanted him to tell me about them. So he accurately separated the two groups. One group of Apaches acted like aboriginals, and the other group acted like poor whites—100 percent. And so I started sending Rorschachs of individuals and families, and we went to Carmel, where he was living, for a couple of weeks and learned how to better administer and something about interpreting Rorschachs. That's how I became interested in the Rorschach. And he was so marvelous. I handed him a protocol from a little 4-year-old girl who just pointed, and did a little bit of talking. And he looked at us, and he looked at the Rorschach, and said, "You want to adopt this child." He was right. He could tell about the personalities of the individuals so perfectly by looking at the Rorschach that I actually developed the idea that the shortest way to determine the modal personality of the tribe, if you didn't have time to spend two years among them, was to get the Rorschachs. If they're properly administered and if they're properly interpreted. So that I became very interested in the Rorschach, and I'm very interested now. That's what I'm using as my major research tool in the Boyer House Foundation.

SvB: While you were working on the reservation, the Apaches declared you a shaman. How do you see the differences between being a shaman and being a clinician?

LBB: I don't really know what a shaman is. I think a shaman is someone in whom other people put a lot of trust. They project into him all this, all of the magical strength they hoped they had themselves. The man or woman who is designated as a shaman also believes he possesses supernatural power, and uses it in culturally defined ways. I have been designated to be a shaman, but I have never behaved as one. I've been a shaman by telephone and cured people that way, and the only thing I've done, I haven't done a goddamn thing but to make a psychoanalytic interpretation. That's all I ever did, as a shaman, was to say, "You feel guilty about that," or such and such.

SvB: Do you have a proudest moment?

LBB: I don't know, I've had so many proud moments. Proudest moment? A proud moment was when the 11th International Symposium for Psychotherapy of Schizophrenia, in their thirty-third year, for the first time created, for me, a Lifetime Achievement Award. Before that I was stunned when the Argentine Psychoanalytic Association struck a medal for me. Maybe my proudest moments have concerned my children, especially identification with their achievements. One was when I delivered my first son, or rather he fell out into my arms, and lived. I was supremely proud when my younger son cured himself of the heroin addiction I had been so blind as to not know he had. I am immeasurably proud that my daughter never complained, although she suffered terribly and eventually died of multiple sclerosis.

I must be one of the most, one of the happiest and most fortunate people who ever lived. I've had such a breadth of experience with so many different kinds of people and I've learned so many things that most people don't have the foggiest notion about, you know? And they are part of me, and I have a family who adore me, and I have a lot of students who think very highly of me.

SvB: Has being a father influenced your work?

LBB: I think that it has—my relationships with my children have materially influenced my relationships with my patients, who often seem like my children to me. The same kinds of philosophies are applicable. That I can, and I allow myself—without having to act on it—I can allow myself almost the same degree of love for my patients that I have for my sons, which is limitless.

Credits

The author gratefully acknowledges permission to reprint material from:

Chapter 1, "Countertransference: Brief History and Clinical Issues with Regressed Patients": *Master Clinicians on Treating the Regressed Patient, Vol. 2*, ed. L. B. Boyer and P. L. Giovacchini, pp. 1–22. Copyright © 1993 by Jason Aronson Inc.

Chapter 2, "Psychoanalytic Treatment of the Borderline Disorders Today": *Contemporary Psychoanalysis* 23:314–328. Copyright © 1987 by the William Alanson White Institute.

Chapter 3, "Regression and Countertransference in the Treatment of a Borderline Patient": *The Borderline Patient, Vol. 2*, ed. J. S. Grotstein, M. F. Solomon, and J. A. Langs, pp. 41–59. Copyright © 1987 by The Analytic Press.

Chapter 4, "Christmas 'Neurosis,' Reconsidered": *Depressive States and Their Treatment*, ed. V. D. Volkan, pp. 297–316. Copyright © 1985 by Jason Aronson Inc.

Chapter 5, "On Man's Need to Have Enemies": *Journal of Psychoanalytic Anthropology* 9(2):1–120. Copyright © 1986 by the Institute for Psychohistory.

Index

Abend, S. M., 172
Abraham, K., 5, 59
Adler, A., 81
Adler, G., 115
Aizenberg, D., 172
Analytic tolerance, regressed patients, 120–122
Anthony, E. J., 45
Anthropology, x–xi, xiv, xxi, 10, 86, 88–95, 192, 245, 247–248. *See also* Cross-cultural psychotherapy
Anzieu, D., 151, 179, 180, 188
Apache people, enemies, 88–95
Arbiser, A., 27
Arco, C. M. B., 45
Arieti, S., 76, 127, 148
Aristotle, xiii
Arlow, J. A., 177
Ast, G., 176
Atkins, N. B., 41, 123

Bach, J. S., 183
Backman, L., 105
Balint, E., 8, 14, 227
Balint, M., 1, 14, 114, 149, 203
Balter, L., 155, 193

Barchillon, J., 24
Bascom, W., 85, 94, 106
Basehart, H. W., 89
Bastide, R., 104
Belfer, M. L., 45
Bellak, L., 30
Belvianes, M., 74
Benedek, T. F., 193, 228
Benedict, R., 105
Bennett, S. L., 45
Bergeret, J., 25
Bergler, E., 123
Berliner, B., 73, 244
Bernfeld, S., 73, 244
Best, E., 105
Bick, E., 150, 179, 180, 188
Binswanger, H., 2
Bion, W. R., xx, 7, 27, 28, 121, 140, 141, 142, 148, 150, 176, 204, 205, 217, 226, 228
Bird, H. R., 104
Blank, M., 45
Blatt, S. J., 119
Bleger, J., 149
Bleuler, E., 24
Bodkin, T., 74

Bollas, C., 3
Borderline treatment, 23–37. *See also*
    Regressed patients
    countertransference, 26–29
    diagnosis, 25
    historical perspective, 24–25
    psychopathology, 25–26
    regression and countertransference,
        39–58
        analyst emotional response as
            facilitator, 50–53
        case presentation, 42–50
        overview, 39–42
    treatability issue, 23–24
Bornstein, M., 173
Bourgignon, E., 192
Boven, W., 118
Bowlby, J., 149
Boyer, L. B., ix–xii, xiii–xv, xx, xxi, xxii,
    1, 2, 9, 10, 12, 24, 25, 27, 28, 29,
    30, 39, 40, 41, 42, 46, 59, 60,
    62, 63, 65, 66, 71, 72, 76, 77, 82,
    84, 85, 88, 91, 93, 94, 103, 104,
    105, 106, 115, 117, 118, 120,
    122, 128, 129, 141, 142, 155, 172,
    173, 174, 176, 177, 179, 180,
    181, 189, 192, 193, 203, 204, 210,
    225, 226, 227
    conversation with, 241–250
Boyer, R. M., x, xiv, 88, 94, 106
Brenner, C., 177
Bromberg, P. M., 8
Brunswick, R. M., 114
Buie, D. H., 114
Bullard, D. M., 29
Bychowski, G., 173, 217

Canino, I., 104
Carpenter, W. T., 115
Carpinacci, J., 28
Carta, I., 173
Carter, L., 41
Casement, P., 226
Cesio, F. R., 28, 106

Chavira, J. A., 104
Cheng, H. W., 172
Chiozza, L. A., 206, 212
Chittenden, H. M., 89
Christie, A., 75
Christmas neurosis, 59–80
    cases, 61–71
    cases discussed, 61–71
    overview, 59–61
    regressions, use of, in treatment,
        75–77
Christmas season, sibling rivalry,
    xxiii–xxiv, 10
Claude, H., 24
Clements, W. W., 90
Cobliner, W. G., 45
Cohen, M. B., 114
Comas-Diáz, L., 104
Conran, M., 14
Costa, G. P., 192
Countertransference, 1–21, 203–224
    borderline treatment, 26–29, 39–58.
        See also Borderline treatment
    case discussed, 215–219
    case material, 206–215
    interpretation, 205–206
    introjection and, 7–14
    Klein, M. and, 6–7
    music and, 171–201. *See also* Music
    orientation toward, xix–xxiv
    overview, 1–6, 203–204
    regression, 154–155
Creativity, potential space, 11
Cremony, J. G., 89
Cross-cultural psychotherapy, 103–
    112. *See also* Anthropology
    discussed, 106–108
    faith healing and psychotherapy,
        105–106
    overview, 103–104
    shamanistic philosophies, 104–105
Cross-cultural study, 10
    enemies, 88–95

Dan, Y., 233
Darwin, C., 81
Davis, D. M., 1
Demers-Desrosiers, L., 151, 206
De Paola, H. F. B., 13
Depression. *See* Christmas neurosis
Depressive position, countertrans-
    ference, 11–12
Deri, S. K., 218, 228
de Rio, J., 104
Deutsch, H., 25, 61, 62
Deutsch, L., 173
Devereux, G., 4, 105
De Vos, 10
Diagnosis, borderline treatment, 25
Doty, L., 226, 234
Dream, therapeutic interview as,
    139–146
Ducey, C., 179

Einstein, A., 82
Eisenbud, J., 3, 59, 71, 72
Eisenstein, V. W., 24, 25
Eissler, K. R., 147
Eissler, P. R., 23
Ekstein, R., 25, 50, 82, 114
Eliade, M., 179
Emde, R. N., 149, 154
Enemies, 81–102
    overview, 81–83
    social solidarity needs, 88–95
    targets of externalization, protection
        of self through, 83–88
Epstein, L., 1, 27
Erikson, E. H., 86, 88, 91, 124, 244
Esman, A. H., 173
Etchegoyen, R. H., 1, 6
Evans, P., 73
Externalization, targets of, protection
    of self through, 83–88

Facilitating environment, regressed
    patients, 119–120
Faimberg, H., 8

Fain, M., 206
Fairbairn, W. R. D., 27, 41, 121, 150,
    176
Faith healing, psychotherapy and,
    cross-cultural psychotherapy,
    105–106
Feder, S., 173
Federn, P., 4, 5, 27, 30, 41, 122
Feiner, A. H., 1, 27
Fenichel, O., 5, 27, 41, 59, 119, 122,
    142
Ferenczi, S., 2, 27, 191
Fernald, A., 172
Ferreira, A. J., 62
Fine, B. D., 171
Flarsheim, A., 121, 123
Flemming, J., 193
Fletcher, R., 81
Fliess, R., 4, 27, 41, 122
Folklore, 10
Fraiberg, S., 41, 149, 173
Freud, A., 87, 120, 148
Freud, S., xx, xxii, 1, 2, 3, 4, 5, 6, 10,
    14, 25, 26, 27, 41, 59, 66, 76, 81,
    82, 84, 87, 88, 127, 139, 140,
    141, 148, 149, 150, 154, 155, 191,
    205, 225
Freyre, G., 104
Fried, J., 74
Friedman, S. M., 172
Fromm, E., 82
Fromm-Reichmann, F., xiv, 25, 30,
    113, 114, 117, 177
Frosch, J., 25, 140
Furst, P. S., 105

Gabbard, G., 177, 179
Gaddini, E., 9, 148, 151, 153, 157, 189
Gaddini, R., 9, 150, 152, 153, 157, 180,
    189
Galenson, E., 152
Galileo, xiii
Ganzarain, R., 179

Garma, A., 25, 29, 59, 114, 121, 143, 203
Garrison, V., 104
Geertz, C., 86
Geleerd, E. R., 25
Gill, M. M., 11, 114, 178
Ginsburg, L., 233
Giovacchini, P. L., xiv, xx, 5, 25, 26, 27, 28, 29, 30, 40, 41, 60, 76, 106, 114, 117, 121, 150, 172, 176, 177, 192, 204, 206
Glass, J. M., 176
Glover, E., 1, 27, 217
Goethe, J. W. von, 74
Golden, K. M., 104
Gonzalez-Wippler, M., 104
Green, A., 192, 205
Greenacre, P., 46, 65, 85, 117, 173
Greenberg, J., 30
Greenson, R. R., 106, 119, 149, 176
Grimm, J. L. K., 183, 191, 233
Grimm, W. K., 183, 191, 233
Grinberg, L., 7, 24, 28, 106, 114, 121, 142, 173, 192, 205
Grinker, R., 25
Grolnick, S. A., 85, 179, 228
Grosskurth, P., 6
Grotstein, J. S., xiv, 2, 25, 28, 120, 121, 142, 188, 192
Gruhle, H. W., 27
Grunberger, B., 203
Gunderson, J. G., 25, 41
Gunderson, J. T., 121
Gunnarson, D. A., 89
Guntrip, H., 27, 41

Hall, E. T., Jr., 89
Hann-Kende, F., 5, 26, 114, 155, 192, 204
Hartmann, H., xix, 25, 27, 41, 84, 117
Hegel, G. W. F., 81
Heimann, P., 2, 13, 14, 192, 203
Hendricks, I., 25
Hermann, I., 77

Herskovits, M., 104
Hilgard, J. R., 60, 104
Hoedemaker, E. D., 122
Hoffer, W., 84
Hoijer, H. J., 89
Holding environment, regressed patients, 119–120
Hollós, I., 4
Hughes, C. H., 24
Hultkrantz, A., 105
Huscher, B. H., 89
Huscher, H. A., 89

Idel, M., 233
Internalization, object relations, 148–154
Interpretation, countertransference, 12–13, 205–206
Intersubjectivity, countertransference and, 8–9
Introjection
    countertransference and, 7–14
    of loving object, xxi–xxii
    means of, 4–5
Isakower, I., 142
Isakower, O., 189, 193
Itzkowitz, N., 86

Jacobs, T. J., 205
Jacobson, E., xiv, 25, 29, 30, 59, 62, 83, 84, 114, 150
Jaffe, D. S., 122, 173
James, W., 81
Janet, P.-M.-F., 3
Jekels, L., 59, 74
Jones, C. W., 73
Jones, E., 2, 3, 60, 75, 82, 139
Joseph, B., 7
Juni, S., 172

Kahlbaum, K., 24
Katz, G., 192
Kelly, K., 85
Kern, J. W., 140

Kernberg, O., xiv, 23, 24, 25, 27, 28,
    29, 30, 41, 44, 61, 83, 85, 114,
    121, 123
Khan, M. M. R., 120, 192, 203, 205
Kiev, A., 104
Klein, M., xi, xx, 6–7, 13, 25, 28, 121,
    141, 142, 150, 188, 244
Knight, R. P., 24
Kohut, H., 25, 83, 172
Kojeve, A., 81
Kolb, J., 25
Kraepelin, E., 24
Kris, E., 62
Kusnetzoff, J., 27

LaBarre, W., 72, 105
Lacan, J., 13
LaForgue, R., 29, 114
Lalanne, L., 73
Landauer, K., 114
Langer, S., 172
Langs, J., 1, 24, 27
Language, regression and, 9–10
Layton, N. D., 88
Leach, M., 74
Leacock, R., 192
Leacock, S., 192
Lehrman, R. P., 62
Leininger, M., 104
Leonard, M., 5
Levy, K., 123
Lewin, B. D., 5, 29, 46, 59, 62, 114,
    139, 141, 143, 180, 188, 227, 244
Lichtenberg, G. C., 81
Lidz, R. W., 25, 117
Lidz, T., 25, 117
Lindon, J. A., 41, 177
Little, M. I., 13, 106, 114, 122, 155,
    178, 204
Little Hans case (Freud), 82
Loewald, H. W., xx, 27, 41, 46, 63, 76,
    118, 119, 120, 130, 149, 203,
    205, 219, 228
Lommel, A., 179

Loomie, L. S., 123
Lorand, S., 244
Lorenz, K., 82, 86, 128, 149
Love, psychoanalysis, xxi–xxii
Lubin, A. J., 69, 70, 72
Luckert, K. W., 105

Maccoby, M., 82
Macfarlane, D., 244
Mack, J. E., 24, 39, 83, 121
Magnan, V., 24
Mahler, G., 182
Mahler, M. S., 25, 26, 41, 77, 83, 84,
    117, 152, 154, 176, 228, 235
Mails, T. E., 89
Malcolm, R. R., 5
Maldovsky, D., 27
Malin, A., 25
Maloney, C., 90
Maltsberger, J. T., 114
Marcondes, D., 106
Marmor, J., 161
Marty, P., 151, 173, 206
Mason, J. C., 106
Masterson, J. F., 41, 117
McCluskey, K. A., 45
McDermott, J. J., 81
McDevitt, J. B., 228
McDougall, J., 3, 114, 151, 173, 205,
    206
McDougall, W., 81
McLaughlin, J. T., 9, 51, 172
Mehler, J., 172
Meissner, W. W., 4, 23, 24, 27, 106,
    115, 172
Meltzer, D., 4, 7, 140, 150, 193
Menzies-Lyth, I., 4
Merenciano, M., 25
Merkur, D., 179
Mester, R., 45
Millan, I., 82
Milner, M., 114
Mintz, I. L., 173
Mitchell, S., 30

Modell, A. H., 27, 40, 118, 149, 226
Moerman, D. E., 104
Mohr, D. V., 90
Monday, J., 173
Money-Kyrle, R. E., 7, 174
Moore, B. E., 172
Moore, H., 192
Mordo, E., 28, 121
Morel, B., 24
Mozart, W. A., 184
Music, 171–201
    background data, 172–173
    course of analysis, 173–184
    current status, 184–187
    discussed, 187–193
    overview, 171–172
M'Uzan, M. de, 140

Nacht, S., 13, 177, 203
Nadel, S. F., 105
Nadelson, T., 27
Narcissistic neuroses, psychoanalysis
    and, xx, 147
Neilson, W. A., 233
Neumann, E., 192
Newman, M. F., 60
Niederland, W., 172
Novick, J., 85
Nunberg, H., 30

Object relations
    countertransference, 6–7
    internalization, 148–154
Ocko, F. H., 73
Ogden, T. H., xi, xiv, xx, xxii, 8, 11, 12,
    25, 41, 85, 118, 119, 120, 121,
    149, 150, 176, 188, 189, 192, 204,
    205, 226, 228, 234, 245
Onwuejeogwu, M., 192
Opler, M. E., 89, 90, 93, 104
Ornstein, A., 41, 176, 211
Ornstein, C. H., 176
Ornstein, P., 41, 211

Orr, D. W., 1, 27, 106
O'Shaughnessy, E., 6, 7

Pao, P.-N., 176
Papousek, H., 172
Papousek, M., 172
Parin, P., 105
Paz, C. A., 24, 39, 121
Penis envy, xi
Peto, A., 25
Pinderhughes, C. A., 86
Pistol, D., 150
Plazak, D. J., 90
Poggi, R., 179
Poland, W. S., 172
Potential space, creativity, 11
Prado Galvao, L. de A., 27, 106
Pruyser, P. W., 121
Psychoanalysis
    love, xxi–xxii
    narcissistic neuroses and, xx
Psychopathology, borderline
    treatment, 25–26
Psychosis
    regression and, 9–10
    treatability issue, 23–24
Psychosomatic syndrome, regression,
    147–170. See also Regression

Racker, E., 3, 6, 7, 13, 14, 24, 28, 114,
    121, 123, 126, 173, 180, 187, 234
Racker, H., 106, 203, 204, 205
Rascovsky, A., 59, 90
Rascovsky, M. W., 90
Rechardt, E., 172
Regressed patients, 113–137. See also
    Borderline treatment
    analytic tolerance and, 120–122
    background data, 118
    case material, 123–129
    countertransference, 203–224. See
        also Countertransference
    discussed, 129–131

holding or facilitating environment, 119–120
overview, 113–118
technical modifications, 122–123
working alliance, 119
Regression, 147–170
borderline treatment, 39–58. *See also* Borderline treatment
case material, 155–164
Christmas neurosis, use of, in treatment, 75–77
music and, 171–201. *See also* Music
overview, 147–154
psychosis and, 9–10
trauma, xxiii
treatment implications, 154–155
Reich, A., 1, 13, 27, 192
Reider, N., 244
Reik, T., 123, 155, 173, 192
Reik, W., 6
Reinach, S., 74
Religion, sibling rivalry, xxiii–xxiv, 10. *See also* Christmas neurosis
Ribeiro, R., 104
Rinsley, D. B., 41
Robbins, M. D., 121
Rockwell, W. J. K., 104
Rodrigues, N., 104
Róheim, G., 90, 105, 128, 187
Roiphe, H., 152
Rosenfeld, A., 234
Rosenfeld, D., xi, 28, 121, 150, 157, 179, 180, 188
Rosenfeld, H. A., 7, 13, 25, 41, 114, 116, 121, 122, 176, 177, 178, 190, 192, 211, 217
Rosenfeld, H. R., xx–xxi
Rosenfeld, S. K., 25
Rosse, I. C., 24
Rycroft, C., 62

Sarnoff, C., 87
Schafer, R., 27, 41, 106

Scharff, J. S., 1, 4
Schroeder, A. H., 89
Schwaber, E. A., 177
Searles, H., xiii, xiv, 5, 27, 28, 30, 40, 106, 114, 116, 121, 122, 124, 155, 177, 178, 192, 203, 204, 205
Segal, H., 7, 11, 13, 141, 154, 179, 192
Self, protection of, through targets of externalization, 83–88
Settlage, C. F., 41
Shamanistic philosophies, cross-cultural psychotherapy, 104–105
Shapiro, E. R., 25, 41, 63, 120
Shapiro, R. A., 25, 28
Sharpe, E. F., 5
Shils, E., 86
Shirokogoroff, S. M., 105
Sibling rivalry, Christmas season, xxiii, 10, 59. *See also* Christmas neurosis
Simburg, E. J., 73
Singer, M. T., 25, 121
Siquier de Failla, M., 28
Skinner, B. F., 82
Smith, H. F., 177
Snow, L. F., 104
Sperling, M., 173
Spiegel, L. A., 155
Spillius, E. B., 11
Spiro, M. E., 182, 192
Spiro, R. H., 41
Spiro, T. W., 41
Spitz, E. H., 173
Spitz, R. A., 45, 149, 244
Sprince, M. P., 25
Spruiell, V., 149
Squiggle game, xxiii, 11, 225–240
case discussed, 233–235
case material, 228–233
described, 227–228
overview, 225–227
Stanton, A. H., 115
Stärcke, A., 1, 5

Stekel, W., 3
Stern, A., 27
Stern, D. N., 84
Stone, L., 119
Suicide, Christmas neurosis, 73
Sullivan, H. S., 30
Szalita-Pemow, A. B., 114

Tähkä, V., 150
Taraporewala, I., 74
Targets of externalization, protection
　of self through, 83–88
Taylor, G. J., 206
Taylor, G. T., 151
Telepathy, 3–4
Therapeutic interview, as dream,
　139–146
Tienari, P., 185
Timsit, M., 25
Tinbergen, N., 82, 149
Tinling, D. C., 104
Torres, M., 82
Tourney, G., 90
Trauma, regression, xxiii
Treatability issue, borderline
　treatment, 23–24
Trehub, S. E., 172
Trotter, R. T., 104
Tustin, F., 85, 129, 150, 173, 175, 189,
　193

Vajda, L., 105
Van Gogh, V., 70
van Ophuijsen, J. H. W., 5
Verbal squiggle game. See Squiggle
　game
Vereecken, J. L. T., 90

Volkan, V. D., xiv, 5, 27, 41, 45, 63,
　64, 76, 83, 84, 86, 114, 116, 121,
　176, 211
von Baeyer, S., xix
Von Domarus, E., 76

Waelder, R., 29, 114
Wagner, R., 183
Waldhorn, H. F., 123
Waldinger, R. J., 204
Wallerstein, J., 25
Warfare. See Enemies
Weigert, E., 4, 27, 41
Wexler, M., 149
Will, O. A., Jr., 30
Williams, J. J., 104
Wilson, C. P., 41, 114, 173
Winnicott, D. W., xi, xx, xxiii, 7, 8,
　11, 12, 13, 24, 26, 40, 42, 77, 83,
　84, 85, 114, 118, 119, 125, 142,
　149, 150, 152, 177, 179, 180,
　193, 203, 205, 228, 233, 235
Wintrob, R., 104
Wohlcke, M., 104
Wolberg, A. R., 24
Worcester, D. E., 89
Working alliance, regressed patients,
　119

Yuletide depression. See Christmas
　neurosis

Zelig, M. A., 123, 180
Zetzel, E. R., 106, 119
Zilboorg, C., 24
Zinner, J., 25, 28, 41
Zusman, W., 140